CREATION WITHOUT COMPROMISE

A CHRISTIAN WORLDVIEW RESPONSE TO EVOLUTIONARY
CHALLENGES TO THE FAITH

CREATION WITHOUT COMPROMISE

A CHRISTIAN WORLDVIEW RESPONSE TO EVOLUTIONARY
CHALLENGES TO THE FAITH

DONALD D. CROWE

Cover Design: Rik Hilverts

Layout: Jessica Spykerman

CREATION
BOOK PUBLISHERS

Printed by Creation Book Publishers
www.creationbookpublishers.com

Creation Ministries International
PO Box 4545 Eight Mile Plains QLD 4113 Australia

Please visit our website for further information on the Christian world-view and the creation/evolution issue.

CREATION.com

To my wife Carol, to our children and grandchildren, and to all who in every place call on the name of Jesus Christ our Lord. That many generations would be encouraged to contend earnestly for the faith that was once for all entrusted to the saints.

INDEX

FOREWORD

A wakeup call that resonates

With all the materials now available on the creation-evolution debate, books for Christians about compromise on Genesis risk being seen as one more beating of the same old drum.

So when I was asked to read the manuscript of Donald Crowe's *Creation Without Compromise*, I was surprised to find myself physically leaning forward after just a few dozen pages. It was as if I was anticipating the pleasure of the next round of his foray.

Crowe draws together a host of threads from the work of other writers in this field, threads I recognize from decades of involvement in the battle—as well as insights from his own literary research for a theological thesis. But he does so in a way that is fresh and appealing, peppered with some really delightful turns of phrase that help grab the reader's attention and drive the points home.

Given the author's Reformed background, it is perhaps not surprising that several chapters are devoted to the positions on Genesis adopted by the Princeton Theologians, notably Warfield and Hodge. The lessons he draws, though, are universal ones, for Bible-believers of all Christian traditions. This work manages to highlight the tragedy of their progressively increasing yielding of the ground, without detracting from the due owed to such giants of the faith.

The book's aim, in addition to edifying God and His Word, is to help us avoid similar mistakes in our day. Part of this involves giving us a sweep of complex history and philosophy made refreshingly easy to read. We can see for ourselves how the tactics of God's opponents, in this battle for hearts and minds, have not really changed from ancient times. Knowing what went wrong in this 'battle for the Bible' is the surest way to set things right in our own sphere of influence

I was wrong in thinking that it might be the same old drum. Instead, it is a clarion wakeup call to the church, one with a disarming style that deserves to get the attention of many.

Dr. Carl Wieland
Founding editor, *Creation* magazine
Creation Ministries International

PREFACE

In the creation vs evolution debate it is customary for the evolutionists to frame the issue as 'religion' versus 'science.' Sometimes creationists, along with Intelligent Design advocates, frame the issue as 'science' versus 'science.' This has the advantage of placing the debate on level ground, but is problematic due to the shifting definition of science. Science in its broadest meaning denotes a systematized knowledge in any field, but is usually applied to the organization of objectively verifiable sense experience. Neither the creationist nor the evolutionary view of origins is ultimately based on verifiable sensory observations. On the other hand, both claim to give a comprehensive system of viewing every area of study. The real issue is the biblical worldview versus the evolutionary worldview. The historical question of origins must be approached and dealt with in terms of worldviews and the kind of evidence appropriate to historical study.

Ancient Greek philosophy provides a typical example of evolutionary-type thinking. Epicurus (341–270 BC) was honest enough to admit that the driving force behind his evolutionary worldview was that the thought of a personal Creator-God, who held all men responsible for their actions, was too troubling to tolerate, and too disturbing to his highly valued tranquility. There was no pretence of scientific evidence; it just had to be true. Modern evolutionists have sometimes been honest enough to express a similar relief at the thought that there will be no sanctions for their behavior.

Epicurean and other philosophies were present in New Testament times. Like Paul at Athens (c. AD 50), the early church largely overcame the Epicurean philosophy. But the seventeenth-century Enlightenment reintroduced similar thoughts. The Enlightenment was also concerned to separate the Bible from the study of science. Francis Bacon (1561–1626) and Galileo Galilei (1564–1642) maintained a Christian profession, but were key advocates of separating the study of science from any biblical input.

The separation of the Bible from science was not enough for those of the evolutionary worldview. The authority and relevance of the Bible had to be undermined. This task was undertaken by those from Benedict (Baruch) Spinoza (1632–1677) to Ferdinand Christian Baur (1792–1860), and beyond, who although they do not biblically qualify even for church membership, let alone teaching offices in the church, posed as experts in the reinterpretation of Scripture. Starting with the presupposition that the Bible could not possibly be true, they set out to devise some new spin. They were particularly zealous to destroy the historical objectivity of biblical revelation and replace that solid foundation with arbitrary and subjective 'moral lessons' that we might learn from these ancient documents. Too often the church's response was to 'defend' Christianity by man's common 'reason' and to let some pagan philosopher (either Plato (428/427–348/347 BC), or Aristotle (384–322 BC)) form the framework for the church's worldview.

The sad history of the church on this issue is one of progressive compromise. Christians would draw a line in the sand as they were rapidly retreating. It was not long before the line would be redrawn again and again, each time accepting more of what had been previously unacceptable. At first it might seem that there was plenty of room in the Christian tent for both the camel's nose of the evolutionary worldview and a kind of Christian theism.

The first casualty was biblical chronology. The notion of millions of years for geology, as decreed by the uniformitarians James Hutton (1726–1797)[1,2], and Charles Lyell (1797–1875)[3], seemed harmless enough. We will accept that much, said the compromisers, but no more. They might have said, 'Our Christianity is not concerned with the age of rocks, but the Rock of Ages.' Then the common idea that

God specially created every species and variety of animal that we see today was challenged by Darwinism. Now the church typically said, 'Maybe the animals evolved, but not man.' We draw a new line in the sand. The next generation of churchmen (e.g. Warfield) would say, 'We concede that the animals evolved, and maybe the body of man as well, but not the soul of man.'

Biblical chronology is obviously fatal to the evolutionary worldview. Scholars of an evolutionary worldview were obsessed with dismissing it. Most conservative scholars, failing to think in terms of a biblical worldview, easily agreed to postulate many gaps in the Genesis genealogies to accommodate evolution's imagined millions of years. The historical issue of what happened at the beginning of the earth was transformed into a 'scientific' question. Evolutionists were permitted to do 'history' without any historical documents, and practice a brand of 'science' without real-time empirical observations.

Charles Darwin (1809–1882) was able to capitalize on the church's slide toward evolution. He was able to put a scientific façade on the ancient evolutionary philosophy. The Epicurean insistence that there could be no accountability after death was combined with detailed and recorded observations and measurements of many unfamiliar creatures. The old belief that God had specially created each individual species seemed very unlikely. This view was common among churchmen and other theists, although the Bible had only used the general popular term 'kind' and not the specific narrow category 'species.'

The Princeton theologians, particularly Charles Hodge (1797–1878) and Benjamin Breckinridge ('B.B.') Warfield (1851–1921), were champions of reformed orthodoxy. Although they were outstanding Christian scholars, who left us great literary output, they did not consistently apply the Bible to areas reserved for 'science'. If anti-biblical philosophies appeared disguised as science, Princeton left the door open to them. Highly improbable spins were put on the historical record of Genesis so as to accommodate some parts of the evolutionary worldview. The Princeton apologetic[4] would content itself with throwing up isolated neutral 'facts' to refute particularly offensive elements of evolution. The foundational worldview presuppositions of evolution were not adequately addressed. Even more serious than the chronological issue itself was the 'treatment' the Bible was given in order to assure conservative Christians that we could still salvage the biblical account as long as we accommodated evolutionary ages of time. This meant that five thousand years of straightforward understanding of Genesis had to be set aside.

The conservative scholars were pleased with their ingenious compromises, but the unmistakable message had gotten out: We can make the Bible say whatever we need it to say. This was destructive to the authority of Scripture. If the true meaning of Scripture is covered over in obscurity, if its understanding requires the sophistry of the elite, then the understanding of Scripture becomes impossible. The one plain reading of Genesis became a dozen competing sophistries.

There were a few voices opposing the evolutionary tide. Robert Lewis Dabney (1820–1898) and other outstanding Southern Presbyterians defended the biblical account in opposition to the evolution-driven compromise views. (Unfortunately, even giants of the faith have feet of clay. Dabney defended Confederate slavery despite noting its grave cruelties and injustices.[5]) The scriptural geologists of England (see Chapter 9) also opposed the new geology, with its 'slow and gradual' assumptions that were based on the rejection of the authority of Genesis and led to millions of years. They did so on scientific grounds, and sometimes on biblical grounds as well. Since they could not be refuted, the opposition either ignored or attempted to discredit them.

A careful exegetical study of Scripture renders the compromise views, all of them, untenable. The sooner Christians learn to place absolute trust in the perspicuous Word of God, the sooner they can successfully resist vain philosophies like evolution.

It should already be obvious that I am not using 'evolution' to refer simply to 'Darwinism' or other theories of biological change. It is the mindset, going way back in recorded history, that rejects the notion of a transcendent Creator. Therefore, all things must have made themselves. Such naturalistic (i.e. rejecting the supernatural) presuppositions were behind the 'millions of years' in astronomy and geology which laid the foundation for Darwinism.

Evolution in this sense was never designed to be confined to a hypothetical explanation of geology, or biology; it was to be an anti-biblical worldview through which all data could be viewed. The acceptance of the fruits of this uniformitarian[6] naturalistic worldview (i.e. millions of years) may have seemed harmless enough to the early nineteenth century compromisers. Thomas Chalmers' 'gap theory,' although exegetically incompetent, at least left the rest of Genesis intact. The genealogies could still be taken at face value, the flood covered the whole earth, and the days of Genesis Chapter 1 continued to be ordinary calendar days. The slippery slope of compromise would soon lead to other compromises that would deny the calendar days, the worldwide Flood, and the value of the genealogies.

The sin of preferring the anti-theistic worldview had far more devastating consequences than the easy-compromise churchmen ever dreamed. Man is always underestimating the harmful and permanent consequences of sin. The evolutionary worldview's cheapening of the value of human life paved the way for the acceptance of abortion, eugenics, infanticide, genocide and other atrocities. Accepting the evolutionary view of man did not absolutely require Hitler to adopt his murderous agenda, but the pseudo-scientific cover of evolution was necessary to support his views. Racism now had a cloak of 'science' to cover its depraved prejudice. There can be no doubt that all these evils are much more comfortable with the evolutionary view of man as a mere mutated ape, than they would be with the biblical view of man as created in the image of God.

History has reinforced the lesson of Scripture. Our apologetic must be a comprehensive biblically based worldview presenting an antithetical challenge to the naturalistic worldview. The arbitrary and inconsistent character of naturalism must be contrasted with the consistent and objectively revealed worldview of the Bible. The deadly fruit of the evolutionary worldview must be brought out into the light. Only by building on the foundation of the revelation of the Omniscient Creator, can we have true knowledge and be able to successfully bring down the stronghold of evolutionary naturalism.

1. Tas Walker, 'The man who made the wedge: James Hutton and the overthrow of biblical authority' (Review of The Man Who Found Time: James Hutton and the Discovery of the Earth's Antiquity by Jack Repcheck (2003)), TJ (now Journal of Creation) 18(2): 55–57, 2004.

2. John Reed, 'St Hutton's Hagiography', Journal of Creation 22(1):121–127, 2008.

3. See how Lyell fudged some of his results to make them fit his theory in Larry Pierce, Niagara Falls and the Bible, Creation 22(4):8–13, 2000; <creation.com/niagara>.

4. An apologetic is a tool used in apologetics = defense of the faith, derived from απολογία (apología). meaning defence. The Greek term comes from words meaning 'out of logic/reason', so refers to a reasoned defence that would be given in a court of law. The classic example is Plato's Apology, Socrates' defence against the charges of atheism and corrupting the youth.

5. See Gary DeMar, 'Does the Bible support slavery? <www.americanvision.org/articlear-chive/04-28-06.asp>

6. Uniformitarianism, as popularized by the 19th Century lawyer and amateur geologist, Charles Lyell, postulated that all geological processes happened at essentially the same rates as observable today. Based on an a priori rejection of the catastrophic global Flood of Genesis, this inevitably meant that vast ages were required to explain sedimentary layers, for instance. Today, there is increasing recognition that many deposits at least must have formed rapidly, but the millions of years remain firmly entrenched.

CHAPTER 1

THE HISTORICAL ROOTS OF EVOLUTIONARY THOUGHT

To use a phrase made famous in another context, Darwin's nineteenth century evolutionary theory fell like a bombshell on the playground of theologians. Yet it was a centuries old philosophy. There were at least two factors that created the climate of acceptance for a philosophy long rejected by the Christian West. One factor was that evolution was 'in the air.' Several nineteenth century men were proposing evolutionary theories. The second factor, equally important, is that the Scripture had been 'declawed,'[1] and thus crippled in the defense of the faith, through neglect of a presuppositional apologetic—i.e. presupposing the truth of the Bible, and interpreting the data through its light.[2] We will say more of this second factor later.

A. ANCIENT EVOLUTION MYTHS[3]

The Bible tells us that Babylon is the mother of harlots, the source of the religious error common to the nations. Thus the likely starting point of evolutionary cosmologies (which will not have God in

---

1. Benjamin Wiker, Chapter 7, 'The Taming of Christianity, or Scripture Declawed,' in *Moral Darwinism* (Downers Grove, Illinois: InterVarsity Press, 2002).

2. 'Neutrality' or 'lack of bias' is a convenient myth—*all* data is interpreted through a worldview, which is based on unprovable presuppositions. It's like saying to the objector, 'Suppose Genesis history were true; what would you expect to find, and let's see how it squares with reality.'

3. See also David Green, 'The long long story of long ages', <creation.com/article/759>, as well as Paul James-Griffiths, 'Evolution: an ancient pagan idea,' *Creation* **30**(4):34–36, 2008.

their knowledge and suppress the truth in unrighteousness) is the Sumerian/Babylonian civilization. According to biblical chronology the Tower of Babel, confusion of languages, and scattering of people groups took place about 2242 BC As far as specific evolutionary theory preserved in writing, we look to the Milesian School of Greek philosophy in the sixth century BC (600–501 BC).

The sixth century BC Milesian School produced Thales, Anaximander, and Anaximenes. Anaximander taught a theory of evolution over two thousand years before Darwin. Colin Brown summarizes his views:

'Anaximander imagined an original state of formless matter which gradually evolved into the universe as we know it. Things came into being through a process of separating out. Living things originated from a primeval slime…he seems to have believed that human beings originally came from fishlike creatures.[4]

Henry Morris summarized their thought as follows:

'Both Thales and Anaximander taught that men evolved from animals, animals from plants, plants from inorganic elements, and all these from water. Xenophanes argued, on the basis of fossil shells on mountains, that land animals had evolved from marine animals.'[5]

Evolutionary myths found their way into the religions, philosophies and mythology of countries from Egypt to China. The religions of Confucianism, Taoism, and Buddhism reflect evolutionary cosmology. In short, all who are cut off from biblical revelation fall into this error.

---

4. Colin Brown, *Christianity & Western Thought* (Downers Grove, Illinois: InterVarsity Press, 1990), p. 21ff.

5. Henry Morris, *The Long War Against God* (Grand Rapids, Michigan: Baker Book House, 1990), p. 217.

B. EPICURUS AND LUCRETIUS

Epicurus (341–270 BC) was a Greek philosopher whose materialistic philosophy became known as Epicureanism. The Greek atomists built their materialistic theories of cosmology from ideas suggested by Democritus. The unique contribution of Epicurus was to 'make physics subservient to ethics.' For Epicurus the feelings of pleasure and pain are the supreme test in matters of morality and conduct.[6] Since the feeling of pleasure and the avoidance of pain were the chief 'virtues,' Epicurus sought to rid himself of all troubling thoughts, those that would disturb his tranquility. Among the most disturbing thoughts were the thought of an afterlife where someone might be punished, and the thought of a god who might concern himself with human accountability. Epicurus designed a materialistic philosophy so as to systematically exclude any such disturbing thoughts. Thus he presupposed that only the material is real. For him the study of science was not a search for truth, but a way of achieving a certain state of mind. He says, 'If our suspicions about heavenly phenomena and about death did not trouble us at all and were never anything to us…then we would have no need of natural science.'[7] Epicurus had not even the pretence of scientific proof for his theories. They were simply presupposed assertions of his preferences. This leads to the possibility that similar evolutionary theories may have been adopted for the same reasons. As Socrates is known in greater detail from the writings of Plato, Epicurus became much better known in the Western world through the writings of Lucretius.

Lucretius (99–55 BC) was a Roman poet and philosopher. In his epic-didactic poem, *De Rerum Natura,* Lucretius' mission was to bring the philosophy of Epicurus to the Western Latin-speaking world. He speaks of Epicurus as 'a god he was who first discovered that reasoned plan of life which is now called Wisdom.'[8] Martin

---

6. Lucretius, *De Rerum Natura,* ed. Martin Ferguson Smith, trans. W.H.D. Rouse (Cambridge, Massachusetts: Harvard University Press, 1992), p. xxxi.

7. Wiker, *Moral Darwinism,* ref. 1, p.33.

8. Lucretius, *De Rerum Natura.* Book V, line 7.

Smith notes that 'Epicureans felt justified in calling their master a god, because, although he was mortal, his discoveries were seemingly superhuman: he had saved men from ignorance and misery, and enabled them to live lives as peaceful as those of the gods.'[9]

Lucretius allowed for the existence of gods if they were conceived of as wholly material and wholly indifferent to human activity. For, as Epicurus had taught before, the gods must have supreme tranquility. If they were to concern themselves with human behavior their peace of mind would be disturbed. This was unthinkable. More relevantly, we need not concern ourselves with the aloof deities. Philosophically he could escape the charge of being an atheist by allowing these deities to exist. Practically, to deny the only God there is, the true and living God revealed in Scripture, is equal to atheism. Biblically there is no partial credit given for believing in a man-created deity; that would be nothing but the sin of idolatry.

According to Lucretius, the sun and rain caused Mother Earth to bring forth, by spontaneous generation, first the plants and then the animals. All life forms came about through the random motion of atoms accidentally assembling themselves into a particular temporary life form. To quote Lucretius:

> 'Certainly the atoms did not post themselves purposefully in due order by an act of intelligence, nor did they stipulate what movements each should perform. As they have been rushing everlastingly throughout all space in their myriads, undergoing myriad changes under the disturbing impact of collisions, they have experienced every variety of movement and conjunction till they have fallen into the particular pattern by which this world of ours is constituted. This world has persisted many a long year, having once been set going in the appropriate motions. From these everything else follows...Bear this well in mind, and you will immediately perceive that *nature is*

9. Ref. 6, p. 379.

free and uncontrolled by proud masters and runs the universe by herself without the aid of gods.' (emphasis in original)[10]

Wiker summarizes the essential ingredients of Darwinism found in Lucretius:

1. Random variation at the atomic level brings about a diversity of creatures at the level of species.

2. Monsters (later called monstrosities by Darwin) do not survive because they cannot defend themselves, nor provide sustenance, nor procreate by 'the ways of Venus.'

3. Whatever animals have survived must have been the most fit, having greater cunning, courage or quickness (or greater utility to human beings), and so are 'able by procreation to forge out the chain of the generations.'

4. Like the monsters, those species that are less fit do not survive, for they 'lay at the mercy of others for prey and profit...until nature brought that kind to destruction,' that is, extinction.[11]

Again, there is no pretence of his Epicurean theory having some demonstrable proof or scientific evidence; Lucretius need only assert his preferences. Yet it all sounds so much like Darwinism. Those Christians who naively thought that cosmology is a peripheral issue, were blinded to the fact that cosmology shapes ethics. It makes a great deal of difference whether we are merely a random collection of atoms on the level of animals and plants or whether we were specially created in the image of God. Christianity has no place for random chance; evolution has no place for God's design. There should never be an attempt to blend these two incompatible views. As Stephen Hawking said in his *A Brief History of Time*, the universe has 'no

10. Henry M Morris, *The Long War Against God* (Grand Rapids, Michigan: Baker Book House, 1990.), p. 212 (Morris cites the R. E. Latham translation of Lucretius).

11. Wiker, *Moral Darwinism*, p. 63f.

beginning or end in time, and nothing for a Creator to do.'[12] From a Christian perspective we could say, 'The universe has a beginning, the Creator controls all things, there is nothing for evolution to do.' Since evolution has become a worldview, a way of looking at all things, nothing less than a thoroughly Christian worldview can meet and defeat its challenge. The Christian worldview can only be weakened by adding elements of anti-Christian evolutionary views or attempting to synthesize them.

Lucretius attacked Greek and Roman religion as the source of evil. Like moderns, he was anxious to relieve us of the fear of hell. Darwin would later use the fact of the Christian teaching on hell as a reason to reject biblical Christianity. 'For Lucretius, Epicurean presuppositions determined every detail of his entire evolutionary account.'[13]

The early church struggled with and overcame Epicureanism. The Renaissance brought back an interest in all things Greek and Roman. Through gradual, subtle and even devious methods Christianity was weakened by injecting this ancient materialistic philosophy. First Plato, then later Aristotle, became attractive to intellectual Christian apologists because these philosophers believed in a First Cause, an Unmoved Mover and an immortal soul. They even had 'proofs' for the existence of 'God.' Instead of developing a foundationally biblical view, church Fathers used Plato to defend Christianity against the clearly atheistic philosophies.

C. THINKING BIBLICALLY ABOUT THE EVOLUTIONARY MYTHS

We learn from biblical history that there is a unity to the human race. All men descended first from Adam, then again from Noah. The Sumerian/Babylonian mythology would perhaps be most significant from a biblical view, since the Tower of Babel represents the last time all peoples shared a common culture. In the biblical account, Nimrod

---

12. Ref. 11, p. 39.
13. Ref. 11, p. 73.

organized the cities of Nineveh and Babylon. Babylon is identified as the Mother of Harlots and Abominations, so would seem to be the source of widespread false religion. Many believe that the Tower of Babel was a ziggurat with some sort of temple or worship area at its top. Morris cites Santillana and von Dechend whose research shows that:

> '...astrology has provided man with his continuing *lingua franca* through the centuries. But it is essential to recognize that, in the beginning, astrology presupposed an astronomy...The trail, pursued necessarily by induction, leads around the world through many lands. ...It also recedes in time until the beginning is reached several millennia ago in Mesopotamia. ...all the great myths of the world have a common origin. ...Myth, in short, was a language for the perpetuation of a vast and complex body of astronomical knowledge.'[14]

Perhaps Babylon's tower was the center from which astrology went out into all the world. It is a remarkable thing to have such consistency, considering there is no resemblance between the actual appearance of constellations and the zodiac names. Other signs of the unity of the human race include the common occurrence of flood narratives. Biblically this is explained by the fact that the Flood actually happened. Although confused in language at the Tower of Babel, the people groups took their rebellious religion with them. Romans Chapter 1 indicates that their substitution of evolutionary myths for God's creation of the world was a deliberate act of rebellion rather than a simple forgetfulness about the details.

> Romans 1:18–23: For the wrath of God is revealed from heaven against all ungodliness and unrighteousness of men, who suppress the truth in unrighteousness, because

14. Ref. 10, p. 247.

what may be known of God is manifest in them, for God has shown *it* to them. For since the creation of the world His invisible *attributes* are clearly seen, being understood by the things that are made, *even* His eternal power and Godhead, so that they are without excuse, because, although they knew God, they did not glorify *Him* as God, nor were thankful, but became futile in their thoughts, and their foolish hearts were darkened. Professing to be wise, they became fools, and changed the glory of the incorruptible God into an image made like corruptible man—and birds and four-footed animals and creeping things.

CHAPTER 2

THE MODERN REVIVAL OF EPICUREAN MATERIALISM

A. CHRISTIANITY VS EPICUREANISM

Although Epicurus stressed peace of mind or freedom from disturbing thoughts, his followers gave Epicureanism the reputation of sensual pleasure seekers. This made it a foregone conclusion that Christianity would set itself firmly against such a philosophy. Tertullian, Athanasius and Augustine were just three of the prominent Christian writers who opposed Epicureanism. However, the (partial) misunderstanding of Epicurus would be exploited by Renaissance thinkers eager to show that Epicurus was not that bad and had been misunderstood. Yet Christianity must oppose the cosmology and ethical system of even 'Epicurus the ascetic.' There must be conflict because the Christian cannot confess that creation came into being by accident, while the Epicurean cannot confess it came into being by design. A sovereign Creator who gives us revealed law yields a fixed absolute morality. A random universe yields an ethic that is nothing more than a temporary social convention. For example, if one is an absolute monarch he need not suffer any pain or punishment for violating mere social conventions. He may get great pleasure in violating these artificial standards. Epicurus has no basis to condemn such actions. The monarchs got the message. As created beings in the image of God we look to our Creator for directives. Where would we look if we are but mutated slime?

Another strategy that seemed successful in the short run was to make use of other Greek philosophies to oppose Epicureanism. Stoicism, Platonism and Aristotelianism all seemed friendlier to Christianity than Epicureanism. From these other philosophies they could set forth the ideas of self-sacrificing service, the immortal soul, and the proofs for the existence of God. As an apologetic, throwing these pagan philosophies at the unbeliever is like throwing a boomerang at him. All the unbiblical baggage attached to these philosophies will come back to haunt the eclectic apologist. Using Aristotle to prove that a god of some sort probably exists does not necessarily move us past Epicurus. He allowed for the existence of some sort of gods. Christians would have to do better than Aristotle to meet the coming storm of the Renaissance.

B. FROM MEDIEVAL TIMES TO THE REFORMATION

Of Medieval scholars none excelled Thomas Aquinas (1225–1274) in influence and ability. The thirteenth century in which Aquinas lived saw the revival of Aristotle as his works became available to the Western World, primarily through Muslim scholars. Aquinas, the Dominican monk, was extremely loyal to the Roman Catholic Church and to the Pope. He supported even the unbiblical inventions of purgatory, indulgences, and the infamous Inquisition with its torture and murder. He wanted to maintain much of Augustine, and explicitly taught a literal Creation Week,[1] but also wanted to show how Christianity was agreeable to the insights of Aristotle. Aquinas used Aristotle's arguments for the existence of 'god' in his famous 'Five Ways' of proving God's existence. These arguments appeared in both his *Summa Theologica* and the *Summa Contra Gentiles*. Aquinas tacked on to the conclusion of Aristotle's arguments, 'And everyone understands this to be God.' This does not seem to follow, since Aristotle himself did not conclude with the biblical God.

The famous *Summa Theologica* follows a set pattern of raising and answering hundreds of questions. Every question and answer

---

1. See <creation.com/Anglican>.

takes the same format. Once Aquinas has stated the question, the answer is always in three steps.

1. First the 'It would seem…' section gives three to five points that seem to support an opposing position.

2. The 'On the contrary' section is a brief quote setting forth Aquinas' own view. The source of the quote may be Scripture, Augustine, or 'The Philosopher' referring to Aristotle. Other sources are quoted less frequently.

3. The final section is always entitled 'I answer…' with perhaps three to five points supporting his answer.

Aquinas, of course, says many good things: creation *ex nihilo*, every sin deserves infinite punishment, and more. But there are several errors and weaknesses in his presentation. In addition to supporting all Rome's invented doctrines, he has no clear teaching on man's fallen nature, holds only a hypothetical necessity for the Atonement, and compromises the doctrine of justification by speaking only of *infused* righteousness rather than imputed righteousness.

One particular problem that Aquinas caused for Christian theology was the issue of how much could be known by natural reason, and how much is known only by divine revelation in Scripture. Francis Schaeffer wrote of the role of Thomas Aquinas in opening the 'nature and grace' discussion.[2] In answering the question, 'Whether God can be known in this life by natural reason?' Thomas embellishes Romans 1:19 as follows 'That which is known of God,' namely, what can be known of God *by natural reason*, 'is manifest in them.' He further says, 'God is known by natural knowledge through the images of His effects.' Grace, says Aquinas, can give us a more perfect knowledge of God than we could acquire by natural reason.[3]

---

2. Francis Schaeffer, *Escape From Reason*, vol. 1, in *The Complete Works of Francis A. Schaeffer* (Westchester, Illinois: Crossway Books, 1982), p. 209.

3. Thomas Aquinas, 'How God is Known,' in *Summa Theologica*, vol. 1 (Books for the Ages; Albany, Oregon: Ages Software, 1997), pp. 142–45.

In another section of the *Summa*, the same sentiment is expressed, 'Therefore without grace man of himself can know truth.'[4] He is speaking of truth about God.

The nature/grace tension meant that man could discover many things in Christian theology by natural reason alone, but needed grace (revelation) to understand such things as the Trinity or the way of salvation. When man introduces such a nature/grace division, the result is much the same as the unwarranted sacred/secular division. What was done with the nature/grace dichotomy, even if Thomas would not have approved, was to give more and more intellectual 'territory' to man's reason and an ever-shrinking portion to God's revelation. The Bible could be regarded as less and less important as man's knowledge advanced. This is a very destructive influence, which must be combated by the Christian worldview. Sadly, Thomas only abetted this destructive influence. Could he have seen the consequences of opening this door to 'reason'? That is doubtful. It is all the more reason we must not compromise the biblical witness to absolute truth—we simply cannot imagine what consequences will follow such a compromise. A synthetic apologetic will bring unexpected consequences, quite opposite of those hoped for. Thomas should not have tried to synthesize his apologetic with Aristotle's philosophy. He should have confronted even Aristotle's philosophy with the antithetical worldview of the Bible.

C. MARTIN LUTHER

Among the many remarkable advancements of the Reformation was the grammatical-historical interpretation of Scripture. This stood in contrast to the Roman method of frequent allegorization. The Protestant Reformation gave an objective meaning to Scripture, instead of leaving the meaning up to the imagination of an interpreter.

Martin Luther (1483–1546) is known for his strong conviction of 'Sola Scriptura.' Scripture alone is our absolute authority, not

---

4. Thomas Aquinas, 'Treatise on Grace,' in *Summa Theologica*, p. 1314.

popes and councils. His rejection of Scholasticism is clear, as seen in this statement:

> 'At the Council of Constance John Huss and Jerome of Prague, those genuine, holy children of God and saints, were condemned and burned; but Thomas Aquinas, the fountainhead and dregs of all heresy, error, and extirpation of the Gospel (as his books prove him to be) was exulted.'[5]

On the question of whether Thomas Aquinas was saved, Luther answered in his usual outspoken way,

> 'For as to Thomas Aquinas I hesitate very much to say whether he is damned or saved ... Thomas wrote much that is heretical, and he is the one who brought about the rule of Aristotle, that devastator of pious doctrine. What does it mean to me that the bishop of bulls has canonized him?'[6]

We are not surprised to find that Luther believed very strongly in creation *ex nihilo*. The creation involved all three Persons of the Trinity and took place in the space of six ordinary days. All this can be easily gathered from his commentary and lectures on Genesis. The only controversy regarding the six-day creation that Luther faced was what to do with the speculations of some church fathers, notably Augustine, that the creation took place in one instant. Luther replied,

> 'We must understand that these days were actual days (*veros dies*), contrary to the opinion of the holy fathers. Whenever we observe that the opinions of the fathers disagree with Scripture, we reverently bear with them and

5. Martin Luther, 'Churchmen,' in *What Luther Says, A Practical In-Home Anthology for the Active Christian*, comp. Ewald M. Plass (St. Louis, Missouri: Concordia Publishing House, 1959), p. 316.

6. Ref. 5.

acknowledge them to be our elders. Nevertheless, we do not depart from the authority of Scripture for their sake.'[7]

It is important to note that when modern advocates of figurative interpretations cite Augustine, they do not really have an ally. Augustine tended to compress the six days into an instant and firmly believed in a 'recent' creation about 4000 BC. He is certainly not a Hebrew expert, nor does he lend any support to those trying to adjust Scripture to the 'millions of years' demanded by evolution.

Luther spoke quite clearly on how long the work of creation took:

> 'When Moses writes that God created heaven and earth and whatever is in them in six days, then let this period continue to have been six days, and do not venture to devise any comment according to which six days were one day. But if you cannot understand how this could have been done in six days, then grant the Holy Spirit the honor of being more learned than you are. For you are to deal with Scripture in such a way that you bear in mind that God Himself says what is written. But since God is speaking, it is not fitting for you wantonly to turn His Word in the direction you wish to go.'[7]

D. JOHN CALVIN

Calvin, in his commentary on Genesis, affirms the *ex nihilo* creation in six days. He says,

> 'He [Moses] moreover teaches by the word 'created' that what before did not exist was now made...Therefore his meaning is, that the world was made out of nothing. Hence the folly of those is refuted who imagine that unformed matter existed from eternity...'[8]

---

7. Ref. 5, p. 1523.

8. John Calvin, 'Chapter One,' in *Commentaries on The First Book of Moses Called Genesis*, trans. John King (Grand Rapids, Michigan: Baker Books, 2003), p. 70.

On the days of Genesis, Calvin leaves no doubt where he stands. Commenting on the phrase 'The first day' he says,

> 'Here the error of those is manifestly refuted, who maintain that the world was made in a moment. For it is too violent a cavil to contend that Moses distributes the work which God perfected at once into six days, for the mere purpose of conveying instruction. Let us rather conclude that God Himself took the space of six days, for the purpose of accommodating his works to the capacity of men.'[9]

We see in the Reformers a bold confidence in the Word of God, understood in a straightforward exegetical manner. The meaning is not to be determined by the speculations of men being brought into the text (eisegesis) and imposed upon the text. When the speculations of men govern the interpretation of Scripture, our confidence in Scripture is undermined. This was indeed the consequence of the lesser interpreters who, in later centuries, attempted to force Scripture to speak 'evolutionese.' There can be no doubt that the Reformers regarded Scripture as absolute truth, far more to be trusted than any word of man. Without the light of Scripture men do not come to know the God of Holy Scripture. While the light of nature is clear enough to leave man without excuse,

> 'Yet it appears that if men were taught only by nature, they would hold to nothing certain or solid or clear-cut, but would be so tied to confused principles as to worship an unknown god [cf. Acts 17:23].'[10]

And on the superiority of the Word,

> 'For by his Word, God rendered faith unambiguous forever, a faith that should be superior to all opinion....no one can

---

9. Ref. 8, p. 78.

10. John Calvin, 'The Knowledge of God The Creator,' in *Institutes of the Christian Religion*, ed. John T. McNeill, trans. Ford Lewis Battles, vol. 1 (The Library of Christian Classics; Philadelphia: The Westminster Press, 1960), p. 66 (I.V.12).

get even the slightest taste of right and sound doctrine unless he be a pupil of Scripture.'[11]

The ancient evolutionary mythology is thoroughly rejected by the Reformers. Calvin specifically rejects the evolutionary view of Lucretius, and of course, opposes Lucretius' rejection of creation *ex nihilo*.[12] Calvin clearly believes that the genealogies of Genesis present a continuous history, and that the Flood was a worldwide deluge. If the reformers had wanted to discard the plain meaning of the Bible so as to accommodate evolutionary worldviews, they could have done so. They refused to do so and stood confidently upon the Scriptures. The clear testimony of the Bible stood squarely against the various evolutionary worldviews. It would take centuries of erosion of this confidence in Scripture for the Christian world to entertain the possibility of evolution.

E. THE RENAISSANCE

The Renaissance was a period of renewed interest in learning. The special motto was 'back to the sources.' There was a new interest in reading the Greek and Roman classics in their original languages. In northern Europe, though not without some negative effects on their thinking, this led to many scholars learning New Testament Greek and Old Testament Hebrew. Particularly in southern Europe, many turned to the ancient Greek and Roman pagan writings. Poggio Bracciolini acquired a copy of Lucretius' *De Rerum Natura* and proceeded to publish the writings of Epicurus and Lucretius.

The question arises, 'How could this reintroduction of Epicurean thought be tolerated in a Christianized society?' Benjamin Wiker gives us three strategies used to gradually and subtly inject elements of paganism into Christianity.

1. The 'not-so-bad-guy' approach: We are not advocating these men. We are merely letting their original writings

11. Ref. 10, p. 71 ff. (I.VI.2).

12. Ref. 10, p. 56 (I.V.4)..

be known. Epicurus himself was not a sensual pleasure seeker; he was ascetic. We want to increase learning. We do not necessarily agree with all the authors we introduce to students.

2. The 'honey on the rim' approach to Lucretius. We are presenting this as a sample of good Latin poetry, not for its specific content.

3. Using Epicurean terms to redefine Christian teaching. We could say pleasure is our highest goal, if our pleasure is in being with God for eternity. We might be able to accept Lucretius' theory of atoms, if God directed the atoms. We don't have to accept all of Epicurus' philosophy; we can still believe in immaterial reality.[13]

Regardless of what their motives were, they uncritically introduced antichristian elements into the Christian West.

F. THE ENLIGHTENMENT: THE LIGHT DIMS

The Age of Enlightenment of the seventeenth and eighteenth centuries brought a renewed interest in materialistic[14] cosmology, usually without the Christian veneer thought necessary in the Renaissance. Influential Christian thinkers of the age include Galileo (1564–1642) and Isaac Newton (1642–1727). These men never intended that a materialistic cosmology should lead us to accept an Epicurean morality. This represents a failure to develop a specifically and explicitly biblical cosmology. It must be remembered that Epicurean cosmology was especially designed to exclude all thoughts of a Creator God. Ethical concerns and presuppositions dictated his cosmology. But many did not see the connection.

---

13. Wiker, *Moral Darwinism*, p. 108.

14. Materialism here refers not to the accumulation of material goods, but to the philosophy that matter/energy is all there is, essentially synonymous with naturalism.

Consider Galileo, famous for opposition to the geocentric model of the solar system.[15] Four centuries earlier, Thomas Aquinas found it quite useful to employ Aristotle in the defense and presentation of Christian teachings. But in the seventeenth century the Church was badly burned because they were standing so close to Aristotle.[16] For it was not a careful exegesis of Scripture that made the geocentric view seem certain, but the confidence in Aristotle's cosmology. In the thirteenth century the Bible could be allegorized into irrelevance to this world, but Aristotle had to be taken seriously. The 'Angelic Doctor' (as Aquinas was known) and the best of the philosophers stood together and would fall together. To attack Aristotle and the allegorical interpretation of Scripture was to attack the official position of the Roman church. Galileo, astronomer, mathematician, and rhetorician was seen as attacking the Church and, presumably, the Scriptures. If Aristotle was wrong, perhaps the Church was also wrong. If Galileo could discover four moons of Jupiter, the universe was much larger than thought. Perhaps Lucretius was right in supposing the universe to be infinite and eternal, though quite changeable. There were natural, mathematical explanations for the universe. The supernatural explanations could be dispensed with.

Wiker cites a famous statement of Galileo:

> 'Natural philosophy is written in a great Book, which holds itself at all times open before our eyes—I mean, the universe itself. But no one can understand it unless to begin with he sets himself to master the language, and recognize the characters, in which it is written. It is written in mathematical language, and the characters are triangles, circles, and other geometric figures.'[17]

---

15. Earth stationary at the center, with the sun revolving around it.

16. For more information refuting the commonly believed misinformation about the Galileo controversy, see Schirrmacher, T., 'The Galileo Affair: history or heroic hagiography?', *TJ* (now *Journal of Creation*) **14**(1):91—100, 2000; <creation.com/gal-affair>.

17. Wiker, *Moral Darwinism*, p. 119.

By finding the key to understanding in mathematics, the universe could be seen in naturalistic, even materialistic terms. The point, smallest unit in geometry, could be compared to the atom, or the stars in astronomy. As similar features were discovered on the moon or other planets, the earth was declared to be not such a special place. Perhaps Earth had lost both its centrality and its uniqueness. Although Galileo maintained his Christianity, his cosmology could do just fine without it.

Isaac Newton received accolades rather than opposition for his work in the eighteenth century. Christians often praise Newton as an example of a Christian prominent in the field of science. Quotations from Newton can be cited to reinforce such a conclusion, e.g.

'This most beautiful system of the sun, planets, and comets, could only proceed from the counsel and dominion of an intelligent Being. ... This Being governs all things, not as the soul of the world, but as Lord over all; and on account of his dominion he is wont to be called "Lord God" Παντοκράτωρ [pantokratòr], or "Universal Ruler." ... The Supreme God is a Being eternal, infinite, absolutely perfect.'[18]

Sir Isaac Newton was a six-day creationist and did not allow for millions of years since the creation, but only thousands. Nevertheless, whether he was a biblical Christian has been called into question, with the claim that he was not a Trinitarian.

R.E.D. Clark agrees that Newton believed the Scripture taught Arianism,[19] but T.C. Pfizenmaier argues that likely he held to the Eastern Orthodox view of the Trinity rather than the Western one held by Roman Catholics, Anglicans and most Protestants.[20]

---

18. Sir Isaac Newton, *Newton's Philosophy of Nature: Selections from His Writings, Principia*: Book III, ed. H.S. Thayer (New York: Hafner Library of Classics, 1953); see also cited in the article by Ann Lamont: 'Sir Isaac Newton (1642/3–1727): A Scientific Genius', *Creation* **12**(3):48–51, 1990; <creation.com/Newton>.

19. R.E.D. Clark, 'Newton, Sir Isaac (1642–1717),' in *The New International Dictionary of the Christian Church*, 1974 ed., p. 704. J.D. Douglas, General Editor.

20. T.C. Pfizenmaier, 'Was Isaac Newton an Arian?' *Journal of the History of Ideas* **68**(1):57–80, 1997.

Regardless, one does find Newton taking the Bible very seriously in his detailed study of chronology, *The Chronology of Ancient Kingdoms Amended*. He worked out a chronology of world history similar to that of Archbishop James Ussher. Those who so easily and ignorantly join in the ridicule of Ussher are strangely silent about the almost identical conclusions reached by Newton. He also took a great interest in biblical prophecy, writing *Observation upon the Prophecies of Daniel and the Apocalypse of St. John*.[21]

Unbelievers in later times would take Newton's mechanistic model and draw atheistic conclusions that would have offended Newton. Newton spoke of God as particularly necessary to create the atoms, to order the atoms, and to make adjustment in the system as necessary. Later thinkers would deny that God was necessary at all.

'Newton saw God as the masterful creator whose existence could not be denied in the face of the grandeur of all creation. But the unforeseen theological consequence of his conception of God, as Leibniz pointed out, was that God was now entirely removed from the world's affairs, since the need for intervention would only evidence some imperfection in God's creation...'.[22]

This idea of 'no imperfections' came in any case from deistic visions of the world, not the biblical worldview which incorporates the Fall. The atheistically inclined materialists found they could adopt Newton's cosmology as supportive of their 'atoms in motion' view. Newton agreed that atoms were very hard and never wear out. For the materialists, God was not needed to order the atoms, because there were vast ages of time for the random motions to consolidate into a given pattern. What God could do in an instant, 'chance' could do given enough time. In some minds, the God of Newtonianism became merely the 'God of the gaps.' The advancing scientific knowledge would push Him back into an ever-shrinking reservation. In the mind

---

21. These two books are available at www.gutenberg.org.

22. Wikipedia essay, 'Isaac Newton's Religious Views' <en.wikipedia.org/wiki/Isaac_Newton%27s_religious_views> accessed 13 November 2008.

of secular enlightenment thinkers, the dispelling of ignorance would increasingly make God an unnecessary hypothesis. Those of the Epicurus–Lucretius persuasion easily incorporated Newton's laws of motion. Matter in motion was seen as the key to understanding all things. Even human thought could be reduced to these terms. The famous astronomer Edmond Halley celebrated this new knowledge in his ode to Newton that reads in part:

> In reason's light, the clouds of ignorance
> Dispelled at last by science…
> Then ye who now on heavenly nectar fare,
> Come celebrate with me in song the name
> Of Newton, to the Muses dear; for he
> Unlocked the hidden treasuries of Truth…
> Nearer the gods no mortal may approach.[23]

Man's delusion of omniscience reached a new peak in 1846, when the planet Neptune was discovered right where mathematical calculations predicted there must be another planet. The mid-nineteenth century was an age of unbounded optimism regarding the potential for mankind. This was the intellectual context in which Charles Darwin lived and absorbed that culture.

G. METHODOLOGY AND MORALITY

Epicurus could begin with his 'ethical' concerns, and then devise a cosmology agreeable to those concerns. As developed in the West, it was first a materialistic cosmology that was promoted, then the ethical implications followed. Biblical cosmology (i.e. Genesis creation) yields an accountable, created man with absolute moral standards derived from the Creator. To undermine biblical cosmology or the doctrine of creation is to undermine biblical morality. In order to subvert the Christian worldview, it was necessary to first devise an

---

23. Isaac Newton, *Mathematical Principles of Natural Philosophy*, trans. Leon J. Richardson (Berkeley, California: University of California Press, 1934), xiii–xv. cited by Wiker, *Moral Darwinism*, p. 138.

Epicurean-like method of gaining knowledge about the creation. It was also necessary to devise a strategy of Machiavellian gradualism in order to subvert Christianity by deception and by small steps designed so as to not provoke strong reaction.

Niccolò Machiavelli (1469–1527) was an amoral Italian political philosopher. His name is synonymous with duplicity, cunning, and ruthlessness in the pursuit of political goals. His 'masterpiece' was his book *Il Principe (The Prince)*, where a 'prince' meant an absolute monarch who need not have any hesitation about committing certain acts because a prince can avoid social punishments. This renders the cautions of Epicurus unnecessary for an absolute monarch. His philosophy is relevant to the promotion of the evolutionary faith in that atheists can put on a public face that says there is no necessary conflict between evolutionary 'science' and Christian 'faith.' Evolutionists often hide their own militant atheism and the atheism of those who devised, developed and promoted their particular faith through the centuries.[24] It is understandable that liberal evolutionized churches would support the chance appearance of life on Earth, but it is dismaying to see alleged evangelicals trying to synthesize the opposing worldviews of evolutionism and creationism.

Sir Francis Bacon (1561–1626), English philosopher and lawyer, is considered the father of the modern scientific method. Science as a systematic study was made possible on the assumption that we live in an orderly universe made by our Creator. Bacon confesses his own personal belief in a recent literal six-day creation.[25] Bacon speaks respectfully, even reverently, of the Scriptures. He relates the Flood and the confusion of tongues as historical. He commends Moses and Job as follows:

'To descend to Moses the lawgiver, and God's first pen: he is adorned by the Scriptures with this addition and

---

24. In a September 2004 PBS series on evolution, militant atheist Eugenie Scott tries to soothe the opposition by saying there is no conflict between evolution and religion, or between evolution and God.

25. Francis Bacon, *Advancement of Learning: Novum Organum*, Encyclopaedia Britannica, Inc., Chicago, 1952 ed., p. 17 ff, published in *Great Books of the Western World*, Hutchins, R.M., editor in chief, No. 30, Francis Bacon

commendation, "That he was seen in all the learning of the Egyptians"…As in the law of the leprosy…and very many other places in that law, there is to be found, besides the theological sense, much aspersion of [natural] philosophy… So likewise in that excellent book of Job…it will be found pregnant and swelling with natural philosophy…'[26]

Bacon made an erroneous statement that would prove quite destructive to Christian worldview thinking. Not only did he oppose building science on the foundation of Greek polytheism, but also went on to oppose the use of the Bible in the acquisition of scientific knowledge. He said:

'Yet some of the moderns have indulged this folly with such consummate inconsiderateness, that they have endeavored to build a system of natural philosophy on the first chapter of Genesis, the book of Job, and other parts of Scripture; seeking thus the dead amongst the living. And this folly is the more to be prevented and restrained, because not only fantastical philosophy, but heretical religion spring from the absurd mixture of matters divine and human.'[27]

How can Bacon say this after what he said about Scripture elsewhere? We might wish he were merely warning us about the danger of clinging to theories on nature derived from allegorical interpretations, church tradition, or Greek philosophy; but Bacon seems to be saying more than this. He sounds so modern with his two-source, two-story, two-book view of acquiring knowledge. Consider what use he makes of Matthew 22:29:

'For our Saviour saith, "You err, not knowing the Scriptures, nor the power of God"; laying before us two books or volumes to study, if we be secured from error; first the Scriptures, revealing the will of God, and then the creatures expressing his power; whereof the latter is a

---

26. Ref. 25, p. 20.
27. Francis Bacon, *Novum Organum*, p. 114.

key unto the former: not only opening our understanding to conceive the true sense of the Scriptures, by the general notions of reason and rules of speech; but chiefly opening our belief, in drawing us into a due meditation of the omnipotency of God, which is chiefly signed and engraven upon his works.'[28]

Further, Bacon begins his *Novum Organum* with these words:

'MAN, as the minister and interpreter of nature, does and understands as much as his observations on the order of nature,…permit him, and neither knows nor is capable of more.'[29]

Now we have a more complete picture. We have two books: the book of nature and the book of revelation. Man must first study nature by his observations alone, without resorting to Scripture. His understanding of nature is the key to understanding Scripture. The book of nature is more tentative, based on our observations. The book of Scripture is to help us meditate on the perfections of God and give us wisdom for living. A more consistently Christian worldview would see that although Scripture is not a textbook on science, it is far better. We need to understand and interpret every observation, 'scientific' or not, in the perfect light of the God-breathed Word. We are not entitled to arbitrarily exclude any area of life or thought from the Lordship of Jesus Christ.

Historically, when a great man stumbles, the lesser men who follow will hold more tenaciously to his errors than to the truths he held. The evolutionary theorists would discard Bacon's praise of Scripture and hold fast to his notion that Scripture should not be used in building our natural philosophy or science. Of course, evolutionists continued to build their science on ancient Greek religious philosophies; but Christians inexplicably were largely persuaded to forsake the only infallible source of truth and adopt

---

28. Francis Bacon, 'Book One, Sect. 9–10,' *Advancement in Learning*, p. 20.

29. Bacon, *Novum Organum*, p. 107.

Epicurean materialism as the true scientific explanation of origins. This pernicious error was used to imply that Christians must forsake any revealed truth that belonged in the arena of 'science.' The Bible retained value only for religious or moral concerns. Where Scripture touches history or cosmology, it was up to the historians and the scientists to decide on its validity. Without the allowance of this false dichotomy, the subversion of the Christian worldview would not have been possible.

If the Christian Francis Bacon could so easily lay aside the fountain of truth that is Scripture, how much more would the French positivist Auguste Compte (1798–1857) set aside (*a priori*) theological explanations as a source of knowledge? The atheistic philosopher postulated three stages through which every branch of knowledge passes. The first stage is the theological or fictitious stage in which events are explained by appealing to God or gods. The second stage is the metaphysical stage in which abstract concepts replace the supernatural beings. The metaphysical stage would include concepts such as social contract, popular sovereignty, and equality of persons. The final stage of intellectual evolution is positive or scientific. This positivistic stage cannot be surpassed. Abandoning the search for origins, we content ourselves with describing and solving human problems.[30]

While the way of pure empiricism may seem attractive, it proves impossible to maintain. No one can settle for a barrage of unrelated sensory data. Everyone has to have a framework into which the data fit or a 'story' to tell in order to understand the data, and to explain both the observed data and their relationship to other data. Neither the creationist nor the evolutionist got their 'story' from sensory experience. Only if the Creator would tell us His account of origins, could we have a sure foundation for knowledge. The way of wisdom is this: Proverbs 9:10 'The fear of the LORD *is* the beginning of wisdom, and the knowledge of the Holy One *is* understanding.'

---

30. 'Compte, Auguste,' in *Funk and Wagnalls New Encyclopedia*, 1996 ed.

CHAPTER 3

THE TAMING OF CHRISTIANITY—OR 'SCRIPTURE DECLAWED'[1]

Since Christianity was the chief obstacle to the acceptance of the Epicurean–Lucretian religious and philosophical views, some way had to be found to undermine the authority of Scripture. For those with an evolutionary worldview, all things are to be viewed through the evolutionary lenses, the Bible included. The first concerted effort was not to openly reject the Bible, but promote various 'interpretations' of the Bible that would point us to the acceptance of the humanistic philosophy. Perhaps we could thank the Medieval Scholastics whose allegorical interpretations of Scripture allowed the Bible to be used for almost any purpose. It should also be noted that early opponents of Christianity, especially Celsus and Porphyry, stated criticisms of the Bible that were taken up by later critics. In the more modern era (seventeenth through nineteenth centuries) three sample critical approaches will illustrate the process of undermining the ability of Scripture to resist the atheistic cosmologies: Thomas Hobbes, Benedict Spinoza, and the Baur–Strauss Tübingen school.

---

1. Benjamin Wiker, 'SEVEN: The Taming of Christianity or Scripture Declawed,' in *Moral Darwinism* (Downers Grove, Illinois: InterVarsity Press, 2002).

A. HOBBES, SPINOZA, AND BAUR

Thomas Hobbes (1588–1679) was a well-known philosopher and promoter of a reinterpretation of Scripture. In order to have his atheistic philosophy accepted, he preferred to reinterpret the Bible rather than openly reject it. Since a false interpretation of Scripture is no longer Scripture, he could reject the Bible under the guise of reinterpreting it. In Hobbes' political Epicureanism, the whole society, not just the individual, should be free of disturbances. The Thirty Years War (1618–1648) immediately preceded Hobbes's *Leviathan* of 1651. This provided Hobbes an opportunity to overlook all the maze of political motives and blame religion for the world's troubles. He called for a new way of looking at Scripture and a new non-traditional religion. Hobbes dealt with those ancient concerns of avoiding any thought of being held accountable in an afterlife. He rejected both Protestant and Roman Catholic Christianity.

Benedict (aka Baruch) de Spinoza (1632–1677) was a Continental rationalist philosopher whose philosophy is relevant to this work only because he put forward a method of biblical interpretation. The fact that Scripture as revealed knowledge plays no part in his system of thought reveals one of his major presuppositions. Like all unbelievers, he operates on the presupposition that the God revealed in the Bible cannot exist. Human reason is his key to knowledge.

Spinoza published *Tractatus Theologicio-Politicus* anonymously in 1670. The Roman Catholic Church considered the book dangerous and placed it on the Index (of prohibited books). Spinoza claimed to liberate us from the theologians by taking a fresh impartial look at the Bible, without any prior assumptions concerning it. Using a two-realities, two-source theory of knowledge, he concluded, 'I became thoroughly convinced that the Bible leaves reason absolutely free, that it has nothing in common with philosophy.'[2]

While Spinoza has some common sense observations on the interpretation of Scripture, (such as paying attention to the nature of

---

2. Robert M. Grant, 'The Rise of Rationalism,' in *A Short History of The Interpretation of the Bible* (New York: The Macmillan Company, 1966), p. 148.

language, the time and occasion of writing, and structure of the book), he wastes little time in undermining the authority of Scripture. He ridicules both the hypocrisy and the reliance on pagan philosophy that he saw in theologians and common Christians. Of theologians he says,

> 'I cannot discover that they teach anything but speculations of Platonists and Aristotelians, to which (in order to save their credit for Christianity) they have made Holy Scripture conform.'[3]

Of the ordinary Christians he says, 'When people declare ... that the Bible is the Word of God ... they evidently do not mean what they say; for the masses take no pains at all to live according to Scripture.'[4]

Spinoza's interpretations made the miracles of the Bible disappear into the credulity of the ignorant. The rationalists of the time felt they needed to put on a public face that appeared more favorable to Christianity than they actually were in their private lives. He said that since God had made perfect laws of nature, it would be absurd to think He would ever need to act contrary to Nature. People in the Bible were simply ignorant of natural causes and considered what they could not explain to be a 'miracle.' In private correspondence with Henry Oldenburg, Spinoza more openly expresses his unbelief. He speaks of the incarnation as absurd. He considers the apostles deceived for believing in the Resurrection and Ascension of Christ.[5] The Bible was reduced to a book of moral guidelines.

Although it would not seem likely that Christians would allow an apostate Jew turned pantheist to interpret Scripture for them, later generations found his methods attractive. Robert Grant says,

---

3. Baruch Spinoza, 'Preface,' in *The Philosophy of Spinoza*, ed. Joseph Ratner (New York: The Modern Library, 1954), p. 9.

4. Ref. 3, p.11.

5. Ref. 3, p. 43ff., footnote.

'Spinoza's method is very much like that followed in
modern introductions to the books of the Bible… It avoids
all the theological questions involved in the interpretation
of scripture; for the scripture has no authority over the
interpreter's mind… Spinoza was the most important
advocate of the primacy of reason over scripture.'[6]

In response to Spinoza's charge of hypocrisy, we should seek a
biblical approach. While we could admit that hypocrisy has occurred
frequently, we know it is a sin only on the basis of the Word of God
in Scripture. The foundational question is, how does Spinoza know
there is anything wrong with 'hypocrisy'? By what standard does he
come to this conclusion? Spinoza himself, along with many fellow
rationalists, seems to actually value hypocrisy as a strategy to gain
a hearing for his ideas. Then is hypocrisy for Spinoza a valuable
strategy or a vice? But Spinoza did have a valid criticism of medieval
allegorizing to make the Bible speak the language of Aristotle.

A piecemeal apologetic borrowed from anti-Christian philosophy
will not stem the tide. Nothing but a foundational, presuppositional
apologetic is adequate to keep us from being deceived by the
challenges of unbelieving philosophers. There is no reason we should
accept a statement as truth, just because Spinoza, or any other human
being, says so. This kind of authority is reserved for the God who
speaks His Word to us in Scripture. Let Spinoza repeat his claims
one hundred times with a great show of authority; we may count it
one hundred lies. Sometimes we must say with the apostle Paul, 'Let
God be true, but every man a liar.' (Romans 3:4)

By the nineteenth century negative biblical criticism was being
promoted from within the church, led by the German universities. One
of the most influential of these critics was F.C. Baur of the Tübingen
school. Baur's student Strauss also applied Hegelian philosophy to
biblical studies. The Bible was strained through a naturalistic filter
to find what little was left of value. Strauss wrote a well-known book
on the *Life of Jesus*. He rejected all miraculous elements in Scripture,

---

6. Ref. 2, p. 150.

including the resurrection of Christ. He preferred his rationalism and naturalism to divine revelation. His work should be viewed as anti-Christian and an example of the distortion wrought on Christianity when it is viewed through evolutionary lenses. Strauss finally gave up the façade of Christianity. After having done his best to inflict damage on the faith, he became an open materialist instead of a covert one.

B. JOHN LOCKE (1632–1704)

For those thinkers who considered themselves Enlightenment elite, reason reigned supreme. All of Scripture must be subject to reason. Those who professed some variety of Christianity often tended toward Unitarianism or Deism. For such thinkers the chief value of the Bible was not in its presentation of the sovereignty of God and the salvation of sinners; it was in the high moral system that should guide our conduct. Those unfortunate souls who lacked acuity of reason needed Scripture to find that moral system that these elite had already found through reason. Even those who were thought of as defending the Christian religion felt compelled to show that Christianity was 'reasonable.'

John Locke's *The Reasonableness of Christianity* (1695) is an example of this central concern for reason. Locke believed that reason alone could discover morality, but revelation was a surer and shorter way for the unlearned to know the required duties.

> 'And 'tis at least a surer and shorter way, to the apprehensions of the vulgar, and mass of mankind, that one manifestly sent from God, and coming with visible authority from him, should, as a King and law-maker, tell them their duties, and require their obedience, than to leave it to the long and sometimes intricate deductions of reason, to be made out to them: such strains of reasonings the greatest part of mankind have neither leisure to weigh, nor, for want of education and use, skill to judge of.'[7]

---

7. John Locke, *The Reasonableness of Christianity*, ed. I. T. Ramsey (Stanford, California: Stanford University Press, 1958), sect. 241. cited by Wiker, *Moral Darwinism*, p. 203.

This quotation puts the emphasis of Christ's coming on the conveying of morality to those who were incapable of sophisticated reasoning. In another work, Locke asserted more clearly the primacy of reason: 'Reason must be our last judge and guide in everything.'[8] Locke's ambiguous theological views, his emphasis on the Scripture as a system of morality, and his confidence in man's reason were all picked up by those who considered themselves Locke's followers. The Irish philosopher John Toland (1670–1722), in 1696, wrote *Christianity Not Mysterious, Or a Treatise Shewing, That There Is nothing in the Gospel Contrary to Reason, nor ABOVE it*. This was followed in 1730 by the English deist[9] Matthew Tindal (1657–1733), in *Christianity as old as the creation, or the Gospel a Republication of the Religion of Nature*. Thus deists and pantheists[10] were eager to employ Locke in their cause by ignoring his belief in miracles, but running with his statements on the supremacy of reason.

It is a sad spectacle in the history of the church to see leaders entrusted with the defense of the faith, trying to model their philosophy after Plato or Aristotle. Many have thought they had to choose between one pagan philosophy and another. Instead of presenting an antithetical biblical worldview, from the foundation up, they settle for some non-biblical expedient designed to persuade the unbelieving world to accept one particular point of Christianity. They may settle for the use of these pagan philosophers to 'prove' the existence of God. The church does not stand in need of any pagan philosophy; it has been given all that is needed to construct a biblical worldview. Instead of challenging the higher critics with the biblical, antithetical worldview, there were far too many attempts at synthesis. Seemingly desperate for academic respectability, even evangelicals were ready to concede some 'unimportant issues' to the higher critics. Such is the academic atmosphere of the nineteenth

---

8. John Locke, *Essay Concerning Human Understanding* (n.p.: Prometheus Books, 1994), IVxix.14. Cited by Carson, *The Gagging of God*, p. 63.

9. Those who believe that some undefined deity created the world, then left it to its own devices like an absentee landlord. In practice, it is barely indistinguishable from atheism.

10. Those who believe that everything (i.e. nature, the created world itself) is God.

century that surrounded Charles Hodge. When he came back from Germany after postgraduate studies, he perceived himself to have returned unharmed. Perhaps he was mistaken in this optimistic self-evaluation.

CHAPTER 4

CHRONOLOGY AND GENEALOGY

A. WILLIAM HENRY GREEN AT PRINCETON

William Henry Green (1825–1900) was Professor of Old Testament at Princeton Seminary from 1851 until his death. He was also a graduate of Princeton Seminary. He is known as a defender of the reliability of the Old Testament, as seen in his *The Higher Criticism of the Pentateuch*. The book was written in 1895 to refute the documentary (JEDP) hypothesis concerning the authorship of the Pentateuch. He shows an awareness of the importance of presuppositions when he is discussing a biblical or 'religious' subject. He says,

> 'It is noteworthy that the partition hypotheses in all their forms have been elaborated from the beginning in the interest of unbelief. The unfriendly animus of an opponent does not indeed absolve us from patiently and candidly examining his arguments, and accepting whatever facts he may adduce, though *we are not bound to receive his perverted interpretation of them*. Nevertheless we cannot intelligently or safely overlook the *palpable bias against the supernatural*, which has infected the critical theories that we have been reviewing, from first to last. *... Their theories are all inwrought with naturalistic presuppositions*, which cannot be disentangled from them

without their falling to pieces...It is only recently that there has been an attempt at compromise on the part of certain believing scholars, who are disposed to accept these critical theories and endeavor to harmonize them with the Christian faith. But *the inherent vice in these systems cannot be eradicated.* The inevitable result has been to lower the Christian faith to the level of these perverted theories instead of lifting the latter up to the level of a Christian standard.' (emphasis mine)[1]

In late nineteenth and early twentieth-century America, Darwinism was all the rage. It so swept the universities that it was difficult for Christians to oppose it. For an educated person to deny evolution in those days would be as socially unacceptable as for an early seventeenth-century man to deny Aristotle. Both Aristotle and Darwin were wrong, but both were hard to deny in scholarly circles. Princeton's defense was weakened both by the desire for intellectual 'respectability' and even more by an apologetic that did not take seriously enough the fallen mind of man. It seldom occurred to them that scientists too are men with fallen minds and false presuppositions. If 'science' could invent the telephone, telegraph, the cotton gin, and the reaper—how could 'science' be wrong about the millions of years? Of course, the technological advances and inventions actually owed nothing at all to speculations about humans evolving from the slime. Modern science was actually founded on the Christian worldview of a regularly ordered universe, not a random accidental one. In fact a truly random world would make scientific study impossible. Nevertheless, Princeton apologists felt they had to accommodate the latest 'scientific' knowledge. From then on it would be the next atheistic theory to catch on that would dictate our interpretation of Scripture. Without realizing it, the Princetonians were changing hermeneutics from an exact science to an *ad hoc* or *ad lib* device to make the Scripture say whatever was required.

---

1. William Henry Green, 'The Bearing of the Divisive Criticism on the Credibility of the Pentateuch and on Supernatural Religion,' in *The Higher Criticism of the Pentateuch* (New York: Charles Scribner's Sons, 1898), pp. 157–158.

Terrified that they might repeat the error of the Roman Church, they were rather uncritical of chronological aspects of evolutionary thought. But there are great differences between the Galileo affair and Darwinism in relationship to biblical interpretation. The question of the motion of the earth or the sun is not addressed in Scripture. As for the sun, in the common language of appearances, we may speak of 'sunrise' and 'sunset' without postulating a particular theory of astronomy. Even in the twenty-first century there is no substitute for these expressions. The other type of description of the sun's 'motion' is in the poetic genre of biblical literature. The sun is like a 'bridegroom coming out of his chamber...' (Psalm 19:4–6)[2] Interestingly enough, if someone refuses to recognize the poetic genre, or the language of appearance, and boorishly insists that the verses propound an astronomical hypothesis, the verse would still be correct. In the late 18th Century, the great astronomer William Herschel mathematically verified that the sun itself moves through space, as a part of our Milky Way galaxy.

Therefore, even if we violate all hermeneutical rules and force a literalism upon a poetic writing, it is still technically true that the sun moves! Since both the earth and the sun are in motion, we may arbitrarily consider either the earth or the sun as a fixed point for the purposes of mathematical calculations. To land a man on the moon, the earth may be considered as a fixed point as far as the necessary calculations are concerned.

This being the case, someone might be tempted to use this passage as a precise scientific description, the exact opposite to the purposes of the critics. Nevertheless, it would be a violation of sound hermeneutical principles to insist that Psalm 19 spells out, over 2,700 years in advance, Herschel's discovery. It would be an even worse violation of sound hermeneutics to insist that Psalm 19 teaches a false astronomical theory.

---

2. This psalm, utilizing the same language of appearance as when we refer to the sun moving lower in the sky, may be referring to the sun's annual circuit through the constellations, given that verse 3 seems to refer to the stars.

One must resort again to poetic passages to deduce a principle of a stationary earth. Thinking that the Bible taught a stationary earth is a result of the common experience of our senses, and the academic insistence that Aristotle's *Physics* was the standard of scientific knowledge. Should we interpret the following (bold mine) as an astronomical theory affirming the earth's motion, or its non-motion, or neither?

> Psalm 99:1 The Lord reigns; Let the peoples tremble! He dwells *between* the cherubim; **Let the earth be moved**!

Or should we interpret this passage as an astronomical theory that the earth does not move?

> Psalm 104:5 *You who* laid the foundations of the earth, So *that* **it should not be moved** forever,

And if Psalm 104 'proves' the earth to be totally without motion, what does the following verse mean?

> Psalm 62:6 He only *is* my rock and my salvation; *He is* my defense; **I shall not be moved**.

Is this a technical statement that David had been turned into a statue, or a tree? Of course it is not. The earth continues seemingly little changed from generation to generation. David resolves to remain steadfast because the Lord is his Rock upon which his life is founded.

Let us leave the poetic genre for the moment, and focus on historical narrative passages. The chronologies of the Bible, particularly Genesis 5 and 11, are set in historical narrative passages. They are distinguished from other genealogical listings by including detailed numbers of years associated with each generation. Now the hermeneutical error in this case would be to attempt to force some imaginative figurative interpretation on a straightforward historical narrative. The indicators of Hebrew grammar identify the passages as historical narrative, not poetry.[3] The meaning is easy to discern; the passages mean what they say.

What Green's approach accomplishes is to repeat the Roman Church's hermeneutical error in the other direction. Instead of forcing a literalized interpretation upon a poetic passage, Green wants us to force a highly figurative interpretation on an historical narrative. His interpretation is one which is impossible to believe could have been the original intent of the author, or the universal understanding among the Hebrews. Green had become convinced by the evolutionary worldview that man was of great antiquity. Therefore, instead of seeing Genesis 5 and 11 as God-breathed and the only absolutely reliable chronological data we will ever have, he sees Genesis as an embarrassment or problem to be explained away. Green admits that the genealogies look like they give us chronological data, but he cautions:

> 'But if these recently discovered indications of the antiquity of man, over which scientific circles are now so excited, shall, when carefully inspected and thoroughly weighed, demonstrate all that any have imagined they might demonstrate, what then? They will simply show that the popular chronology is based upon a wrong interpretation, and that a select and partial register of ante-Abrahamic names has been mistaken for a complete one.'[4]

Green is not sure these theories are correct. They are merely what 'any have *imagined* they *might* demonstrate...' But just in case there might be a conflict, the Bible must give way at once. While the Christian world should insist on a hermeneutically sound interpretation of Genesis 5 and 11, Green will not or cannot give us one. In the Christian worldview, nothing is more certain than a correctly exegeted passage of Scripture. For William H. Green,

---

3. See for example Don Batten *et al.*, 'Is Genesis poetry / figurative, a theological argument (polemic) and thus not history?' <creation.com/fh>, 30 November 2007.

4. William Henry Green, 'Primeval Chronology,' *Bibliotheca Sacra,* April 1890; available <www.geocities.com/athens/thebes/7755/PrimevalChronology.html>.

we should abandon the biblical chronology at once, just in case someone, some day, gets proof of man's antiquity.

Many since have followed Green's unsound method of ascertaining the meaning of Genesis 5 and 11. In place of a credible exegesis of Genesis 5, we are directed to other passages that contain only sketchy genealogical information. In order to ignore the Hebrew grammar and syntax of Genesis, the reader's attention is misdirected to the English translation of the Greek New Testament. Matthew Chapter 1 is brought to our attention. There are three names omitted in Matthew 1:8. They are Ahaziah, Joash, and Amaziah.[5] The only way we know there are names missing is from the Old Testament's more complete information. In other words, the Hebrew record is more complete than the Greek New Testament summary. Our thesis that the Old Testament presents a complete chronology remains undisturbed by such irrelevant misdirection away from the text. Matthew One needs to be exegeted in its own context, not merely abused in order to discredit Genesis. Continuing to ignore Genesis, Green next directs us to 1 Chronicles 26 where we are told there is a 'most striking' example of how biblical genealogies omit names. But, of course, 1 Chronicles is merely a list of names with no numerical information, as everyone acknowledges.

Toward the end of the article Green finally takes notice of the difference between the detailed genealogies of Genesis and the other mere list of names he has been dealing with elsewhere in Scripture. But now, Green supposes he has established an 'analogy of Scripture' that shows that *all* genealogies in Scripture omit names. But what of the great difference between detailed information on the age of the patriarch at the birth of the son, the number of years lived after the birth of the son, and the total number of years of his life? Is that not significantly different from a general listing of selected ancestors? Green speculates that the genealogies were not given for

---

5. For a complete explanation of Matthew 1, see F. N. Jones, *The Chronology of the Old Testament*, 36–41. Matthew 1:8 may omit the three monarchs whose 'Davidic' line was most contaminated by Omri's daughter Athaliah. Matthew 1:17 can speak of the 17 monarchs as only 14 generations, since 3 of them ruled for three years or less, hardly enough to count as a 'generation.'

the purpose of constructing a chronology. He says they merely give us individual examples showing how the lifespan of humanity was gradually reduced.

B. A BIBLICAL SOLUTION

What can the Christian worldview say in response to these assertions? We should learn to distinguish between assertion and proof. Only God's 'assertions' should be taken as absolutely conclusive proof. All that is necessary to 'refute' Green's assertion is to make a counter-assertion. Here is one from Henry Morris regarding Genesis 5:

> 'The record is perfectly natural and straightforward and is obviously intended to give both the necessary genealogical data to denote the promised lineage and also the only reliable chronological framework we have for the antediluvian period of history.'[6]

One major difference is that Green makes no attempt to provide a credible or even understandable exegesis of Genesis 5, but Morris does give us an exegesis consistent with normal hermeneutical principles. No special pleading is necessary for Morris; he does not have to ignore the context before him.

Green has two alleged justifications for his assertions: First, the supposed analogy of Scripture and secondly, the alleged purpose of the genealogies. The genealogies are asserted to have no chronological purpose. What evidence do we have of that? All we have is the fact that the genealogies neglected to sum up a 'grand total' of the years from Creation to the Flood. This would be a significant observation if it can be established that divine revelation is required to perform simple addition. But mathematics requires only the created order God has given us, not a special revelation for each addition problem.

It is quite true that the genealogies of Genesis are representative rather than complete, but in a totally different way than that

---

6. Morris, Henry M., 'The Lost World,' in *The Genesis Record* (Grand Rapids, Michigan: Baker Book House, 1976), p. 154.

asserted by critics. The genealogies are complete *chronologically*. Their representative nature is only in their interest in tracing a line from Adam to Noah, then from Noah to Abraham. Only one son is mentioned, because only one son was a progenitor of Abraham through Noah. The father had others sons and daughters. The purpose of the genealogy in tracing the ultimately Messianic line is met by mentioning only the son who is a link to Abraham. The progenitor was not always the first-born son and seldom, if ever, the only son.

Green also makes the commonly observed statement that there is not perfect agreement among the Masoretic text, the Septuagint, and the Samaritan Pentateuch. This is an extremely weak objection. Four examples will be given to demonstrate the weakness and irrelevance of Green's objections to the Genesis chronology.

First, what does Green think of the value of the Samaritan Pentateuch when he is working in his Old Testament specialty? '...in our present argument no significance can be attached to the Samaritan Pentateuch...'[7] Why then, is it so important to bring up the less reliable Samaritan Pentateuch to oppose the Masoretic text of Genesis? Does it now suddenly have 'significance' in the book of Genesis that it lacks elsewhere? Similarly, the LXX (Septuagint) shows a pattern of altering the numbers in the genealogy that, once again, shows it less reliable than the Masoretic text.

The second weakness is the irrelevance of the observation. Even if we take the least accurate account (LXX) we have the time from Adam to Abraham as 3,312 years instead of the more accurate Masoretic figure of 1,946 years. But what is the purpose of abusing the Scripture in such a way? Will the evolutionist now be happy with the extra thousand years, when he insists on millions of years?

The third weakness is Green's superficial understanding of biblical chronology. Christians should by now be weary of those with a superficial understanding of biblical chronology who so easily dismiss the meticulously detailed work of Archbishop Ussher. In the twenty-first century, Floyd Nolen Jones, as the subject of

---

7. William Henry Green, *The Higher Criticism of the Pentateuch*, p. 45.

his doctoral studies, has done a painstakingly meticulous study of biblical chronology. The Christian world is well advised to invite critics of Genesis chronology to come back later, after they have refuted the careful work that has been done in support of Genesis. Ignorance and ridicule should never be accepted as a refutation of biblical chronology. The present time cries out for Christians to be more skeptical of man's fallible theories and totally accepting of God's infallible Word.

A fourth great weakness of Green's presentation is by far the greatest. What happens to biblical interpretation when Green's assertions trump sound hermeneutical principles? Not one person in ten thousand would think Genesis 5 to be devoid of chronological information. Is that information valid? Of what use is our defense of biblical authority if the 'interpretation' of the text must constantly change in order to conform to whatever atheistic philosophy is currently popular? If the Scripture is said to get it wrong on earthly things, how are we to trust it on 'spiritual' things? Since the Bible is not a *textbook* on history or science, is it therefore unreliable when it touches on those areas of life? Is there something more compelling about constantly outdated textbooks over the biblical God-breathed record?

There are some indications of Green's lack of understanding of biblical chronology. He asserts that biblical chronology would have to say '…Noah was for fifty-eight years the contemporary of Abraham, and Shem actually survived him thirty-five years…'[8]

There are two things that must be said in reply. First, if that is what the biblical chronology actually said, that is *precisely* what we should believe. Second, the biblical chronology does not say any such thing. The actual figures are:

Noah: 2948 BC to 1998 BC
Shem: 2446 BC to 1846 BC
Abraham: 1996 BC to 1821 BC.

---

8. William Henry Green, 'Primeval Chronology,' p. 303.

In reality, then, Noah was a contemporary of Abraham exactly *zero* years, not 58 years. Shem did not survive Abraham at all, let alone by 35 years. William H. Green made some very valuable contributions to Old Testament study, but offers little of value on the topic of biblical chronology. Green was a godly scholar, caught up in the evolutionary euphoria. He has a better excuse for his compromising view than do Christians of the twenty-first century. We would be far more culpable to follow his error than he was to propose it.

What about the biblical chronology? Are there gaps in the genealogies?

Oxford Hebrew professor James Barr has said,

'Probably, so far as I know, there is no professor of Hebrew or Old Testament at any world-class university who does not believe that the writer(s) of Genesis 1–11 intended to convey to their readers the ideas that…the figures contained in the Genesis genealogies provided by simple addition a chronology from the beginning of the world up to the later stages in the biblical story.'[9]

This statement from Barr should alert Christians that a strategy of accommodation will not be a successful apologetic with intelligent unbelievers or liberals. Barr knows what Genesis says; he simply does not believe it. An apologist who wants to agree with Barr that the biblical chronology is false, but that the Bible did not 'really' *mean* to give a chronology, is bound to fail.

Although the great theologian and church father Augustine had but scanty knowledge of both Hebrew and science, he is often seized upon by neo-evangelical 'old-earth' proponents as an ally. But regardless of his confusion regarding the days of creation (that they were what we would call milliseconds in duration), he totally rejected the 'old-earth' view. This can be seen in a largely overlooked passage in his *City of God.*

---

9. James Barr, 'Letter to David C. C. Watson,' 1984; available at <creation.com/barr>, accessed 20 September 2008.

'Consequently, how utterly unconvincing is the presumptuous prattling of those who maintain that Egyptian astronomical science has a history of more than 100,000 years!...we know from Holy Writ...6,000 years have not yet elapsed from the days of Adam, the first man, should we not ridicule, rather than bother to refute, those who strive to convince us of a temporal duration so different and so utterly contrary to this established truth?... We, on the other hand, have the support of divine authority in the history of our religion. Accordingly, whatever in secular histories runs counter to it we do not hesitate to brand as wholly false...'[10]

The straightforward reading of Genesis 5 and 11 prevailed universally in Christendom for more than eighteen centuries. Only when one was convinced by ancient evolutionary thought (Babylon, Greece, Egypt) or modern evolutionary thought (Darwin), was any other 'interpretation' suggested. Most of those today who advocate a non-literal view of Genesis admit that their view did not arise from the text itself (exegesis), but was determined by outside ('scientific') considerations. Those who try to fit millions of extra years into the genealogies, usually also deny the worldwide flood of Noah, and the literal days of Genesis One. These are indications that for them so-called 'science' is a higher authority than divine revelation. This triumph of empiricism over Scripture is destructive to maintaining a consistent Christian worldview. It also makes the interpretation of Scripture an impossible task, since they can make a word mean what they want it to mean. This only reinforces the unbeliever's dogma that the Bible can be made to say anything. Although fatally false, such a view is encouraged by compromises with the current cultural consensus.

---

10. Augustine, 'About the Most Mendacious Vanity of the Egyptians, in Which They Ascribe to Their Science an Antiquity of a Hundred Thousand Years,' in *City of God*, ed. Vernon J. Bourke, trans. Walsh, Zema, Monahan. and Honan (Garden City, New York: Image Books, 1958), Book 18, Chapter 40.

The errors of Green's article on chronology were perpetuated by Warfield and are still uncritically cited by many others today. For this reason it merits discussion and refutation. By equating the schematized listing of Matthew 1 with the detailed genealogy of Genesis 5, we get an unwarranted expansion of the word 'begat'. By a similar hermeneutic error the word 'son' has been stretched beyond the breaking point. The same error has been employed to distort the meaning of 'day' in Genesis 1. The error involves searching the whole semantic range of *possible* meanings of a word, selecting the meaning most suited to your purpose, then insisting that your selected meaning applies to the Genesis passage—regardless of contextual factors. This is eisegesis, not exegesis. Because some other context uses a word in a rare figurative way, does not warrant imposing the figurative meaning on the Genesis context.

One argument against the biblical genealogies is the supposition that both Genesis 5 and Genesis 11 list ten names, the last of whom had three sons. This is supposed to show that Genesis genealogies are just like Matthew One's list of names. If the supposition were correct (that there is a list of ten in each chapter), it could be explained by ten being exactly (perhaps coincidentally) correct. But the lists do not appear in such a pattern. The 'pattern' has to be imposed on them. Adam to Noah (Gen. 5) has ten names with Noah having three sons. Gen. 11 lists nine names from Shem to Terah who had three sons. In order to manufacture a parallel, one has to count in a different way in each chapter. Green, for example, wants ten in each list. He must then *not count* one of Noah's sons as the final name, for that would make eleven. Next he *must count* one of Terah's sons in order to make ten, because there are only nine names. This pretended parallel seems born out of desperation rather than exegesis.[11]

Let us consider the usage of the word 'father' (*'ab* or אב) Hugh Ross claims that because a word can have an extended meaning such as 'grandfather' or rarely further extended to descendant, we

---

11. Travis Freeman, 'The Genesis 5 and 11 fluidity question', *Journal of Creation* **19**(2):83–90, 2005 <creation.com/fluidity>.

should take the extended meaning in the genealogies of Genesis. Actually, the word 'father' is not even used in the genealogies of Genesis. Without casting any doubt on Ross's Christianity or his knowledge of modern astrophysical theories, it is not hard to see that his attempted use of Hebrew examples is quite faulty. This is just one of many of Ross's erroneous claims about the Hebrew text, demonstrating how his claims should be greeted with skepticism and checked carefully.

So let us consider the word actually used in Genesis 5, ילד (*yālad*) meaning 'to be born'. In the genealogies the verb appears in a causative (*hiphil*) form meaning 'to beget, or **cause to be born**'. Some translations have translated the verb form as 'became the father of' which leads to discussion of the absent Hebrew noun 'father'. If we discuss the verb actually used, a different conclusion is even more apparent. [YLT]**Genesis 5:7** 'And Seth liveth after his **begetting** Enos eight hundred and seven years, and **begetteth** sons and daughters.' The verb beget is followed by a direct object indicator (*'et*) and the name of the son begotten. This means that the begetting occurred when the father was X number of years old. Even if we assume without evidence that the begotten one was a grandson, the birth still occurred when the progenitor was X years old. The *hiphil* stem used constantly in the genealogies 'communicates the subject participating in [the] action that caused the event'.[12] In other words, the father 'caused' the birth of his son.

Further supporting evidence is found in the constant refrain following the mention of the one particular son, 'and begat [other] sons and daughters'. This is unmistakably referring to natural sons and daughters, not remote descendants.

The interlocking formula of Genesis 5 is not a simple 'A begat B' as in Matthew 1, but a more complex and interlocking format, 'When A had lived x years, he begat B. After the begetting of (becoming the father of) B, A lived y years. All the days of A were z years.'

---

12. Jonathan Sarfati, 'Biblical Chronogenealogies,' *TJ (now Journal of Creation)* **17**(3):14–18, 2003 available <creation.com/chronogenealogies>, accessed 20 September 2008.

'The interlocking nature of the information provided is forceful internal evidence that, instead of having a broken or discontinuous line of descent, the material in Genesis 5 and 11 presents a continuous line of descent.'[13]

The remarks of Gerhard Hasel of Andrews University highlight the importance of our presuppositions in dealing with such issues.

'There is a scholarly tradition that argues that wherever and whenever the conclusions of historians, scientists, sociologists, etc., are in disagreement with the Bible, the Bible will have to be reinterpreted to be brought into harmony with these conclusions. Another scholarly position is not so ready to yield everything outside of faith and conduct to the norms of the investigator, but maintains that where the Bible impinges on subjects such as history, geography, ethnology, botany, astronomy, etc., it is trustworthy. Thus the Word of God is seen to impinge on historical, scientific and other phenomena. For them the subordinating of biblical reports to modern scientific reconstructions and interpretations remains highly problematic and reverses the structure of authority.'[14]

To insert even 10,000 years into the genealogies, it would be necessary to add at least 250 names to them. It is inconceivable that such detailed information as is presented to us in Genesis is so shot full of holes. It would render a genealogy useless to have the vast majority of descendants omitted. Further, the apologetic concession made would be worse than useless, as the evolutionist would not be satisfied with a mere 10,000 years.

We have in the chronologies of Genesis a fatal blow to the evolutionary philosophy. The chronologies absolutely exclude such common myths as 'prehistoric times,' since Adam was the first human being and his history is recorded. To take the Scripture seriously is to exclude the possibility of evolution and the evolutionary time scale. The Christian worldview is squarely opposed to evolutionary thought and must not twist the Bible to accommodate it.

---

13. Gerhard F. Hasel, 'The Meaning of the Chronogenealogies of Genesis 5 and 11,' *Origins* 7, no. 2 1980 available www.grisda.org/origins/07053.htm, accessed 10 January 2007.

14. Ref 13.

All the indications are that the genealogies have no gaps. Evolutionary interpretation would demand hundreds of gaps in a list of ten names; this is unbelievable. Where would the gaps be inserted, if there were any? Jonathan Sarfati provides these examples of direct father-son relationships:

Seth: Seth is definitely a direct son of Adam and Eve, and seen as a replacement for Abel. (Genesis 4:25)

> Enosh: must be a son of Seth, because Seth named him (Gen. 4:25)
>
> Enoch: Jude 14 says Enoch was seventh from Adam, which indicates a straightforward father-son relationship from Adam to Enoch.
>
> Noah: Lamech named him, so Lamech must be his father, not just an ancestor. (Gen. 5:29)
>
> Shem, Ham and Japheth were definitely ordinary sons of Noah, since they accompanied him on the Ark.
>
> Arphaxad was plainly a son of Shem, because he was born two years after the Flood. (Gen. 11:10)
>
> Abram, Haran, and Nahor were Terah's ordinary sons, since they journeyed together from Ur of the Chaldees. (Gen. 11:31)[15]

Since it is a well established historical fact that Abraham lived about 2000 BC, all the imaginary 'gaps' would have to fit into those very places that we know are listing the direct literal sons. If we are really interested in an analogy of Scripture, there can be no reason to guess that the few remaining names have millions of years between them. The biblical record makes perfect sense as it is; the figurative

---

15. Sarfati, Ref. 12.

guesswork varies wildly. Does the Bible have an objective meaning or does each person impose his own unique meaning on the text? When the one objective historical-grammatical meaning is set aside, a dozen speculations rush in to fill the void. Shall we render the whole Bible meaningless just to 'rescue' the Bible from this conflict with naturalistic philosophy?

The case of Methuselah provides further evidence of the accuracy of biblical chronology. Methuselah: Enoch, a pre-Flood prophet (Jude 14), gave his son a name meaning 'when he dies it shall be sent', and the Masoretic chronology without any gaps would place his death in the year of the Flood.

It should be noted that, for our purposes, the important point about Methuselah is not the meaning of his name but the number of years he lived. If the chronologist had been simply making up numbers and had made Methuselah 5 years older, it would have meant Methuselah lived through the Flood. This would conflict with the account that only Noah and his family survived, just eight people. As it is, the biblical chronology shows that Methuselah died in the year of the Flood.[16] This would be an example of the precision of the chronology, rather than a collection of vague allusions to distant descendants.

Since most people are quite unfamiliar with many of these individuals, it is easy to imagine them as living with centuries between each name. But when we take a closer look at what the Scripture says about them, another picture emerges. Every time we know the background and detail about the persons named we find a father-son direct relationship. It would be totally arbitrary and unreasonable to assert that the few remaining names have huge gaps between them. Everything we know for sure about them verifies the grammatical-historical interpretation of the genealogies.

Chronology is to history as the skeleton is to the body. Chronology provides the framework of history. Chronology is one of the most important distinctions between history and mythology. Since the revelation of Scripture is so profoundly rooted in history,

---

16. For a discussion on the meaning of Methuselah's name, see Sarfati, 'Biblical Chronogenealogies,' Ref. 12.

it is almost incredible that Christians would so easily discard it. Indeed, it is discarded for extremely superficial reasons. As with the related issues, it is not the text of Scripture, but outside influences that have created the impression that the chronology of Scripture is not worth the effort it takes to study it. The outside influence is the uniformitarian time scale that forms the foundation of evolutionary thought. The biblical record tells us of Adam and Eve, the first human beings. Those who lightly (and ignorantly) discard the biblical chronology are forced to fill the 'vacuum' thus created with pagan mythology, commonly known as 'prehistoric times' or 'ape-men' or other mythologies. Destroying biblical chronology inevitably leads to the destruction of the essential historical foundation of revelation.

Floyd N. Jones has performed the tedious exhaustive study of biblical chronology for Christians of the twenty-first century. He describes the attack on the consistent Christian worldview as Satan's trident, a three-pronged fork. The central fork is evolutionary thought; the other two forks are derived from it. Those other forks are, he says, textual criticism (perhaps better stated as 'higher criticism' to avoid tarring the legitimate enterprise of trying to understand what the original text said) and the attack on the chronological framework of Scripture. The theory of evolution will not and cannot remain a biological hypothesis. To its adherents it is a worldview. It is the glasses through which every aspect of life and thought is viewed. Jones introduces his work by establishing the correct foundation. Will it be a man-centered worldview or a God-centered worldview?

Dr. Jones provides answers to many of the chronological issues that have been raised in Old Testament study. While the man-centered worldview will always err, the God-centered worldview offers us the hope of arriving at the truth. Jones builds on the right foundation. He defends the biblical account against alleged errors or contradictions, making the book valuable in that regard as well. Dr. Jones himself had once held the man-centered view. Speaking of himself, he says:

'Until his thirty-sixth year, the humanistic uniformitarian-evolutionary beliefs held sway over his life. However, he now candidly acknowledges to hold the God centered world view... [and is] firmly committed not only to special creation of the universe, earth, and man but to all the other supernatural and miraculous events as recorded in Scripture.'[17]

The Princetonians are not alone in their attempt to make the biblical chronology seem hopeless by bringing up the Samaritan Pentateuch and the Septuagint. These have some differences with the Masoretic text. Usually, the mere mention of these differences is assumed to be sufficient excuse to dismiss the biblical record as unreliable. Yet both of these texts indicate the authors were trying to 'fix' the Hebrew text. The Samaritan Pentateuch writers rid the text of 'embarrassing' reports that some antediluvians waited 100 years or more to have the son named in the genealogy. It is usually overlooked that the son named in the genealogy is not necessarily the first child, nor the only son. For example, Seth follows Adam in the genealogy of Genesis 5. But we know that Seth was no less than the third son of Adam. We do not know how many other sons—and daughters—preceded Seth. The genealogies of Genesis, as well as the narrative itself, are primarily interested in following the Messianic line of descent, first down to Noah, then to Abraham. Besides all this, the Samaritan Pentateuch abounds in inaccuracies.

When the Samaritan Pentateuch was rediscovered for the Western world in the seventeenth century, it was met with the usual enthusiasm reserved for new discoveries. Several critical scholars of the 18th century were extravagant in their praise for it.

'Here the matter rested until 1815, when Gesenius (*De Pent. Samuel Origine, Indole, et Auctoritate*) abolished the remnant of the authority of the Samaritan Pentateuch. So masterly, lucid, and full are his arguments and his proofs that there has been, and will be, no further question as to the absence of all value in this recension, and in its

---

17. Floyd Nolen Jones, 'Establishing the Correct Foundation,' in *The Chronology of the Old Testament* (Green Forest, Arkansas: Master Books, 2005), p. 3.

pretended emendations. In fact, a glance at the systematic arrangement of the variations, of which he first of all bethought himself, is quite sufficient to convince the reader at once that they are for the most part mere blunders, arising from an imperfect knowledge of the first elements of grammar and exegesis. That others owe their existence to a studied design of conforming certain passages to the Samaritan mode of thought, speech, and faith...'[18]

The Septuagint, contrary to the Hebrew text, seemed to impose a gradual and continuous decline in the age spans of the postdiluvian patriarchs. For the antediluvian patriarchs, the LXX frequently adds 100 years to the age at begetting the son mentioned, then subtracts 100 years from the years lived afterward, leaving the total lifespans as they are in the Masoretic Hebrew text. For the postdiluvians, the LXX tends to add 100 again to the age at begetting the son named, but leave the years after the begetting the same. This leaves the post-flood patriarchs with longer total life spans. Thus they achieve the desired pattern of gradual and continuous decline, rather than the sharp drop in life spans reported in the Hebrew text.[19]

Augustine explains the Septuagint's systematic changes as due to a rationalistic belief that the Genesis patriarchs could not have lived as long as recorded in the Hebrew text. Therefore, they speculated that one of our years equaled ten of the biblical years. That rationalistic interpretation allowed them to think that Methuselah lived only 96.9 years, rather than 969 years. This speculation ran into an absurdity in Gen. 5:12 and 5:15 where their theory would have a father be only 7 years old in one case (where the text said 70), and 6 ½ in another (where the text said 65). One false theory usually requires several more false theories to prop it up. To rescue their theory, they added 100 years to the time of begetting the listed son, so as to make the

---

18. James Strong, and John McClintock, 'Samaritan Pentateuch,' in *Cyclopedia of Biblical Theological and Ecclesiastical Literature*, Ages Digital Library ed., p. 335ff.

19. For a detailed study of the LXX see Floyd N. Jones, *The Septuagint: A Critical Analysis*, sixth ed. (The Woodlands, Texas, 2000).

father at least 16 years old. See chart on page 76. Such is the folly of attempting to 'rescue' the God-breathed record with rationalistic theories.[20]

It should be noted that critics of biblical chronology also reject the chronologies of the LXX and the Samaritan Pentateuch. Bringing them up appears to be nothing more than a smokescreen to cover the fact that they have adopted an evolutionary chronology and really do not accept *any* version of biblical chronology. The conclusion of C. F. Keil is that the Hebrew text is the only reliable account:

> 'That the principal divergencies of both texts [Samaritan Pentateuch and LXX] from the Hebrew are intentional changes, based upon chronological theories or cycles, is sufficiently evident from their internal character...No such intention is discernable in the numbers of the Hebrew text; consequently every attack upon the historical character of its numerical statements has entirely failed, and no tenable argument can be adduced against their correctness.'[21]

When the chronology of Scripture is dismissed as irrelevant or likely to offend a scientific consensus, unforeseen consequences follow. Compromising the Bible to accommodate an alien worldview (the 'scientific' consensus) leads to an inability to understand history. The first eleven chapters of Genesis exclude the evolutionary worldview so absolutely that from a biblical worldview, evolution is 'DOA'. But evangelical compromisers are doing their best to give evolution 'CPR'. The Christian world is far overdue to be offended at the cavalier treatment of the Word of God, and far less concerned with whether the absolute truth of the written Word offends the

---

20. Augustine, Book 15, Chapter 14, 'That The Years in Ancient Times Were of The Same Length As Our Own.' in *The City of God*, ed. Philip Schaff, trans. Marcus Dods (Nicene and Post-Nicene Fathers: First Series, Volume 2; reprint, Albany, OR: Ages Software, 1997), pp. 631–33 (page citations are to the reprint edition).

21. C.F. Keil, and F. Delitzsch, 'The History of Adam,' in *Commentary on the Old Testament*, trans. James Martin, Volume 1, The Pentateuch (Grand Rapids, Michigan: William B. Eerdmans Publishing Company, 1976), p. 123.

COMPARISON OF HEBREW TEXT WITH ALTERED TEXTS OF THE SEPTUAGINT AND THE SAMARITAN PENTATEUCH
THE AGE OF THE PATRIARCH AT THE BIRTH OF THE NAMED SON

NAME	HEBREW TEXT	SEPTUAGINT	SAMARITAN
Adam	130	230*	130
Seth	105	205*	105
Enosh	90	190*	90
Cainan	70	170*	70
Mahalaleel	65	165*	65
Jared	162	162	62
Enoch	65	165*	65
Methuselah	187	167	67
Lamech	182	188	53
Noah	500	500	500
Shem	100	100	100
Arphaxad	35	135*	135
Shelah	30	130*	130
Eber	34	134*	134
Peleg	30	130*	130
Reu	30	130*	130

Septuagint (LXX), As explained by Augustine: The rationalistic principles of the LXX made 1 ordinary years equal to 10 "Bible" years so that patriarchs who were said to live 900 "years," really lived only 90 years. Because this formula make the father too young, (some as young a 3 years old !) the LXX felt free to add 100 years to the biblical age (marked with *) wherever they thought necessary.

Samaritan Pentateuch's rationalists believed some father waited too long to have children. Working from the LXX version they adjusted the figures so that the father would be between 50 and 150 years old at the birth of his named son. The well known Noah was left as in the correct Hebrew text. They must have assumed in error that the son was the firstborn, which is not true in many cases. The one son mentioned is the one who is the ancestor of Noah, then Abraham, and ultimately Christ.

unbeliever. After all, the Scripture plainly tells us that the unbeliever will not have God in his knowledge—we should not be so surprised to find it is true. Compromise views frequently tell us that the Bible is not really interested in giving us chronological information. One might wonder if one who makes such statements has ever read the Old Testament with their eyes open. Consider just this one example of many from the Biblical revelation:

> Genesis 7:1: In the six hundredth year of Noah's life, in the second month, the seventeenth day of the month, on that day all the fountains of the great deep were broken up, and the windows of heaven were opened.

Can anyone seriously suggest that God was not concerned to give us chronological truth? If the compromisers had written Genesis, it would read something like this: 'Long, long ago, in a land far away there lived an old man we call Noah...' That is, of course, what we definitely do not find.

C. THE IMPORTANCE OF THE ISSUE

So far from being insignificant, the historical framework provided by Genesis 5 and 11 is one of the most outstanding features distinguishing the Genesis narrative from pagan mythology. Mythology lacks a chronological framework. Mythology tells of imaginary people who lived an unspecified time 'long ago' in some unspecified place. The great theological truths that the allegorizers say they are so interested in are rooted in history. The twenty-first-century Westerner may be easily convinced that the chronology of Scripture is insignificant, but that is not the biblical view. When the biblical chronology is rejected, we are left with nothing but mythology. We can state it this way: When one generation throws out biblical chronology, it will not be long before the following generations call the narrative mythology. This is logical consistency. If the biblical record lacks a chronology, its historical nature is immediately thrown into question. This march toward mythology has been demonstrated in the history of the church.

When compromisers must finally give up the eisegesis of desperation, they are faced with a choice. Will they humble themselves, repent, and return to the biblical record? Sometimes they do, but too often they either search for another bit of hermeneutical sophistry or they give up and deny that the Bible gives us an historical account. We can see this decline in the continuum of 'Reformed Orthodoxy' from Old Princeton to Westminster East. Princeton was willing to discard the biblical chronology, but wanted to maintain the historical reliability of the Genesis record. But a purported 'history' that lacks a chronological framework will inevitably be considered mythical. That is the way of myths.

The problem for the allegorizers is compounded when they finally give up on the various eisegetical attempts to harmonize creation with evolution. We can see what happened in the short span from the renowned Old Testament scholar E. J. Young (1907–1968) to his son Davis Young. E. J. Young valiantly defended Genesis 1–3. He argued powerfully against day-age and framework schemes as exegetically flawed. He defended everything about the Genesis narrative *except* the chronology. His son, Davis Young, went from one figurative compromise to another, finally denying that the account gave us any reliable real history.

Meredith Kline (1922–2007) hung on to his hypothesis, but at the cost of putting in doubt the reality of the events recorded. Calling them 'upper register' events is a bit of sophistry worthy of Karl Barth. Barth is reputed to have said words to this effect, 'It is not important whether the serpent existed or not; the important thing is what he said.' Once a person has adopted the evolutionary chronology, no amount of sophistry can harmonize that view with Scripture.

To complete the downward slide into mythology, we see that Westminster's Old Testament professor (until he agreed to resign on 1 August 2008), Peter Enns (1961–), has chosen to label the early chapters of Genesis as mythology. He arrived at this conclusion during his graduate studies at Harvard under non-Christian scholars. He did not confront and refute the evolutionary view of Genesis but surrendered to it. He says in an attempt to salvage something from the Bible:

> 'But one might ask *why* it is that God *can't* use the category *we* call 'myth' to speak to *ancient* Israelites....We must begin our thinking by acknowledging the ancient Near Eastern myths are almost certainly older than the versions recorded for us in the Bible.'[22]

There are several things of note here. Enns' 'Why can't' question is similar to the question, 'Why can't God use evolution?' Of course the issue was never about the ability of the omnipotent God, but the truthfulness of His revelation in Scripture. We could better ask, 'Why can't God reveal what He actually did in time and space history to bring this universe into being? And why won't we believe Him?' Enns calls the biblical revelation a *version* of pagan myths of the Near East.[23] Fortunately, Westminster suspended him,[24] and he resigned on 1 August 2008.[25]

We must choose between the Bible and the evolutionary philosophy falsely called science. The mistake of Christians who tried to accept the scientific part of Darwinism, while rejecting the atheistic part, was to think that any of its broad historical claims were scientific fact. The initiators of the mythical view were motivated by their evolutionary presuppositions to deny Mosaic authorship of Genesis, and give priority to pagan myths. Not only is the JEDP late composition theory in error; but Moses used the much earlier patriarchal *toledoth* passage form[26], which predates the pagan mythology. The Bible affirms the linguistic ability of the first man Adam. The long lives of the early patriarchs guaranteed a continuity

---

22. Peter E. Enns, *Inspiration and Incarnation: Evangelicals and the Problem of the Old Testament*, (Grand Rapids, Michigan: Baker Academic, 2005), 49–50. Cited by Paul Elliott in *Christianity and Neo-Liberalism*, p.104.

23. G. K. Beale is professor of New Testament and Kenneth T. Wessner Chair of Biblical Studies, Wheaton College, reviews the book in *Journal of the Evangelical Theological Society*, June 2006.

24. Sarah Pulliam, 'Westminster Theological Suspension: Peter Enns's book Inspiration and Incarnation created a two-year theological battle that resulted in his suspension', *Christianity Today* 52, April 2008; <www.christianitytoday.com/ct/2008/aprilweb-only/114-24.0.html>.

25. Joint Statement by WTS and Professor Enns, <www.wts.edu/stayinformed/view.html?id=187>, 23 July 2008.

in the preservation of the historical records. What similarities there are in pagan mythology can be explained from the fact that all peoples are descended from Adam and again from Noah. Therefore we are not surprised to find accounts of creation, the fall, and the Flood in corrupted form. Pagan mythology may picture the world on the back of elephants or giant tortoises, so we may recognize that the omniscient Creator did not inspire those accounts.

The Bible preserves the only absolutely accurate historical account of the creation by divine inspiration. Pagan mythology either corrupts the recollection of the event, or deliberately distorts the account to favor the 'gods' of their own making. The pagan peoples were disconnected from the godly line by the confusion of language at Babel.

It is vital to preserve the historical nature of the Genesis record. Biblical revelation is rooted in the reality of God's acting in real history. It cannot justly be reduced to an Aesop's fable where an imaginary story teaches us a character lesson. Yet that is where the road leads that begins with a rejection of biblical chronology. As Francis Schaeffer wrote: 'The mentality of the whole Scripture, not just of this one psalm [136], is that creation is as historically real as the history of the Jews and our own present moment of time.'[27] Schaeffer also speaks of the historical reality of the Flood.

'From China to the American Indian and even the pre-Columbian Indians, one finds in strange forms the myth of the great flood. Most of these myths have weird elements—foolish elements, for example the descriptions of the boat that was used. In the Bible these strange and

---

26. The *toledoth* (plural) are the passages that recur in Genesis of the form *'These are the generations of ...'*. Some suggest that this indicates that Moses, under God's inspiration, compiled much of Genesis from ancient texts, and that these *toledoth* mark the boundaries between areas derived from individual such texts, either as a sign-off on the preceding one, or as titles of the segments following, except for the first segment, Gen. 1:1 to 2:3. See.<creation.com/toledoths>. Finally, there are those who accept the *toledoth* hypothesis, but regard them as colophons, that is, as subscripts or bibliographical references at the *end* of each segment, including the first one.

27. Francis A. Schaeffer, *Genesis in space and time, the flow of biblical history*. (Downers Grove, Illinois: InterVarsity Press, 1972), p. 15.

foolish elements are not there. We would say, then, that the Bible gives us the history of the flood; the myths all over the world are contorted, but show that men everywhere have a memory of it. Here in the Bible is the one flood story whose details, including the construction of the vessel, are reasonable.'[28]

D. PAGAN GLOBAL FLOOD STORIES

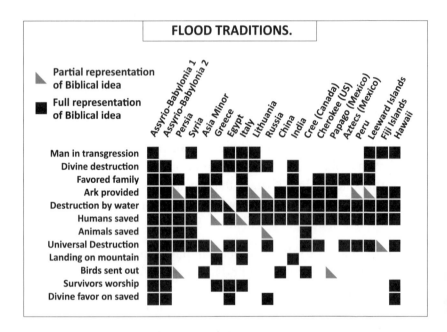

See Jonathan Sarfati, 'Noah's Flood and the Gilgamesh Epic.' <creation.com/Gilgamesh>. Note the following from that article:

1. The best explanation of the widespread Flood stories is that all peoples, being descended from Noah, had some memory of that Flood.

---

2. Only the Bible recorded the events accurately. Others dis-
    torted details, often to favor their own 'gods' or heroes.

3. The Genesis account is older and original as the patriarchs
    were literate and kept records. The inspiration of Scripture
    preserved their accuracy in detail.

Dr. Duane Gish, in *Dinosaurs by Design*, says there are more than 270
stories from different cultures around the world about a devastating
flood. In fact, 'every Amazonian society ever studied has a legend
about a great flood', according to Dr. Alexandra Aikhenvald.[29]

The chart on page 80 shows the similarities that several myths
have with the Genesis account of Noah's Flood. Although there are
varying degrees of accuracy, these legends and stories all contain
similarities to aspects of the same historical event—Noah's Flood.
The modern critical approach assumes that since so many nations
have flood-myths, the Bible must record Israel's flood-myth. The
reality-based biblical worldview sees that there are many stories of
the Flood because the Flood actually happened in space-time human
history, and because all the nations are descendants of Noah. Only
the Bible preserves the events with perfect accuracy. Other accounts
are filled with errors and distortions.

The biblical account of the Ark describes in detailed dimensions
a huge three-deck sea-worthy ship capable of remaining afloat and
stable on the stormy waters. Mythology will usually have a cube-
shaped boat, a canoe, or even raft and all without specific time or
dimension indicators. The Genesis record's details on chronology and
dimensions are the stuff of which history is made. When modern
artists portray the Ark as a large crowded bathtub that would sink
in a minute at sea, they do a great disservice to Scripture. Even if
unintentionally, they inject a mythical and impossible element into
the God-breathed revelation.

In the biblical revelation God the Creator guides and governs
history. In mythology there is no infinite yet personal God. In the

---

29. Cited in Barnett, A., 'For want of a word', *New Scientist* **181**(2432):44–47, 31 January 2004.

biblical worldview, God not only is eternally existent, but He has given us His own word preserved in Holy Scripture. In pagan mythology the gods are silent, and far from sinless. These gods are made in the image of man. In the biblical worldview there is the value of the individual because he was created in the image of God. In mythology the gods are somewhat indifferent to humanity's woes. In the biblical revelation God loved humanity and gave His Son to die for all His people. We can love Him (and others) because He first loved us. The pagan views (including evolution) rob man of freedom, dignity, morality, purpose, meaning, and eternity. Evolutionists may profess that these things do not matter, but find it hard (as image-bearers of God) to live consistently with the presuppositions of their worldview.

CHAPTER 5

CHARLES DARWIN AND THE ORIGIN OF SPECIES

A. DARWIN'S EARLY YEARS

Born in Shrewsbury, Shropshire, England, on 12 February 1809, Darwin was the fifth child of a wealthy and sophisticated English family. His maternal grandfather was the successful china and pottery entrepreneur Josiah Wedgwood. His paternal grandfather was the well-known eighteenth-century physician Erasmus Darwin. After graduating from the elite school at Shrewsbury in 1825, young Darwin went to the University of Edinburgh to study medicine. In 1827 he dropped out of medical school and entered the University of Cambridge, in preparation for becoming a clergyman of the Church of England. There he met two stellar figures: Adam Sedgwick, a geologist, and John Stevens Henslow (1795–1861), a naturalist. Henslow not only helped build Darwin's self-confidence, but also taught his student to be a meticulous and painstaking observer of natural phenomena and collector of specimens. After graduating from Cambridge in 1831, he was taken aboard the *HMS Beagle*, largely on Henslow's recommendation, as an unpaid naturalist on a scientific expedition around the world. He worked on the captain's schedule so was unable to stay as long as he wanted at a particular stop.

B. DARWIN'S RELIGIOUS BACKGROUND[1]

The Darwin family was associated with the Church of England. Their lack of Christian convictions was no hindrance to their attending the state church. Darwin's wife's family, the Wedgwood family, was associated with the Unitarian Church. Since Darwin married his first cousin, Josiah Wedgwood (1730–1795), who first industrialized the manufacture of pottery, was grandfather to both Darwin and his wife Emma. Darwin was baptized in the Church of England, like almost everyone else in Victorian England. He received a degree in divinity from Cambridge although his real interest was in being a naturalist. After his marriage to Emma, he had no problem attending her family's Unitarian Church. Following the death of his favorite daughter, he turned away from the church and began his path toward a religious agnosticism.

The Unitarian corruption of Christianity was in no condition to resist the evolutionary wave already in progress. The Unitarians had a vague concept of a benevolent deity, but took no pains to conform their every thought to the Word of God. Their God had to conform to the standards of an English gentleman, eschewing all manner of wrath and judgment. The innocuous Victorian religion spoke of a God whose goodness could be seen in the wonders of creation. Unitarians and other vague theists were ill prepared for the attack on their faith from the 'problem of evil.' Since they had no concept of the Fall of man and the subsequent Curse on creation, they thought of their deity creating the world just as we find it today. When nineteenth-century critics pointed to the cruelty and wastefulness of 'nature' and nature 'red in tooth and claw', the sentimental religious feelings of vague theists were shattered. Darwin was aware of this, especially after the death of his daughter. The only kind of 'god' Darwin could then imagine was one who was not responsible for creating the world and had no control over events. Nature became a source of skepticism rather than an inspiration to faith.

---

1. See also Russell Grigg, 'Darwin's arguments against God: How Darwin rejected the doctrines of Christianity', <creation.com/darwinvgod>, 13 June 2008.

The Unitarian denial of the Fall of man played into their being deceived further. When the Fall of man is denied, it follows that the world we now see is just as God created it. This conveniently places the responsibility for evil on God and excuses man.

There were other ramifications to the denial of the Fall of man. Previous to the evolutionary revival on the mid-nineteenth century, people knew that the gospel of Christ was responsible for the difference between Western civilization and the condition of pagan peoples. The evolutionary worldview ignored the transforming power of the gospel on the individual and the culture. Their story about the human condition was a story of natural, gradual (even inevitable) progress, not the gospel or the providence of God. The parallel development was a racist attitude that England's better conditions were not due to the influence of Christianity, but to the inherent superiority of the European 'race'. Those in pagan lands were not enjoying an advanced civilization because they were not as highly 'evolved' as the European people. Skin pigmentation and other superficial physical features were cited as evidence that these African, Aboriginal, or other 'races' were simply more ape-like, thus less evolved. Evolutionary thought was also useful to reinforce their prejudice against Christianity. They could now explain 'religion' (by which they meant Christianity) as a mere stage of evolution that was once useful. The nature of Christianity as divinely revealed truth was totally ignored.

The biggest obstacle to the acceptance of evolution in nineteenth-century Victorian England was the influence of Christianity. Christians had always assumed that the earth was created just a few thousand years ago, as the Bible indicated. From Irenaeus in the second century and Augustine in the fifth century, right down to the nineteenth century, the recent creation of the earth was affirmed. Even the wildly allegorical Origen could not imagine the creation being more than 10,000 years old, despite his immersion in Platonic philosophy.

Few evolutionists wanted to directly challenge the Bible or Christianity, but soon discovered what gradual steps could be taken without arousing public outcry. Most evolutionists of that time preferred to call themselves deist or some kind of theist, even if they were privately atheist. Like Epicurus of old, they too could tolerate a vague, uninvolved deity as long as it was not the God of the Bible who holds people accountable. Christians would gradually concede a series of seemingly unimportant issues. These small steps led them to a place that would have been seen as a shocking departure from the faith had they taken one giant step at the start.

Darwin had once taken an interest in William Paley's popular book, *Natural Theology*. Darwin professed to have been an 'orthodox' Christian when the *Beagle* set off on its journey. It is hard to imagine what orthodoxy there could be in a man of Unitarian church attendance, and Darwin does not often speak of his religious views. Nor do religious sentiments arise naturally in his discussion of 'nature'. He also says of that time when he began his voyage,

> 'But I had gradually come, by this time, to see that the Old Testament from its manifestly false history of the world, with the Tower of Babel, the rainbow as a sign, etc., etc., and from its attributing to God the feelings of a revengeful tyrant, was no more to be trusted than the sacred books of the Hindoos [*sic*], or the beliefs of any barbarian.'[2]

This certainly does not sound like any recognizable form of orthodox Christianity.

Already Genesis has been relegated to the realm of irrelevant mythology. A very good question that should have been put to Darwin is, 'How do you know all these things about God since you say you are an agnostic?' When he cannot answer the question of origins, he can plead agnosticism. When promoting his theory, he seems dogmatically certain that God cannot be as He is described in the Bible. Where then does he get his pretended knowledge of God? He does not say.

---

2. Charles Darwin, *The Autobiography of Charles Darwin 1809–1882*, Nora Barlow, ed. (New York: W.W. Norton & Company, 1969), p. 85. With original omissions restored.

Darwin's wife Emma did not want the public to know her husband's religious view for fear of rejection, so edited out some damaging statements from his *Autobiography*. Darwin came to the place where he could not even imagine any kind of evidence that could convince him of the truth of Christianity. Apparently he expects the readers to go along with his unsupported assertions, replacing God's authoritative word with his relatively ignorant opinions.

> 'But I found it more and more difficult, with free scope given to my imagination, to invent evidence which would suffice to convince me. Thus disbelief crept over me at a very slow rate, but was at last complete. The rate was so slow that I felt no distress, and have never since doubted even for a single second that my conclusion was correct. I can indeed hardly see how anyone ought to wish Christianity to be true; for if so the plain language of the text seems to show that the men who do not believe, and this would include my Father, Brother, and almost all my best friends, will be everlastingly punished. And this is a damnable doctrine.'[3]

Recent repetitions of similar sentiments by modern evolutionists show us that while the 'dogmatic agnostic' may be an oxymoron, it is not an endangered species. From a biblical worldview, Darwin's feelings and assertions have no epistemological foundation on which to be accepted as valid truth claims. Then too, the phrase 'damnable doctrine' is rendered meaningless on his presuppositional basis. This is nothing more than ancient Greek philosophy of fallen and rebellious sinners who want to convince themselves that they will never have to give an account to the living God.

Darwin's hostility to Christianity surfaced first at the death of his favorite daughter, and became more and more pervasive. He refused to consider any evidence that Christianity might be true. To his mind, it could not be true because of the doctrine of everlasting

---

3. Ref. 2, p. 86f.

punishment of the unbelieving sinners, of which he was admittedly one. The theological education that Darwin endured (more than pursued) had no answers as far as defending Genesis is concerned. Makeshift compromises created more contempt for the biblical record, since it could be made to say whatever some scientists theorized next. Darwin could not imagine any evidence that could convince him of Christianity, but he imagined quite a bit that could convince him of evolution. He even had to imagine that someday there would be the requisite fossil evidence. Evolutionists are still imagining that magical circumstance. Darwin is an excellent case showing how the presuppositions brought to a question shape the interpretation he would give. The Bible is shown absolutely accurate in its prediction of the natural man's hostility against God.

C. INTELLECTUAL PREDECESSORS

Leaving aside for the moment the ancient predecessors of Greek and Roman times, we will look at the more immediate predecessors whose ideas influenced Darwin in his formation of his version of evolutionary theory.

Darwin's grandfather Erasmus Darwin (1731–1802) was a prominent and erudite physician, poet, scientist and inventor. He founded the Lunar Society as a social club for scientists, industrialists and natural philosophers. Natural philosophers were those involved in what should be called speculative science, such as theories of origin. The Lunar Society was a society of elites including James Watt, Joseph Priestly, Josiah Wedgwood (Darwin's other grandfather), and Samuel Galton. Erasmus was strongly anti-Christian and began devising an evolutionary theory as early as 1770. He was very proficient in Latin, having translated the work of Carl Linnaeus (1707–1778) on plant classification. In 1770 Erasmus Darwin added the Latin phrase *E Conchis omnia* to his family coat of arms. The phrase means 'Everything from shells' and expresses his evolutionary philosophy.[4] The coat of arms appeared on his bookplate and briefly

---

4. Russell Grigg, 'Darwinism: it was all in the family: Erasmus Darwin's famous grandson learned early about evolution', *Creation* **26**(1):16–18, 2003, <creation.com/erasmus>.

on his carriage. The phrase was removed from his carriage, which was used for his medical practice, for fear of offending some wealthy patients. His major work *Zoonomia or the Laws of Organic Life* (two volumes, 1794 and 1796) was his huge medical-biological treatise. It was the first publication of modern times to embrace a comprehensive hypothesis of evolution. This was sixty-five years before Charles Darwin's *Origin of Species*. Although neither Charles Darwin nor his modern believers like to give Erasmus Darwin credit, his *Zoonomia* does anticipate *Origin* in many ways. Erasmus put forward the concept of millions of years of biological development. Erasmus said,

> 'Millions of ages [i.e. thousands of millions of years] before the commencement of the history of mankind… all warm-blooded animals have arisen from one living filament, which THE GREAT FIRST CAUSE endued with animality, with the power of acquiring new parts… and thus possessing the faculty of continuing to improve by its own inherent activity, and of delivering down those improvements by generation to its posterity, world without end!'[5]

Later, in *The Temple of Nature*, (published posthumously in 1803) Erasmus Darwin extends this to read:

> '[A]ll vegetables and animals now existing were originally derived from the smallest microscopic ones formed by spontaneous vitality in primeval oceans…man should eye with tenderness all living forms, his brother-emmets [i.e. ants], and his sister-worms.'[6]

5. Erasmus Darwin, *Zoonomia Or The Laws of Organic Life*, vol. 1 (London: Johnson., 1794), p. 505, as cited by Russell Grigg, ref. 4.

6. Erasmus Darwin, *The Temple of Nature* (1803) from Desmond King-Hele, *Erasmus Darwin: A Life of Unequalled Achievement*. (New York: Charles Scribner's Sons, 1963). Cited by Russell Grigg, ref. 4.

There are several things notable about this quotation. For one thing the vague reference to a deity is gone as evolution now needs no divine help. A type of spontaneous generation is advocated. Holding this theory would become quite foolish after Louis Pasteur (1822–95) disproved the theory, yet even afterward evolutionists resorted to some variation of spontaneous generation to escape thinking about the Creator. The second important thing to notice is that all Erasmus Darwin does is to tell a story, asserting whatever he pleases. The posthumously published work had no reason to fear public reaction, enabling Erasmus to say what he really believed. Charles Darwin had enough predecessors to go ahead of him and 'test the waters' of public reaction. The church at large did nothing in response to the groundless assertions of the evolutionary worldview except to scramble for a new compromise to bring the Bible into line with the latest consensus. This non-presuppositional response guaranteed that the church would lose respect and the Bible would be devalued.

If the Bible must be forced to say whatever the cultural consensus demands, it is no longer of any use. Erasmus Darwin had such an anti-Christian religion (worldview or philosophy) that he included 'Credulity, Superstitious Hope, and the Fear of Hell in his catalog of diseases.'[7] By the time Charles Darwin wrote his books, the Christian world by and large had already conceded so much that they had lost the ability to effectively refute the evolutionary worldview. For the Christian it is folly to try to mix the dross of naturalistic philosophy with the absolutely perfect revelation from the Creator Himself. Yet that was the result of the Christian world's strategy to defend only the so-called core of Christianity, which was ever shrinking. Consider that a significant portion of the church, once capitulating to evolution, also abandoned the doctrine of eternal punishment to further appease the unbelieving social consensus.

So it was that when Erasmus Darwin put forth his theory, he was too plainspoken to be commended by the society of his day. It would

---

7. D. King-Hele, *Erasmus Darwin: A Life of Unequalled Achievement* (New York: Charles Scribner's Sons, 1963), 55,171; cited by Russell Grigg, ref. 4.

take another generation or two of preparation, so that when Charles published similar thoughts it would be well received. Because of the criticism showered on Erasmus, Charles publicly distanced himself from his grandfather, while privately following in his footsteps. Charles' own father Robert Darwin had also imbibed the freethinking of his father Erasmus. Clearly the evolutionary worldview was all in the family.

Even the famous illustration of the finches had already been given by Erasmus Darwin years before. Erasmus had written:

> '...some birds have acquired harder beaks to crack nuts, as the parrot. Others have acquired beaks adapted to break the harder seeds, as sparrows. Others for the softer seeds of flowers, or the buds of trees, as the finches... All...gradually produced during many generations by the perpetual endeavour of the creatures to supply the want of food.'[8]

Charles Darwin drew heavily from his grandfather Erasmus. Atheism was quite intellectually respectable in the Darwin household. Their expression of it was restrained only by their fear of public reaction.

About the same time, the Scottish geologist James Hutton (1726–97), acquainted with his fellow Scotsman David Hume (1711–76), a leading antitheist, imposed a completely uniformitarian model upon the rock formations. He claimed there was no sign of any beginning (or creation) and that the earth was immeasurably old. He also rejected the Flood of Genesis since he thought there had been no major catastrophes in the earth's early history. Because he published in 1795, his *Theory of the Earth* received much criticism. Yet his view (summarized by his later disciple, Charles Lyell, as 'the present is the key to the past') and exclusive use of naturalistic uniformitarian processes to account for all phenomena continued to distort the study of geology with a false chronology. We must be reminded at this point that Hutton is doing nothing more than strongly expressing

8. Erasmus Darwin, ref. 5, p. 504.

his faith-preferences. Also remember that the only way evolutionists have devised to do 'history' without any records and without any testimony is to project present processes back into the distant ages. The biblical reason we know nothing about these 'prehistoric ages' is that they did not exist. Anyone else setting out to give a history without documentation or testimony would be considered to be on a fool's errand. For the evolutionist it is routine. The evolutionists must substitute speculation about the rock formations for actual historical evidence. The biblical worldview already has a perfect explanation of the rock formations involving creation, flood and the associated catastrophes following. The rocks themselves do not tell us which account is correct. Both creation and evolution involve a chosen faith; both are religiously held worldviews.

Charles Lyell (1797–1875) two generations later could again assert the uniformitarian approach to geology. Hutton had taken the flak, but now Lyell found the waters were fine and invited everyone to jump in. The confident repetition of uniformitarianism and its attendant millions of years began to prevail among the 'experts.' Previous generations had believed in a more recent creation and a global flood; the new generation had been conditioned to accept a naturalistic explanation. Because of the church's previous compromises, the Scripture was tacitly assumed to be irrelevant to the truth claims of geology. Instead of evaluating every truth claim by the standard of God's Word, there was an easy adjusting of Scripture to fit whatever theory the scientists might insist was factual. Because the church failed to evaluate truth claims with a presuppositional worldview apologetic, all subjects considered 'neutral' escaped critical examination. If the Bible was written to tell us about the Rock of Ages, we need not concern ourselves with the age of rocks. The other-worldly attitude and anti-intellectual stance of much of the church put up but a weak and futile resistance to the attacks on the Old Testament that were getting progressively severe. After all, the Old Testament had so much this-world material in it that thought-allergic Christians could not be bothered. Thus the foundation was allowed to be destroyed and following generations would act quite shocked at the level of unbelief their road of compromise had reached.

Before his conversion, the popular Scottish pastor Thomas Chalmers (1780–1847) had devised a theory that would leave evolutionary-uniformitarian long-age notions unchallenged and provide Christians a way to avoid biblical worldview thinking. It must have come as a great relief to thought-allergic Christians to have a 'gap' into which to throw all the evolutionary theories that could be devised. They could get back to more spiritual concerns. The once popular Gap Theory proposed that between Genesis 1:1 and 1:2 we could insert a gap of however many millions of years might seem necessary to accommodate the cultural consensus. Chalmers also latched on to Cuvier (1769–1832), whose unbiblical theory of multiple catastrophes sounded like the lesser of two evils.[9] But this merely illustrates the folly of choosing the least harmful pagan viewpoint as our own. Christians are to develop all their thinking on any subject from the foundation of Holy Scripture. An authentic Christian worldview is based only on scriptural considerations. Cuvier, for example, had no concern to have harmony between the Bible and evolutionary-uniformitarian thinking. To him the Genesis Flood, to the extent that it was relevant at all, could only be the most recent in a long series of catastrophes. Although Thomas Chalmers may be rightly honored for his post-conversion pastoral work, his Gap Theory undermined competent exegesis and (unwittingly) compromised the authority of Scripture by discarding the antithetical character of God's revelation versus man's speculation.

It was not long before the Gap Theory received a challenge from Anglican clergyman George Faber (1773–1854). Tragically, it was not a call to a biblical worldview, just another competing compromise. This time it was a day-age theory. The Gap Theory began to lose support among the educated Christians, even though the new compromise was just as exegetically irresponsible as the first. Someone came up with yet another compromise, more absurd than the others, calling it the 'Tranquil Flood' theory. This view claimed that although there was a global flood, it left no traces in

---

9. See also John Reed, 'Cuvier's analogy and its consequences: forensics vs testimony as historical evidence', *Journal of Creation* **22**(3):115–120, 2008.

the geological record. Then the view had to be modified to a local tranquil flood to account for the alleged lack of any trace of it in the layers of *sedimentary* (i.e. rock laid down by water!) rock. Each new compromise, instead of solving any problems, was increasingly absurd. The Scripture could hardly have made it clearer that the Flood was global in extent. To pretend that the Bible said otherwise could only bring the Scripture into contempt. The avoidance of critical presuppositional worldview thinking would have increasingly devastating effects for the following generations.

Thus, thirty-five to fifty years before the Darwin controversy, a large part of the Christian church had already surrendered to 'evolution' without a fight. The only fight was about which pet compromise should be adopted. The biblical chronology, skeletal framework of biblical history, was carelessly tossed aside as inconsequential. Compounding this was the church's thoughtless assumption that the 'kinds' of Genesis are identical to the 'species' as classified by the naturalists. The view that each *species,* rather than each kind, was specially created was an ideal setup for defeat. There is no deliverance from this defeat apart from a full confidence in every word that has proceeded from the mouth of God.

The views of Charles Lyell's *Principles of Geology* (1830–33) had a great influence on Charles Darwin. The millions of years assumed in geology could be assumed in the realm of biology. It was so much easier to imagine that random changes might bring forth advanced complexity, if only millions of years of time were granted. The millions of years, impossible for those believing the biblical chronology, became the life breath of evolution. And evolution would not remain a biological theory, but increasingly overtly show its true colors as a comprehensive worldview involving only naturalism, all the time. What the Creator could accomplish in an instant could maybe be imagined to have happened by chance over millions of years.

Even though Anglican clergy largely staffed Cambridge, Darwin's training there did not include Christian biblical worldview critical thinking. Like most modern seminaries, the worldview was largely absorbed from the cultural consensus, rather than being consciously and consistently built up from Scripture—which takes work. Both Adam Sedgwick of Cambridge and William Buckland of Oxford were leading Anglican geologists popular in the 1820s. They began conceding millions of years, and continued to drift away from scriptural moorings. They would eventually deny all kinds of catastrophism. The stiff resistance that met Erasmus Darwin was largely dissipated by the time Charles was ready to write. The most vigorous opposition to Darwin came from the older generation of scientists, on scientific grounds. The most consistent opposition, that from the scriptural geologists (see Chapter 9), could not be refuted, but could be ignored or ridiculed.

Edward Blyth (1810–73) was an English chemist and biologist. As a Christian he had spoken of 'natural selection' as an aspect of the Creator's design. As modern evolutionist Loren Eiseley claimed in 1979 '…the leading tenets of Darwin's work—the struggle for existence, variation, natural selection and sexual selection—are all fully expressed in Blyth's paper of 1835.'[10] Darwin does mention Blyth several times in *The Descent of Man* (1871), which is written in a much more formal, footnoted style. Blyth is not, however, credited with the specific concept of natural selection. The issue here is neither to charge Darwin with plagiarism, nor to exonerate him, but simply to point out that natural selection (an observable fact that does not require the conclusion of microbe-to-man evolution) was not original to Darwin. Darwin himself says in his Introduction to *The Descent of Man* that his work contains hardly any 'original facts' about man. Blyth had seen natural selection as a conservative weeding out process; Darwin seized on it as the mechanism for evolution.

Alfred R. Wallace (1823–1913) is certainly worthy of mention. His 1858 manuscript on natural selection, 'On the Tendency of Varieties to Depart Indefinitely From the Original Type,' outlined an evolutionary theory nearly identical to what Darwin was formulating.

---

10. Loren Eiseley, 'Charles Darwin, Edward Blyth, and the Theory of Natural Selection,' *Proceedings of The American Philosophical Society* 103, no. 1 February 1959; Cited in Russell Grigg, 'Darwin's Illegitimate Brainchild', *Creation* 26(2):39–41, 2004; <creation.com/brainchild>. Accessed September 25, 2008.

Lyell and other friends of Darwin urged him to rush his manuscript to publication. Because he did, Darwin is a patron saint of evolution by virtue of timing, even though his ideas were not original. One reason anti-Christian crusaders favored Darwin was that Wallace stopped short at human evolution, reserving that last step for divine intervention.[11] Darwin and friends would later ridicule this idea as a 'hankering after miracles.' Darwin was riding the wave of anti-Christian sentiment and the younger generation received his book gladly. But a closer examination reveals that, like his grandfather's *Zoonomia*, his book continued very speculative explanations of his observed data. The observations may have been carefully done and presented in an interesting way, but the explanations were speculative with a predetermined God-excluding naturalism.

D. DARWIN'S *ORIGIN OF SPECIES*

Darwin did not find the family tradition of medicine to his liking. He was for a time attracted to the idea of being a country parson with a steady income and plenty of leisure time. His only degree was a divinity degree, but he was a mediocre and disinterested student. His real interest was in the developing sciences. He especially liked the fieldwork of observing, drawing, and recording the details of his observations. His opportunity for an around-the-world trip on the *Beagle* was enough to cause him to forget about being a country parson. This was probably all for the best, because with his Unitarian and nominal Anglican religion, he had no gospel to preach.

We can well imagine the excitement created by the returning Darwin with his descriptions of strange creatures, never seen by most Englishmen. It was easy to think that such carefully detailed and recorded observations gave a special credence to his particular explanation of the origin of species when it was published many years afterwards. Later he would add drawings to his works, further popularizing his theory. He benefited from the human tendency to extend unwarranted authority to a man because of his relatively

11. Russell Grigg, 'Alfred Russel Wallace—"co-inventor" of Darwinism', *Creation* **27**(4):33–35, 2005 <creation.com/wallace>.

unrelated accomplishments. A modern version of this phenomenon is the 'expert' status accorded to an actress or athlete when they speak on political or environmental issues. Never mind that the just-so story Darwin told about a personified 'Natural Selection' required more credulity than the miracle claims of Lourdes. Nothing was too improbable for the evolutionists if only God could be excluded.

From a biblical worldview we know that no matter how extensive or detailed Darwin's observations, as long as his erroneous naturalistic presuppositions were in place and his ignorance of genetics continued, his conclusions would be as false as his religious-philosophical foundations. The creationist-evolutionist debate is ultimately not about objective observations, but the interpretation of those observations and their relationship to one another. The real issue is historical, philosophical and religious in nature. The real issue is, what standard or frame of reference shall we use to understand and interpret all observations and all truth claims? Darwin was already enamored with naturalism's uniformitarian hypothesis of millions of years. Lyell, in accord with his religious views, popularized uniformitarianism in geological studies; Darwin added uniformitarianism to his biological speculations.

Darwin's *Origin of Species* consists of approximately four hundred pages of mostly correct observations, followed by highly speculative extrapolations presumed to explain the development of the observed species. As an example, take Darwin's treatment of pigeon breeding. He assumed that what the breeder did by intelligent purposeful actions could be accomplished by 'natural selection' provided millions of years were available. Darwin observed that the variations achieved among the pigeons could be great enough for some naturalist, finding such a pigeon in the wild, to announce a new species had been discovered. Darwin made at least two faulty assumptions in order to make his observations seem to count against the biblical record.

1. The first was the commonly held assumption that the Bible taught 'fixity of species.' Therefore, if a naturalist comes up with a new 'species' of pigeon, the Bible must

be wrong. Darwin is not entirely to blame for the 'fixity of species' characterization. Too many Christians eager to show how 'scientifically' up-to-date the Bible was, equated the biblical 'kinds' with the naturalist's 'species.' But the biblical term 'kinds' is not a narrowly defined technical term of modern classification. 'Kind' is simply a common sense way of speaking of various sorts of animals as 'cows, horses, dogs, birds, etc.' Using the word 'dog' as an example, the 'dog kind' might include a whole canine family of wolves, coyotes, foxes, wild dogs, and domestic dogs. How many original pairs had to be created to bring about the present varieties, is a matter that can be investigated by genetic science. God may have created just one pair of 'dog kind' or He may have created a 'wolf kind' and a 'fox kind' from which all others developed. What is forbidden by the biblical account is something like the dog evolving from an amphibian or some other distinct kind.

2.   A second faulty assumption is that the relatively small variations within a kind can be greatly extrapolated to account for vast changes from one kind to a totally different kind. The evolutionary speculation that reptiles evolved into birds is just one example. Since Mendel did not publish the laws of genetics until 1865, Darwin had some excuse for his ignorance of the genetic information mechanism. It turns out that the specialized varieties have less genetic information than the original created kind. This loss of genetic information is exactly the opposite of what is required for upward evolution to occur. Specialized breeds of dogs have less genetic information, less potential for variation, than a wolf in the wild. Mutations do not rescue the theory since they are not only often harmful, but even the rare beneficial ones seem to almost universally involve the loss of genetic information, instead of a gain. Making

random changes in a perfectly functioning organism is, to
say the least, not likely to be helpful or to be passed on.

Darwin's many meticulous observations of pigeons and finches
could never prove that birds came from reptiles. Both the breeder's
skill and natural selection can select only from the available
genetic information. Selection cannot create new information. An
oversimplified illustration of variations within limits is seen in the
large variety of three, four and five-letter words that may be formed
from the pool of letters: SAEPRS. No amount of random selection
can generate the word 'KNOT' from this pool of information. As
Darwin confessed for his time, 'The laws governing inheritance
are for the most part unknown.'[12] Once again ignorance provided a
comfortable shelter for evolutionary speculation. But the ignorance
was inexcusable because God had already revealed the truth that
each animal brings forth after its kind. As the Bible says,

> Genesis 1:21–25: So God created the great creatures of
> the sea and every living and moving thing with which the
> water teems, according to their kinds, and every winged
> bird according to its kind. And God saw that it was good.
> And God blessed them, saying, "Be fruitful and multiply,
> and fill the waters in the seas, and let birds multiply on
> the earth."…Then God said, "Let the earth bring forth the
> living creature according to its kind: cattle and creeping
> thing and beast of the earth, each according to its kind";
> and it was so. And God made the beast of the earth
> according to its kind, cattle according to its kind, and
> everything that creeps on the earth according to its kind.
> And God saw that it was good.

No one doubts the reality of natural selection, nor that variations
occur in living things. However, for the belief that it had in the past

---

12.Charles Darwin, 'Chapter I. Variation Under Domestication,' in *The Origin of Species By Means of Natural Selection Or The Preservation of Favoured Races in The Struggle for Life* (The Modern Library, including *Descent of Man* in the same volume, reprint, New York: Random House, Inc., n.d.), p. 19. Hereafter cited as *Origin of Species* or simply *Origin*.

progressively generated the enormous amount of information in living things to be at least partially intellectually credible, it suited the naturalistic religion for it to be personified and often capitalized. 'Natural Selection'. Darwin and others speak of many amazing phenomena in terms of this Natural Selection. As scientists of his day pointed out, he can provide no hard evidence in favor of these many 'just-so' stories. All Darwin could show us was that dogs brought forth dogs, pigeons brought forth pigeons, and finches brought forth finches. We see a considerable potential for variation within each kind, but no transitions from one kind to another. There is no evidence of transition creatures between, for example, those which reproduce by cell division, those that lay eggs, and those which reproduce as mammals. All we have ever seen are distinct kinds, just as the Bible says.

To illustrate the overuse of speculative language in trying to establish his theory, consider the amount of guesswork on a single page:

> '...we suppose the amount of change...we have only to suppose the steps...I believe...it is probable...I have assumed...the amount of change supposed... after fourteen thousand generations, six new species...are supposed to have been produced.'[13]

Proponents of the evolutionary worldview love to use a kind of 'bait and switch' technique to argue their case. They may define evolution as 'change over time.' When they have demonstrated what no one disputes, they claim to have provided evidence for molecules-to-man evolution. No one doubts that there is 'change over time' but where is the evidence of reptile-to-bird or ape-to-man evolution?

Darwin adapted the language of Malthus (1766–1834) to his theory.[14] Malthus had postulated a geometric growth in the population,

---

13. Charles Darwin, 'Chapter IV: Natural Selection; or the Survival of the Fittest.' In *The Origin of Species* (The Modern Library, New York: Random House, Inc., n.d.), p. 90.

14. Historian Noel Weeks demonstrated the historical context of Darwin's theory including Malthusian ideas in 'Darwin and the search for an evolutionary mechanism', *TJ* (now *Journal of Creation*) **12**(3):305–311, 1998; <creation.com/article/1754>.

but only an arithmetic growth in the food supply. This would create a struggle for survival, leading to widespread suffering, and an inevitable return to subsistence-level existence for most. Population increase was a problem to Malthus. Because of the development of technology, his theory was shown to be false. But in 1859 Darwin could still believe it. Those who believed God's scriptural revelation would know beforehand that the theory was false, leaving Darwin and others without excuse. It is a sad fact that clergyman Malthus was not remembered as a faithful preacher of the gospel of Christ, but as a promoter of a foolish speculation that bore much bitter fruit as 'people' became a problem to be rid of rather than image-bearers to assist in godly dominion, bringing God's solutions to the problems of humanity.

Darwin's chapter on the laws of variation evidences the poor state of knowledge in nineteenth-century science. He seems to think that changing conditions cause the animals to suddenly develop a useful variation. We now know that a particular combination of genetic information can be advantageous in certain conditions. For example, if a specialized breed of dog no longer has any genetic information for short hair, leaving only 'long hair' instructions in its genes, it has an advantage in a cold climate. But this loss of genetic information is not evolution. Evolution requires an increase in genetic information in order to produce an advanced and more complex variety.

Apart from a breeder's purposeful design in bringing out certain traits, there are examples of 'natural selection' in the older sense maintained by Edward Blyth. Isolated population groups may inbreed and have a more limited gene pool from which to select. They have actually lost genetic information and thus reduced the amount of variation now possible to them. There are two 'species' of nearly identical squirrels living near the Grand Canyon. Being on opposite rims of the canyon, they are separated. They have different dominant genes for coloration, but could revert to the same type if not kept apart by the huge canyon. This is another illustration that it is unwise to equate the biblical 'kinds' with the naturalist's 'species.' Both groups are squirrels and will never be anything but squirrels.

Darwin assumes much in his presentation. He asserts that moles once had good eyesight, but lost it through disuse. But the mole looks like it was well designed to do what it does in its underground existence. Where is the evidential specimen of the mole with 20/20 vision before it 'evolved' into a blind mole? The same kind of thing is asserted of the blind fish in caves, though in that case there is considerable evidence that the fish's ancestors could see. This includes breeding two different types of blind fish together, with some descendants now having sight. This indicates that the blindness in the case of each type came from damage to a different type of genetic pathway. Natural selection (lower case) will tend to rapidly favour fish born sightless from such inherited genetic mistakes. Vision is no advantage in a cave, but fish with eyes, bumping into cave walls, are exposed to many more avenues for injury to those delicate structures, allowing infection, for example.[15] But how does their loss of sight help establish the upward progress of evolution? The change is in precisely the wrong direction. Darwin's most accurate statement in the chapter is, 'Our ignorance of the laws of variation is profound.'[16]

Because of the partially Christianized culture of England, Darwin was more open about the difficulties of his theory than are his modern-day dogmaticians. He admitted the widespread lack of transitional forms in the fossil record. According to his theory there should be many more transitional forms than there are distinct modern kinds. This overwhelming paucity of transitional forms Darwin excused because of the deficiency of the fossil record. One hundred and fifty years later that same lack of more than a mere handful of creatures which could even be put forward as candidates for transitional forms argues for a deficiency in Darwin's theory. This lack of evidence has led to much jumping to conclusions about every so-called 'missing link' and even a considerable number of deliberate hoaxes designed to promote the theory. Some modern

---

15. Carl Wieland, 'Let the Blind See: Breeding blind fish with blind fish restores sight', <creation.com/blindsee>, 11 January 2008; Jonathan Sarfati, Christopher Hitchens—blind to salamander reality, <creation.com/hitchens>, 26 July 2008.

16. Ref. 13, p.122.

evolutionists have devised a story known as 'punctuated' evolution, in which the changes from one kind to another take place suddenly. Instead of evolution happening too slowly for us to observe, the new story claims it happened too quickly for us to observe it. This just-so story conveniently allows the theory to continue despite the general absence of evidence in the fossil record. One version of this story explained away the absence of fossil evidence for the reptile-bird transition because one reptile's egg hatched directly into a bird (ignoring the problem of where it would find a mate). Good story-telling skills have more than once overtaken evidence in the crusade for evolutionary religion. Another variation is the story that acknowledges that life is too complex to have evolved originally from raw chemicals as the standard theory maintains. So this new story has aliens from outer space leaving living spores behind to develop into the rich variety of life we have today.

Darwin attempts to explain how the marvelous complexity of the eye could have resulted from random changes:

> '...to suppose that the eye with all its inimitable contrivances for adjusting the focus to different distances, for admitting the different amounts of light, and for the correction of spherical and chromatic aberration, could have been formed by natural selection, seems, I freely confess, absurd in the highest degree.'[17]

Here we find an area of agreement with Darwin; his theory really does seem absurd. Darwin, though, thinks he has solved the difficulties by imagining a story of how the eye might possibly have developed, nonetheless. What if a primitive optic nerve covered by a light-sensitive membrane gradually developed over many generations into an eye? This is indeed a convenient and imaginative tale.

Given the state of knowledge in nineteenth-century science, it was easy to imagine all kinds of things. However, the eye is actually far more complex than people at the time realized. Likewise, they

---

17. Ref. 13 p. 133.

could think of one-celled animals as being as simple as a blob of jelly. It makes a fascinating study to see how modern-day molecular biological research, as brought to public attention by such as Michael Behe,[18] has destroyed the scientific value of Darwin's imaginative just-so stories. There is an amazing complexity even in a one-celled animal. Furthermore, an irreducible complexity[19] at the biochemical level is required for the useful operation of even the 'simplest' known light-sensitive membrane, let alone many other complex systems. The eye we have is incredibly complex, and even though it is possible to still have some sight after removing the lens, for example, really useful vision is only possible if all its many complex parts are present and functional at the same time. And the eye must work in conjunction with the brain in all its complexity, for even a complete, functional eye would be useless without the interaction with the brain to interpret the signals it produces as visual information. Behe, a Roman Catholic professor of biochemistry at LeHigh University, is open to evolutionary theories of origin, and never specifies what kind of intelligence is at work.[20,21] On one thing he is quite clear, though; the typical Darwinian explanation does not credibly account for life's complexity. The more we know about the eye, the harder it becomes to imagine with Darwin how it could come about by random changes over time.

---

18. Michael Behe, *Darwin's Black Box: The Biochemical Challenge to Evolution*, The Free Press, New York, 1996; see review by Carl Wieland, 'The mousetrap man', *Creation* **20**(3):17, 1998; <creation.com/behe>.

19. This means that it is logically impossible to conceive of a simpler system, with any part missing, that would perform that function. Behe uses the example of a mousetrap; with any one of its component parts removed, it could not catch mice. To explain something complex by Darwinian evolution, it is absolutely essential to be able to postulate a preceding step that is functional and hence is selected for.

20. Michael Behe, *The Edge of Evolution: The search for the limits of Darwinism*, Free Press, NY, 2007; see review by Don Batten, 'Clarity and confusion', *Journal of Creation* **22**(1):28–33, 2008.

21. This came in for severe criticism from the evolutionary gatekeepers, e.g. Richard Dawkins, Inferior Design, *New York Times*, 1 July 2007. For refutation, see Jonathan Sarfati, J., 'Misotheist's misology: Dawkins attacks Behe but digs himself into logical potholes', <creation.com/dawkbehe>, 13 July 2007.

The fossil record, the study of genetic information, and the fact of irreducible complexity have one thing in common—the ignorance of them made the evolutionary theory's acceptance much easier. Evolutionary theory 150 years later still thrives on ignorance and suppression of alternative views. The means of suppression include not hiring or not extending tenure to teachers and professors who do not subscribe to the evolutionary dogma, and initiating legal maneuvers and court decisions to silence even the slightest questioning of the evolutionary worldview. On the other side, biblical illiteracy makes it easier for Christians to imagine that there is no conflict between evolution and the Bible. Those who have not bothered to look closely at either evolution or the Bible prefer this easy synthesis to the hard work of constructing a consistently biblical worldview. Finally, the state-controlled educational system, with evolution as the established religion, teaches for social conformity, not critical thinking. In other words the goal is not education but indoctrination, because the slightest mention of an alternative is forbidden.

How could Darwin so strongly maintain his case after admitting ignorance in regard to the fossil record and ignorance of the laws of variation? He simply asserts his case dogmatically, and places the burden of disproof on those who disagree.

> 'If it could be demonstrated that any complex organ existed, which could not possibly have been formed by numerous, successive, slight modifications, my theory would absolutely break down. But I can find no such case.'[22]

Darwin believes he does not actually need to prove his theory. Instead opponents must prove that it 'could not possibly' have happened as his story indicates. As long as he can imagine how it might have possibly happened, his theory is secure. Would the evolutionists mind if creationists used the same kind of defense? Then the creationist could answer something like this, 'If it could be demonstrated that

---

22. Ref. 13, p. 135.

any complex organ exists, which could not possibly have been formed by divine creation, our theory would absolutely break down. But we can find no such case.' Actually, the creationist does not need to resort to such evasive blind faith maneuvers.

Evolutionists constantly cite changes within a kind, then jump to the conclusion of amoeba-to-man evolution over millions of years. One simply does not follow from the other. An interesting example of what can occur from natural selection operating on existing variation within a population is highlighted by the discovery, in the wild, of a 'pizzly' bear. Jim Martell harvested a half polar bear, half grizzly hybrid on 16 April 2006 in the Northwest Territory of Canada. DNA tests have confirmed that the father was a grizzly and the mother was a polar bear. This is thought to be the first of its kind to be documented in the wild.[23]

The fact that a grizzly and a polar bear have been able to produce fertile offspring indicates that both species descended from a common created pair of the bear 'kind.' As far as the biblical record is concerned, there could have been as few as one pair of the bear kind originally created, which developed into the variations we see today. Natural selection has likely played an important role in 'sorting out' the genetic information into the different descendant varieties. However, in each case, the total amount of genetic information is less than in the original created kind. A population of such 'pizzlies', closer to the original created kind, is theoretically capable of generating either polar bears or grizzlies, whereas either one of these do not have the information to give rise to the other. What is not acceptable is the artist's drawing of Darwin's tree of life replacing true scientific investigation.

When Charles Darwin discusses the giraffe, he makes up an imaginative scenario to explain its long neck. Modeled after the story told by Lamarck, it does not qualify as science. Giraffes appear to be

---

23. Andrew Lamb, 'The Pizzly: a polar bear / grizzly bear hybrid explained by the Bible', <creation. com/pizzly>.

designed to do what they do and do very well. There is no compelling fossil evidence that such a transition from short-necked giraffes to long-necked ones ever took place.

Christians need to be constantly aware of the great difference between observational-operational science and historical science, which is the type necessarily involved in the study of origins. The former is what we know of as experimental science, and is applied to finding out how the world works. The latter is the type of science that has to be applied to such historical disciplines as archeology, or forensic science, for example.

The study of origins aims to give an account of, or a history of, the observed data. This means that every observer has an interpretive framework, a presupposed philosophical point of view. Evolutionists constantly repeat their claim that their faith in naturalistic uniformitarianism is 'science' while the Christian's faith in recorded testimony is called 'religion.' Both views should be considered 'religiously' held. Both are ultimately presupposed worldviews by which *all* truth claims are evaluated.

The issue is really a war of worldviews. The Christian worldview refers to God the Creator, not out of a desire to be 'religious,' but because God actually did create the world in six calendar days a few thousand years ago. The evolutionary worldview was motivated in ancient times as well as modern times by those who would not have God in their knowledge. Their rebellion against God is more a religious category than science. That is why it is not enough for the creationist to present more 'data' to the evolutionist. The latter did not arrive at his view via evidence, but by the strong preference of fallen humanity to exclude God from its thinking. The evolutionist's religiously held worldview must be challenged as arbitrary, subjective and self-contradictory.

CHAPTER 6

CHARLES HODGE OF PRINCETON

Princeton Theological Seminary remained for over one hundred years (1812–1929) as a faithful witness to the Scriptures and the Reformed faith. Charles Hodge entered the College of New Jersey (later call Princeton University) in the year the seminary was founded. For more than fifty years of the orthodox life of Princeton, Charles Hodge was the defining force of Princeton theology. Princeton was established to promote a balance of biblical scholarship and personal piety. Charles Hodge was an embodiment of these goals. He and R. L. Dabney were two of nineteenth-century America's great defenders of the faith. Hodge exerted much influence through the hundreds of students he personally taught at Princeton, the many journal articles he wrote, several books, some New Testament commentaries (most notably on Romans) and the most enduring monument of his thought, his Systematic Theology. We will look primarily at his *Systematic Theology* and his book *What is Darwinism?* to discover his response to the controversial theory of evolution.

Like most men of his time, Hodge placed a high value on science and the role of reason. His very first item of business in his systematic theology is to affirm that theology is a science. The process of induction follows that of empirical fact-finding. As a scientist gathers factual data scattered throughout nature in order to formulate a coherent and systematic explanation, so the theologian formulates his theology from the scattered data of Scripture. Systematic theology aims to achieve a consistent explanation of the relationships among various teachings of Scripture. Even though the Bible is not a textbook on systematic theology, it contains all the data or facts necessary to construct a systematic theology.

For the scientific method to function, we must make certain assumptions. Hodge assumed the trustworthiness of man's sense perceptions, his mental operations, and the existence of built-in truth like the law of cause and effect. Even though the theologian must follow the same rules as the scientist, there is an added element in theological understanding. There is the inward teaching of the Holy Spirit, confirming in the believer those objective truths already revealed in the Bible (1 John 2:20). Such teaching does not add to, and is certainly consistent with, the objectively revealed doctrines of Holy Scripture. Hodge says,

> 'This inward teaching produces a conviction which no sophistries can obscure, and no arguments can shake…you might as well argue a man out of a belief of his existence, as out of confidence that what he is thus taught of God is true.'[1]

Hodge's answer to the question, *What is Darwinism?* was 'It is Atheism.' Hodge also spoke of the innate knowledge of God, which every rational mind possesses. Says Hodge, 'The mind is so constituted that it perceives certain things to be true without proof and without instruction.'[2]

Hodge also speaks of intuitions of the intellect and moral intuitions. These are:

> 'Certain truths which the mind perceives to be true immediately, without proof or testimony…[and moral truths] the essential distinction between right and wrong; the obligation of virtue; responsibility for character, and conduct that sin deserves punishment; are examples of this

1. Charles Hodge, *Systematic Theology*, vol. 1 (Peabody, Massachusetts: Hendrickson Publishers, 1999), p. 16.
2. Ref. 1, p. 192.

class of truths. No man needs to be taught them. No one seeks for further evidence of their being truths than that which is found in their nature.'[3]

Knowing some of the things Hodge wrote, we would expect him to be a mighty champion on behalf of the Christian faith as against the evolutionary worldview. But his seemingly powerful attack is weakened by many qualifications. He is unable to deal the deathblow to evolution because the Sword of the Spirit is held back. The areas of confusion are God, reason, and science in particular. Hodge had said that the knowledge of God is innate, seeming to follow Romans 1. Then he makes a fatal qualification, because it is not the God of Scripture! 'It is in the general sense of a Being on whom we are dependent, and to whom we are responsible, that the idea is asserted to exist universally, and of necessity, in every human mind.'[4]

In Romans 1, it is God who makes Himself known to man. It is man, who knowing [the one true] God will not have God in his knowledge. Man suppresses the truth in unrighteousness. This is not the same thing as man acknowledging a god of some sort who probably exists. From Epicurus to the twenty-first century, fallen man will not have the knowledge of the one true and living God of Scripture in his life. Neither Epicurus nor modern haters of God are particularly opposed to a vague concept of a remote deity of some sort. It is certain that the apostle Paul was not speaking of a vague abstraction, 'a god.' It is the constant usage in the Bible to speak of the God of Abraham, Isaac, and Jacob. In his commentary on Romans, Hodge has no hint of 'a general sense of a Being.' All his exegetical work speaks of the one true God. This simply does not transfer to his systematic theology. In his systematic theology, we must begin with Aristotle's arguments for the existence of a god. Men must be convinced by reason to acknowledge a god of some sort whose existence is very likely. But this is a step backward from

---

3. Ref. 1, p. 193.
4. Ref. 1, p. 195.

what Romans 1 says men already know! They already know the One and Only God, but suppress that knowledge out of their love of unrighteousness and hatred of God. Princeton largely ignored the wise counsel of Tertullian , 'What has Athens to do with Jerusalem?' by employing the arguments of Aristotle/Aquinas. Worse yet, Athens will now dictate to Jerusalem how her Scriptures should be interpreted. These arguments were of no profit to the philosophers of ancient Greece, and they accomplished nothing for the cause of Christ. Hodge himself admits that the arguments do not prove 'that this Being is extramundane, much less that it is a personal God.'[5]

Hodge's problem in regard to science is related to a naïve confidence in the reason and mind of fallen man. Princeton was from the beginning concerned with the harmony of science and biblical accounts. But they allowed 'science' to be too broadly defined. Real science involves the more objective part of observations, measurements, and recording of results of experimentation. The scientific method, however, goes on to formulate hypotheses, theories, and eventually laws. The way one accounts for the data observed is more subjectively influenced. The creationist and the evolutionist usually agree (somewhat) on what data has been observed, but differ on how to account for what has been observed and studied. It is the account of the data, the story that is told to explain it, that is so affected by the religiously held presuppositions of the observer. This is not consistently recognized by the Princeton apologetic. As a result, theories proposed to explain data were mistaken for objective science. Instead of bringing every thought into captivity to the obedience of Christ, Princeton was willing to let so-called 'science' dictate the interpretation of Scripture. The biblical approach would have been to examine all things in the light of Scripture. Thus Princeton felt forced, because of this inadequate foundation, to resort to highly unlikely and ultimately self-defeating 'interpretations' of Scripture so as to conform to the story evolutionists were telling about the 'facts.' We need to tell God's story about the facts, not the story of the rebel.

---

5. Ref. 1, p. 215.

This represents a fundamental problem in Hodge's evidentialist[6] apologetic. There is a naïve confidence in fallen man's reason that allows it to pass judgment on revelation. The truth of divine revelation must be 'proved' by reason. The truth of God's existence is not established by Scripture alone, Romans 1 must be 'proved' by the arguments developed by Plato and Aristotle. This type of apologetic will prove problematic when facing questions from 'science.' Often the scientist is incorrectly assumed to be a neutral observer, willing to follow the truth wherever it may lead.[7] If they are recognized experts in their field, their conclusions ('science') must determine our interpretation of Scripture. The Christian community is set up from the beginning for a capitulation to the pronouncements from the scientific community. The mindset becomes fixed that Scripture was not written to instruct us in 'science,' but leaves that field for 'scientists.' The great Baconian divide becomes an axiom for almost all such evidentialists. Scripture has its area of authority in morals and 'religious things' and other specialties have their area of expertise. The evidentialist method regards unbelievers not as 'suppressing the truth in unrighteousness' but as oftentimes authoritative witnesses on their area of study. Foundation-destroying speculations are allowed as possible or even probable explanations of nature, in preference to the biblical record. Profession of biblical authority is maintained, but it is limited in scope. Biblical authority must not wander off the reservation. Our 'interpretation' of Scripture cannot be governed by the historical-grammatical exegetical method and common usage of language. Speculations of 'scientists' impel us to re-interpret the Scripture in exceedingly unlikely ways. The Bible is twisted this way and that in order to fit the latest speculation. In five more years when another speculation gains ascendancy, the Scripture must be

---

6. Evidentialism, the antithesis of presuppositionalism (defined on p. 21), is a method of defending the faith that relies primarily on the presentation of various facts to the unbeliever that are held to be independent of the Bible. But the unbeliever (apart from the grace of God) interprets those very same facts, not in objective neutrality as evidentialism assumes, but in accordance with his anti-supernatural bias and assumptions.

7. This assumes that facts speak for themselves, something that most modern philosophers of science recognize is not the case.

re-twisted. This is a lack of absolute confidence that the Bible is the very word of God, authoritative in every area of life and thought. Historically the results are always the same: a compromise in some seemingly 'unimportant' area, leads to a decline and collapse of the whole system of the Christian worldview. There are always unforeseen consequences that will follow, because all biblical truths are inter-related. When the Bible is rejected (even if by means of an externally imposed hermeneutic) in an 'unimportant' area, rejection of the rest of it cannot be far behind. When the Bible is rejected in those areas we can see and experience (science, history, etc.) how can we expect its acceptance in areas we cannot personally investigate? For example, a rejection of biblical cosmology leads to a rejection of biblical morality. The divine revelation is as a seamless garment, not as a collection of threads from which we may pick and choose so as to craft a different kind of garment.

Once we grant to fallen man that his reason must judge the revelation of God in Scripture, how can we avoid putting Reason above revelation? Hodge's dictum, 'Reason must judge of the credibility of a revelation'[8] is an overestimate of the ability of fallen man's reason. Here is a confusion of the hierarchy of authorities. For example, if a store clerk at the bookstore asks for some ID he assumes that a driver's license has more authority than simply taking the word of the customer. The driver's license is seen as a higher authority to which we may appeal. Now may we say that Reason is a higher authority than the revelation of God in Scripture? How can we demand that the Lord of all creation show his ID? In granting such autonomous authority to the reason of fallen man, the apologist is actually denying those very biblical truths he wants to defend.

The cracks in the foundation of the Princeton apologetics begin to appear. The 'god' they say is innately known turns out to be a vague Being, fallen man's reason is said to be capable of fairly evaluating God's revelation, and theories of scientists are confused with demonstrated observational and experimental science.

8. Ref. 1, p. 50.

Hodge recognizes, in theory, that there is a difference between fact and theory[9]. He says on the question of origins, 'The data for the solution of the problem do not lie within the sphere either of experience or reason. All human theories on this subject are nothing more than conjectures more or less ingenious.'[10] Elsewhere he says again,

> 'The Princeton Review has ever held and taught, in common with the whole Church, that this infallible Bible must be interpreted by science…Science is not the opinions of man, but knowledge…the ascertained truths concerning the facts and laws of nature. To say, therefore, that the Bible contradicts science is to say that it contradicts facts, is to say that it teaches error; and to say that it teaches error is to say it is not the Word of God.'[11]

Even as Hodge is affirming the difference between theory and fact, he is confusing the two. The above statement was in response to an editorial in the *New York Observer* criticizing Princeton for their compromise on the age of humanity, six thousand years according to biblical chronology, millions of years according to evolutionary theory. Hodge was ready to accept the evolutionary speculations of Lyell and Darwin regarding the rock layers and fossils. Instead of giving a biblical explanation in terms of a worldwide catastrophic flood, he was ready to accommodate the God-excluding, judgment-excluding uniformitarian theory of the fossils. Hodge fails to distinguish between demonstrated scientific fact and speculation when he equates the evolutionary speculations of his day with the observational results of Galileo, Kepler, *et al.* He says,

> 'The Church has been forced more than once to alter her interpretation of the Bible to accommodate the discoveries

---

9. The word theory is here used more in the lay sense of hypothesis or conjecture, not as it is often used in scientific circles, as a fairly well-established body of facts, e.g. Atomic Theory, or Gene Theory.

10. Ref 1, p. 550.

11. Charles Hodge, 'The Bible in Science,' *New York Observer*, 26 March 1863, pp. 98–99.

of science. But this has been done without doing any
violence to the Scriptures or in any degree impairing their
authority.'[12]

Hodge thus assumes that the Bible needs to be reinterpreted as to
the antiquity of humanity. He mistakenly places long-age theory
(if in theistic form) on the level of Copernicus' discoveries as 'science.'
But evolutionary thought is more of a metaphysical speculation than
a 'discovery of science.' Has such 'reinterpretation' impaired the
authority of Scripture? It most certainly has. A Bible that can be
made to say anything says nothing. If the Bible cannot be trusted in
the things that are seen, how are we to trust it in the things that are
not seen? The authority of the Bible has been impaired far more by
its accommodating 'friends' than by its openly hostile enemies.

What Hodge meant by the 'more than once' the church was
forced to reinterpret the Bible is unclear. Actually, he seems to
have had only one time in mind, the time of Galileo. This will be
discussed below.

There are at least three profoundly serious errors in Hodge's
statement about always changing our interpretation to accommodate
'science.' The first error is the ready acceptance of atheistically
generated speculation as if it were an actual scientific discovery. The
second error is the underestimation of the importance of the biblical
chronology as the framework of biblical history. To so casually give
away the framework of biblical history is like saying that we cannot
see any importance of the skeleton, because the body is the really
important thing. Hodge regarded this biblical truth as non-essential
and beside the purpose of the Bible. One could compare Hodge at
this point to the group of Philistines thinking how unimportant
were the efforts of Samson tugging at the pillars of their temple.
Once those pillars were gone it was too late for damage control. One
cannot destroy Genesis and expect the rest of Scripture to remain
unharmed. The third major error is the disastrous hermeneutic set

12. Hodge, *Systematic Theology*, Vol. I, p. 573.

in motion by the Genesis compromise. Once the undermining of Genesis destroys the foundations of Christian doctrines, it is too late for damage control. Hodge could have learned so much from the master exegete John Calvin. The historian Philip Schaff calls Calvin 'the founder of the modern grammatico-historical exegesis.'[13] In his commentary on Galatians, Calvin says:

> 'Let us know, then, that the true meaning of Scripture is the natural and obvious meaning; and let us embrace and abide by it resolutely. Let us not only neglect as doubtful, but boldly set aside as deadly corruptions, those pretended expositions, which lead us away from the natural meaning.'[14]

Calvin placed great emphasis on the plain, literal historical meaning of Scripture. And the hermeneutical principle is sound: the intended meaning of Scripture is Scripture and a false interpretation of Scripture is not Scripture. In his Epistle Dedicatory to the Epistle of Romans, Calvin says,

> 'Such veneration we ought indeed to entertain for the Word of God, that we ought not to pervert it in the least degree by varying expositions; for its majesty is diminished, I know not how much, ...And if it be deemed a great wickedness to contaminate any thing that is dedicated to God, he surely cannot be endured, who, with impure, or even with unprepared hands, will handle that very thing, which of all things is the most sacred on earth. It is therefore an audacity, closely allied to a sacrilege, rashly to turn Scripture in any way we please, and to indulge our fancies as in sport...'[15]

---

13. Philip Schaff, 'Calvin's Theology,' in *History of the Christian Church*, vol. 8 (Third Edition, revised; Grand Rapids, Michigan: Wm. B. Eerdmans Publishing Company, 1910), p. 532.

14. John Calvin, 'Chapter IV,' in *Commentaries on the Epistle to the Galatians*, trans. William Pringle (Calvin Translation Society, reprint; Grand Rapids, Michigan: Baker Books, 2003), p. 136.

15. John Calvin, 'The Epistle Dedicatory,' in *Commentaries on the Epistle to the Romans*, trans. John Owen (Calvin Translation Society, reprint; Grand Rapids, Michigan: Baker Books, 2003), p. xxvii.

This is such a stark contrast to Hodge, who under the pressure of current scientific opinion, wishing to be thought scholarly, so nonchalantly turned over the interpretation of Genesis to whatever consensus a group of anti-Christians would come up with. Hodge said we can frequently change our interpretation accordingly with no harm to Scripture. It was the worst and most harmful statement he ever penned. How he could have learned so much from Calvin!

Hodge discusses various theories of creation, or origin of the universe, in chapter ten of his systematic theology. He rightly observes that the question of origins is not something observed or experienced by any human being. This makes man's theories of origins somewhat speculative and subjective. Citing Genesis 1:1, Hodge observes three things:

1. The universe is not eternal. It had a beginning.

2. It was not formed out of any pre-existing material, but created *ex nihilo*.

3. The creation was not necessary. God was free to create or not create.[16]

As Hodge writes in the latter half of the nineteenth century, the Nebular Hypothesis of Kant and Laplace was quite popular. This theory held that clouds of gas broke off into rings, then condensed into planets. Hodge sees this as an inadequate alternative to the Genesis account. The axiomatic statement 'nothing comes from nothing' should be understood to mean that existence cannot *spontaneously* spring from non-existence. The Creator is the only sufficient cause for the existence of the universe.

Hodge sets forth the biblical doctrine of creation.

(Hebrews 11:3) 'By faith we understand that the worlds were framed by the word of God, so that the things which are seen were not made of things which are visible.'

16. Hodge, *Systematic Theology*, Vol. 1, p. 553.

The true explanation of origins, the biblical doctrine of creation, can be known only by revelation. The universe was created by the simple word or command of God. The creation was immediate, instantaneous and not formed of any preexisting material. The account of Genesis is an historical account. It claims to be historical and is written in that form. Genesis 1 through 11 form an appropriate and necessary introduction to the widely acknowledged historical narrative of the following chapters. The creation account is cited in other parts of the Bible as true history. This is seen especially in Exodus 20, speaking of the fourth commandment,

> (Exodus 20:11) ' For *in* six days the LORD made the heavens and the earth, the sea, and all that *is* in them, and rested the seventh day. Therefore the LORD blessed the Sabbath day and hallowed it.'

Hodge gives a final reason why the account of Genesis must be taken as historical.

The facts here recorded, including as they do the creation and probation of man, lie at the foundation of the whole revealed plan of redemption. The whole Bible, therefore, rests upon the record here given of the work of creation, and consequently all the evidence which goes to support the divine authority of the Bible, tends to sustain the historical verity of that record.'[17]

A. HODGE CONSIDERS OBJECTIONS TO THE MOSAIC ACCOUNT

Hodge is overly concessive in his response to objections. The strong confident statements made in setting out the biblical doctrine of creation are replaced by tentative and uncertain responses to criticisms. For example, some had suggested that the 'days' of Genesis 1 might be long ages instead of ordinary calendar days. Hodge had spoken of the six days, even pointing us to the fourth commandment's

---

17. Ref. 16. pp. 568–69.

use of the phrase to describe our weekly cycle. But in response to this criticism, he is quite accommodating:

> 'It is a belief founded on a given interpretation of the Mosaic record, which interpretation, however, must be controlled not only by the laws of language, but by facts. This is at present an open question. The facts necessary for its decision have not yet been duly authenticated. The believer may calmly await the result.'[18]

What Hodge regards as a minor concession is actually quite destructive of sound biblical interpretation. As a Presbyterian minister, Hodge had taken ordination vows, which included his statement of adherence to the Westminster Confession of Faith. The Confession's statement on the interpretation of Scripture reflects the church's faith:

> WCF 1.9 The infallible rule of interpretation of Scripture is the Scripture itself: and therefore, when there is a question about the true and full sense of any Scripture (which is not manifold, but one), it must be searched and known by other places that speak more clearly.

Doubtless, on any Sunday morning, Hodge would affirm the Westminster statement without qualification. Not only that, but his teaching elsewhere in his *Systematic Theology* is quite sound. Under the topic of rules of interpretation, he says:

> The words of Scripture are to be taken in their plain historical sense. That is, they must be taken in the sense attached to them in the age and by the people to whom they were addressed. Scripture cannot contradict Scripture... Hence Scripture must explain Scripture. The Scriptures are to be interpreted under the guidance of the Holy Spirit, which guidance is to be humbly and earnestly sought. ... The unrenewed mind is naturally blind to spiritual truth

---

18. Ref. 16, pp. 557–58

[1 Cor. 2:14]…only those who are spiritually minded can truly receive the things of the Spirit.[19]

It is surprising, in view of the excellence of these statements, that he so easily concedes uncertainty as to the meaning of 'day' in Genesis 1. He also disregards the rules of sound interpretation by saying that, in this case, our interpretation of the Mosaic account must be controlled *not by the laws of language, but by 'facts.'* Here we do not find 'Scripture interprets Scripture' but 'facts' interpret Scripture. Something from outside Scripture may be imposed upon it, so as to destroy the 'plain historical sense' Hodge had previously so skillfully advocated. Here we also find the value-free concept of 'facts' so characteristic of the evidential apologist. 'Facts', so clearly distinguished from 'theories' elsewhere in Hodge, are now confused. Hodge does not specify in this context what 'facts' could thus destroy the plain historical meaning. Elsewhere we see that it is the growing evolutionary consensus among scientists. The intellectual pressure to conform was very great, and remains a strong temptation even now, one hundred and fifty years later. The weak apologetic of the nineteenth century sought desperately to conform to the consensus, even at the cost of setting unsound precedents in the interpretation of Scripture. (At what price intellectual respectability?).

Hodge says that objections to the Mosaic account of creation are of three kinds: critical, astronomical, and geological. He dismisses the critical hypothesis by saying that the biblical account is consistent and it would not affect the historical truth of Genesis if Moses used source documents under inspiration. While in isolation this comment appears to be appropriate, in the context of the hypotheses then being floated, Hodge may have been too accommodating. The critical hypothesis was heading toward the documentary hypothesis (JEDP) and the role of Moses would be denied altogether. But apparently in 1872, Hodge could feel his response was adequate for the critical theory as it then existed. This earlier version of the critical theory had *Moses* using a Jehovah (J) source document and an Elohim (E) source document. (Of course, this version too is false.)

---

19. Ref. 16, pp. 187–88.

Of the objections from astronomy, we have the geocentric view and the problem of light and day/night cycle before the creation of the sun. Of the first Hodge speaks of the ordinary common way of speaking of sunrise and sunset, without asserting a geocentric view. The second objection may be met, he says, by assuming that the fourth day was only the appointment of sun and moon to determine seasons, etc. The sun could have already been in existence. Alternatively, a previous source of light distinct from the sun may be referred to. After all, 'The narrative makes a distinction between the cosmical light mentioned in the earlier part of the chapter, and the light emanating from the sun, specially designed for our globe.'[20]

Hodge considers the geological objections most serious. The commonly received chronology (derived from Scripture) makes the earth only thousands of years old; most geologists say it has existed for countless ages. Genesis 1 says the creation was accomplished in six days, but geology says it took long ages of time to bring our world to its present state.

Typical of an evidential apologist, Hodge does not confront the total worldview of evolution with the antithetic worldview of Christianity. Instead he easily concedes much to the evolutionary worldview. If we considered the Scripture as a department store of infallible truth, and Hodge as the night watchman, we will be in for a surprise. When we return in the morning, we find the store under new management. Although it is no longer *wholly* owned by the Sovereign of the universe, our night watchman encourages us that he has saved a corner booth within the new owner's store for biblical truth. Hodge seems to believe that the absolute authority of the revealed Word of God may extend only so far as humanistic evolutionary scientific consensus will allow.

Concession, not confrontation, is characteristic of Hodge's apologetic. His first comment is, 'Admitting the facts to be as the geologists would have us believe...'[21]

---

20. Ref. 16, p. 550.

21. Ref. 16, p. 570.

Those Christians willing to concede the geologists' view have devised many ways of supposedly reconciling the geologists' view with the biblical record. In Hodge's time the two ways of accommodating evolution were the gap theory and the day-age theory.

The so-called 'Gap Theory' became a popular compromise. Although Hodge does not mention it by name, that is what he is describing. This theory posits an original creation in Genesis 1:1 and then the long geological ages are inserted. Finally, we come to verse two where the re-creation account begins. Thomas Chalmers, a godly preacher from Scotland, developed this theory in 1804. While we can be immensely grateful for his pastoral and preaching ministry, his concessionary apologetic left much to be desired. Christians, panicked by the wide acceptance of naturalism's millions of years, were given an easy way out. Thanks to the gap theory they could be freed from the hard work of developing a Christian, biblically based worldview in every area of life. They could leave geology to the geologists, accept whatever they said, and go on to think about more important spiritual things. Let the astronomers tell us how the heavens go; we will stick to telling how to go to heaven. Let the geologists talk about the age of rocks; we will talk of the Rock of Ages. All the geologic ages, the cavemen, dinosaurs, and all else could be thrown into the virtual black hole between Genesis 1:1 and 1:2.

Although this view was popularized by *The Scofield Reference Bible*,[22] competent exegetes found it impossible to accept. The text could not be made to conform to the gap theory. The Hebrew grammar calls for verse 2 to be explanatory of verse 1, not a chronological sequence to it. Not only is the verb almost always translated as 'was' and very rarely as 'became', but there are also more technical grammatical considerations that rule out a sequential relationship between Gen. 1:1 and Gen. 1:2. The prefixed Hebrew letter *vav* (ו) (also designated *waw*) is a conjunction meaning 'and'

---

22. C. I. Scofield, ed., 'Genesis One,' in *The Scofield Reference Bible* (New York: Oxford University Press, 1917), p. 3.

or 'but.' There are two basic uses of *vav* in Genesis 1. One is the *vav* consecutive, used to show sequential relationship. Examples of this usage are seen in verse 3 '*And* God *said...*' verse 4 '*And* God *saw...*' verse 5 '*And* God *called...*' etc. The *vav* consecutive shows a sequential relationship. The distinctive thing about the construction is that the *vav* is prefixed to a verb. Now notice verse two which also begins with *vav*. Here, however, vav is prefixed to a noun. This construction is a *vav* disjunctive. This is used to describe further detail surrounding the event just mentioned. In Gen. 1 it means that verse two '*Now* the earth *was...*' is a description of the state of things when (in verse one) 'God created' It does not describe something that happened millions of years later.[23]

The gap theory is thus exegetically impossible, besides being scientifically faulty.

As usual, trying to make God's infallible word conform to man's fallible ideas results in both poor science and even poorer exegesis. Hodge did not speak against this view, but quietly dropped it in favor of a day-age type view.

Hodge's second way of 'reconciling' geology and the Bible was what is now called the day-age theory. This he treats more favorably. If only the days are taken to be geologic ages, there is no contradiction. Thus we see that instead of a presuppositional worldview apologetic, Hodge will settle for a piecemeal, non-antithetical apologetic. Whereas the Christian worldview would interpret geology biblically, the piecemeal accommodating apologist insists on interpreting the Bible geologically. In Hodge's own words,

> 'It is of course admitted that, taking this account by itself, it would be most natural to understand the word ['day'] in its ordinary sense; but if that sense brings the Mosaic account into conflict with facts, and another sense avoids such conflict, then it is obligatory on us to adopt that other.'[24]

---

23. Bruce K. Waltke, and O'Conner, M. 'Coordination and Clausal Adverbs,' in *An Introduction to Biblical Hebrew Syntax* (Winona Lake, Indiana: Eisenbrauns, 1990), p. 650ff., see also the NET Bible, Biblical Studies Press, L.L.C. (2005), p. 2.

24. Hodge, *Systematic Theology*, Vol. I, p. 571.

Hodge suggests that since 'day' can possibly mean 'an indefinite period of time' and there are [unspecified by Hodge] examples of it being so used, we can understand the 'days' in Genesis 1 to be geologic ages. This is obviously driven by the acceptance of the uniformitarianism upon which modern geology is founded. It is certainly not driven by the exegesis of Scripture. Because Hodge does not challenge the presuppositions upon which evolutionary geology was built, he allows pseudo-science to force him into faulty exegesis. Actually he does not do any exegesis at all! He totally ignores the context in Genesis, which clearly identifies 'day' as a calendar day. What kind of apologetic says to the unbeliever, we can make the Scripture say anything you want it to say? The result of such an 'apologetic' is that the Christian is encouraged to move (just a little, only on 'unimportant' passages) toward evolution. The evolutionist is encouraged to continue doing without the Bible, since Scripture must be conformed to what he says anyway. Hodge's apologetic 'success' cannot be distinguished from surrender. Subsequent history made clear what he did not clearly see; a few concessions now will result in a total abandonment later. So went Princeton along with the larger Protestant denominations. We must give up the strategy of the guaranteed loss apologetic and have greater confidence in the Word of God written.

The omniscient God 'got it right' in every word He has spoken, even when touching on 'scientific' areas. God's omniscience means that His knowledge is perfect and totally comprehensive. Genuine science can discover nothing more than a few of the things God has known all along.

Hodge tries to show how the days of Genesis and the geologic ages might be correlated. Some apologists even suggested that Genesis had described the geologic ages before geology did. Just as Christians had often felt forced to adopt whatever philosopher's theories seemed closest to Christianity, they now felt forced to look for some compromise interpretation that could salvage the really important core of Christianity. But the uniformitarian 'ages' do not correlate with the days of Genesis, if we take a closer look. They simply do not agree, for example, on the order of creation. The Bible presents birds before land reptiles, just the opposite of evolutionary schemes. The uniformitarian will likely deny that there was a creation at all.

Christians should realize that the evolutionary view was specifically intended to exclude God. It is very strange that Christians should feel a need to incorporate it into their thinking. But if we wanted to make the Bible agree with uniformitarian (evolutionary) geology, our concessions cannot logically stop at Genesis 1.

Hodge affirms that there can be no conflict between Scripture and the *facts* of science, only conflict with the *theories* proposed. One of Hodge's problems is that he accepts too much of the uniformitarian theory as 'facts.' His other major problem is that he thinks that 'facts' can be understood apart from their relation to God. Unless the 'facts' are seen as God-created and God-interpreted, they are a meaningless barrage of unrelated sensations. A presuppositional apologetic would have evaluated the data of science in order to interpret them biblically, seeing the data as God-created. This would avoid imposing anti-Christian theories on the data of science.

But Hodge takes the wrong road regarding the 'facts' of science. To repeat what was previously quoted:

> 'The Church has been forced more than once to alter her interpretation of the Bible to accommodate the discoveries of science. But this has been done without doing any violence to the Scriptures or in any degree impairing their authority.'[25]

This is nonsense. Hodge appeals to the worn-out excuse about the sun going around the earth. He seems to think the Church (Roman Catholic) adopted a geocentric view based on their understanding of Scripture. What if they adopted a geocentric view based on the Aristotelian 'scientific consensus' of the university doctors, then assumed that the Bible should be brought into agreement? The

25. Ref. 1, p. 573.

medieval church, already notorious for allegorical interpretations, forced the 'scientific' philosophy of Aristotle upon some poetic sections of Scripture. The real story is that Hodge *et al.* are repeating in the nineteenth century the error of the Roman Church in the seventeenth century. Then the pressure of the university consensus led to forcing poetic passages of Scripture to conform to Aristotle's scientific views; now the pressure was to make the historical narratives of Genesis into something highly figurative in order to conform to the new university consensus. The common error is attempting to interpret Scripture by the standard of currently popular theories, instead of evaluating these theories by the standard of Scripture. It does irreparable damage to the Bible to twist it this way and that according to the direction the latest scientific speculations are headed. Real scientific investigation in the late twentieth century has given us abundant reason to reject Darwinism. Incredibly enough, some evangelicals hang on to outdated concessions, as if we were still caught up in the evolution euphoria of the late nineteenth and early twentieth centuries. Sadly, Princeton would slide downhill even further in later years.

B. HODGE ON BIBLICAL CHRONOLOGY

We should not suppose that Hodge was a convinced believer in the evolutionary chronology of Lyell and Darwin. He finds every individual argument favoring hundreds of thousands of years of human history to be inconclusive. Finding arguments from lake dwellings, fossil human remains, flint implements, ancient monuments and Egyptian chronology all to be unpersuasive, he says,

'The fact that the monuments of human art cannot pretend to a higher antiquity than a few thousand years, renders it utterly incredible that man has existed on the earth hundreds of thousands or, as Darwin supposes, millions of years.'[26]

26. Hodge, *Systematic Theology*, Vol. II, p. 39.

Even after finding every argument for evolutionary chronology unconvincing, Hodge is still hesitant to have any confidence in the biblical chronology. The paralyzing fear of repeating the Galileo affair leads him to surrender biblical chronology without a fight. This is not because it has been proven wrong, but because Hodge seems to fear that it will some day be proven wrong. He aims to put the Bible out of range of the critics by making the Bible irrelevant to chronology. As far as chronology was concerned, Hodge would put the Bible in a safe but irrelevant place. This kind of method would be used by twentieth century neo-orthodoxy in order to make massive concessions to higher criticism. They would dismiss the Bible's literal history and call it 'salvation history.' Let critics destroy the historical value of Genesis, we will retain the spiritual significance. Hodge is ready to concede every criticism of biblical chronology because: 'the chronology of the Bible is very uncertain...not stated for purposes of chronology...rests mainly on the authority of Archbishop Usher [*sic*].'[27]

Hodge has the standard objections to biblical chronology. The LXX (Greek Old Testament) makes the time of creation slightly earlier, there may be gaps in the genealogies, various chronologists have not reached precise agreement, and the genealogies were not really written to give us a chronology. After raising these questions as if they were unanswerable, he attempts to comfort the friends of the Bible,

> 'If the facts of science or of history should ultimately make it necessary to admit that eight or ten thousand years have elapsed since the creation of man, there is nothing in the Bible in the way [i.e. blocking the way] of such a concession. The Scriptures do not teach us how long men have existed on earth.'[28]

27. Ref. 26, p. 40.
28. Ref. 26, p. 41.

C. EVALUATION OF HODGE'S APOLOGETIC

What shall we say to these things? There are several indications that Hodge's apologetic is both superficial and piecemeal, especially in this area of biblical creation. He helps us to see how anything less than a foundational presuppositional apologetic will be found wanting. His needless concessions had the unintended ultimate effect of encouraging unbelievers to hold on to their evolutionary worldview, and allow Christians to move in the direction of evolution. If the effect of an apologetic is only to permit Christians to move closer to the abyss of unbelief, while leaving the unbeliever unmoved, it is time to look for another apologetic approach.

Hodge's phrase, 'Scriptures do not teach us how long men have existed on the earth,' has become a standard opening for liberals who are about to announce a view contrary to Scripture. Their opening line is usually, 'The Bible says nothing on the subject of...' This means they are about to set forth an unbiblical view of homosexuality, abortion, economics, education, etc. If they must admit that the Bible seems to say something on the topic, they will insist that the Bible was not written for *the purpose* of teaching us about science, history, psychology, chronology, etc. This method provides a way of rejecting biblical teaching by ignoring it rather than directly attacking it.

This leaves us with three basic views on the subject:

- The liberal view: Of course the Bible plainly gives us a chronology, but it cannot be taken seriously in our modern scientific age.

- The trepid neo-evangelical view: Of course we believe the Bible, but we are not woodenly literal in our interpretation. Our faith must be intellectually respectable, in accord with the findings of modern science. We are fearful of another Galileo affair. We must get the Bible out of the range of criticism by not pressing it on non-spiritual issues.

- The consistently biblical view: The Bible plainly gives us a chronology. It is a God-breathed record; nothing is or ever could be more reliable.

Hodge's statement was that the Bible was not written to teach chronology. This is another attempt to avoid the teaching of Scripture by a statement that is true only in a trivial and irrelevant sense. No one says the Bible's main purpose for being written is so we could have a chronology. That is why the statement is irrelevant to the debate. It shows that the person making the statement does not understand the question or does not want the question to be understood. Such people often say, the Bible was written to teach us how to be saved or how to go to heaven. They end up implying that a necessary corollary would be: 'only those statements of the Bible which refer to being saved are reliable.' Hodge and many others have chosen to begin with a statement concerning the (main) purpose of Scripture that is irrelevant to the point in dispute. Christians who affirm biblical chronology are agreed on the first statement, but strongly disagree that the Bible is unreliable on subjects other than theological loci pertaining to salvation or heaven. This would presuppose that the Bible is mostly useless 'filler' with an occasional nugget about something spiritual. One question we should always ask about such assertion is this: What view of the Bible or of God does the statement in question *presuppose*?

Other statements to the effect that the chronology of the Bible is very uncertain, or that we should not rely on Archbishop Ussher, provide a valuable lesson for us. Christians must learn not to accept assertions as proof, unless it is an assertion of God in Scripture. All others must make their case. If there is uncertainty, it is not the fault of Scripture. The biblical account is not *unclear*; it is *uncomfortable* for the modern evolutionized Christian. When Christians feel compelled to grasp in desperation at some naturalistic and uniformitarian explanation of creation, let us remember that the Creation was neither naturalistic nor uniformitarian; it was supernatural and instantaneous.[29]

For a more detailed account of the biblical genealogies, refer to Chapter 4 'Chronology and Genealogy.'

---

29. See for example Genesis 1:3–30 for the constant refrain: "God said…and it was so." God spoke His supernatural Word, and that which He spoke came into being at once.

CHAPTER 7

ROBERT L. DABNEY

D abney's thoughts on evolution are most readily found in his published *Lectures in Systematic Theology* and the four volumes of essays under the title *Discussions*. He makes a crucial statement at the beginning of a lecture on evolution. '*Genera* may begin or end, but never transmute themselves into other *genera*.'[1] It is worth noting that Dabney thinks of the biblical 'kinds' as genera. This is an improvement over the popular tendency to equate the biblical kinds with species, but still carries more risk than using the actual biblical term. Nevertheless, Dabney does give his views on the limits of variation among living beings. We know from breeding practices that many varieties of a given kind are possible, but there are also limits on how much variation is possible.

We could even grant a degree of natural selection, that breeds or variations could occur naturally as well as under the guidance of a breeder. In either case there are definite genetic limits that assure an offspring of the same 'kind.' That is, the horse always remains a horse; the dog remains a dog, although differing in several ways from other breeds of the dog kind.

Dabney is not receptive to the theory of evolution. He is, in fact, far less receptive to it than was Charles Hodge. The evolution hypothesis is, indeed, no novelty.

---

1. Robert Lewis Dabney, 'Evolution,' in *Lectures in Systematic Theology* (Grand Rapids, Michigan: Zondervan Publishing House, 1972), p. 26.

'It is, after all its pretended modern experiments, but a revival of the 'atomic theory' of the Greek atheist, Democritus, adopted by the Epicurean school. Its application to the descent of man from some lower animal has often been attempted, as by Lord Monboddo, who almost exactly anticipated Dr. Chas. Darwin's conclusion.'[2]

'The tendency of this scheme is atheistic. Some of its advocates may disclaim the consequence, and declare their recognition of a God and Creator, we hope, sincerely. But the undoubted tendency of the speculation, will be to lead its candid adherents, where Dr. Leopold Buchner has placed himself, to blank materialism and atheism. For the scheme is an attempt to evolve what theists call the creation without a Creator;...'[3]

Dabney raises many cogent objections against evolutionary theories. By using the term 'natural selection' evolutionists give the impression of intelligent choice. But the whole scheme was designed to exclude any intelligence. The regular permanent selection of favorable features would require intelligence, he claimed.

The fossil record should contain vastly more remains of failed random changes than successful ones. Yet all we find are fully developed specimens. The wide geographical distribution of species argues against their supposed 'survival of the fittest' in response to local conditions. Changes we have actually observed in the process of bringing about new varieties of animals, are the result of intelligent purposeful activity, not random changes. The developed varieties show a natural tendency to revert to their original type. Furthermore, hybrids are frequently sterile.[4]

---

2. Ref. 1, p. 27. Lord Monboddo (1714–99) was a Scottish jurist also known as James Burnett.

3. Ref. 1, p. 27. Leopold Büchner (1824–99) was a German physician and philosopher.

4. Modern creationist arguments point out that hybridization between two different species, whether the offspring are fertile or not, is a likely indication that the two were originally derived from the same created kind.

Evolution cannot account for the mind of man. A comparison of bones and physical remains are not an adequate explanation of the vast differences between man and animals. For example, a fossil leg bone of an ape, if similar in some way, does not prove the ape is an ancestor of modern man. Even if we granted some questionable assumptions made by evolutionists, their theory would still be a mere possibility, not proven. There is a huge gap between observed facts and fanciful inductions. Dabney quotes Dr. Huxley on this matter:

> 'Until either actual experiment or actual observation has verified the expectation of the hypothesis; and verified it in such a way as to make it clear to the mind, that the expected result followed the antecedent as propter hoc and not a mere post hoc; that hypothesis, however plausible, and seemingly satisfying, is not demonstrated.'[5]

The verification of the evolutionary theory is in the nature of the case impossible—the dates proposed for evolution's supposed occurrence greatly precede the experience of mankind. This means that the arena of speculation has been entered.

> 'These speculations are mischievous in that they present to minds already degraded, and in love with their own degradation, a pretext for their materialism, godlessness and sensuality.'[6]

Dabney saw this clearly, but he could not imagine that the evolutionary scheme, so degrading to humanity, would ever prevail among men. How much more surprised he would have been to see it so prevalent in the churches. Dabney saw the theory as libelous and absurd. Dabney contrasts the worthlessness of speculative possibilities with the 'inspired testimony upon the subject, to which the Revealed Theology will soon introduce us.'[7]

---

5. Ref. 1, p. 31.

6. Ref. 1, p. 32.

7. Ref. 1, p. 33.

It is a case of hypothetical evidence versus judicial historical testimony. A defense attorney may argue that person B could possibly have committed a crime, but that would be far less weighty than an eyewitness testimony that in fact person A committed the crime.

> 'Does Revelation bring in the testimony of the divine Eyewitness, because actual Agent, of the genesis of the universe? Is Revelation sustained as a credible witness by its literary, its internal, its moral, its prophetical, its miraculous evidences?'[8]

Evolutionary theory insists on excluding this possibility, even from consideration. The biblical worldview assumes its truth and sees evidence of its truth on every hand. Does the evolutionary theory suppose organisms were produced a certain way? 'God the Agent, tells us that, in point of fact, they were otherwise produced.'[9]

Darwin's theory would have the consequence of doing away with teleology. Dabney saw in Darwin's theory its deeply philosophical and religious motives:

> 'Darwinism happens just now to be the current manifestation, which the fashion of the day gives to the permanent anti–theistic tendency in sinful man. As long as men do not like to retain God in their knowledge, the objection to the argument for His existence will reappear in some form. And the forms will all be found cognate. This recent evolution theory verges every year nearer to the pagan atomic theory.'[10]

Dabney here recognizes the presuppositional roots of evolutionary thought more clearly than did Hodge. After citing the geological data about rocks and fossils that is claimed to show that the earth is more than six thousand years old, Dabney notes that modern theologians

---

8. Ref. 1, p. 33.

9. Dabney, *Lectures in Systematic Theology*, p. 33.

10. Ref. 9, p. 37.

have usually yielded to this as a demonstration. Those who seek to 'rescue Moses' from apparent error include noted evangelicals like Chalmers and Charles Hodge. Some resorted to what was later called the 'gap theory' postulating vast ages of time between Genesis 1:1 and 1:2. Others adopted a day-age theory. Dabney rejects these compromises and gives exegetical grounds for his objections. For example:

1. The sun, moon and light were only created at the Adamic period. Without these there could have been neither vegetable nor animal life before.

2. We seem to learn from Gen. 1:31; 3:17–19; Rom. 5:12; 8:19–22, that all animal suffering and death came upon our earth as a punishment for man's sin; which our conceptions of the justice and benevolence of God seem to confirm.

Dabney knows that advocates of the gap theory have attempted to answer these objections. He is unconvinced, although he believes this interpretation less objectionable than the day-age view.[11] The day-age view was also being promoted in the time of Hodge and Dabney. The days were said to be long geologic ages. Some added that the geologist's succession of fossils corresponded to the order of the days of Genesis.

Again Dabney cites exegetical objections as the most important considerations. Leaving aside that not all geologists had an agreed order of fossils, the order of the days in Scripture is not the same as the geologic column postulated. The vague language of some church fathers provides no convincing evidence for this view. The church fathers did not adopt such a view, and were inclined to greatly shorten the period of creation rather than lengthen it.

'The sacred writer seems to shut us up to the literal interpretation, by describing the day as composed of its natural parts, 'morning and evening.'... And it is hard to see what a writer can mean, by naming evening and morning as making a first, or a second 'day'; except

---

11. Although exegetically unsound, the gap theory at least allows the six day creation, the global flood, and the Genesis genealogies to be read as straightforward history.

that he meant us to understand that time which includes just one of each of these successive epochs: —one beginning of night, and one beginning of day. These gentlemen cannot construe the expression at all. The plain reader has no trouble with it. When we have had one evening and one morning, we know we have just one civic day;'[12]

Dabney will not compromise a sound exegesis of Scripture to accommodate a theory of man. It is obvious that for him Scripture is the highest authority by which all other ideas must be judged. At this point, and others, Dabney is a sounder interpreter and a more faithful defender of Scripture than was Hodge. Hodge could have learned from Dabney that his concessions to evolution were unwise. Hodge ends up defending a discredited theory, adopted only to accommodate an anti-Christian worldview. Distorting the truth of Scripture results in a faulty hermeneutic and a faulty science.

Dabney recognizes the Genesis account as historical narrative, not symbolism. The very nature of creation is a supernatural instantaneous act of God. We cannot keep changing our exposition to match the ever-changing theories of scientists.

'I repeat, if any part of the Bible must wait to have its real meaning imposed upon it by another, and a human science, that part is at least meaningless and worthless to our souls. It must expound itself independently; making other sciences ancillary, and not dominant over it.'[13]

Dabney saw the consequences of tampering with Scripture far more clearly than most of his time. The church would have gone into the twentieth century in far better spiritual health if it had heeded Dabney's advice. The geologist does not dislodge the Bible until he has constructed his own independent, and exclusive, and demonstrative evidence that his hypothesis must be the true one, and the only true one.[14] And that is what Dabney is confident will never happen.

---

12. Ref. 9, p. 255
13. Ref. 9, p. 257.
14. Ref. 1, p. 258.

Hodge himself thought highly of Dabney, even repeatedly urging him to come to Princeton. Dabney shows us that it was quite possible for a Christian to resist the evolutionary enthusiasm of the last half of the nineteenth century. And he saw the evil consequences toward which compromise would lead. He must have wondered why the merely theistic philosopher seems to be 'hankering after atheism' by pushing God's creative act back into the remotest past. We should also note that the theistic evolutionist gets his information about God from his imagination instead of God's own revelation. What God has told us about the method and time of creation forms the boundary lines beyond which our speculations must not pass. Theistic evolution can never rise above the level of an opinion, since it is not grounded in God's revelation of Himself in Scripture.

Dabney points out that the dating of fossils and strata is reasoning in a circle. By this he means that they date the fossils by the strata in which they are found then argue the vast age of the strata from the assumed age of the fossils. A much more comprehensive creation science would not be developed until the latter half of the twentieth century. It is all the more remarkable that Dabney was not swept away by the deceptive philosophy like so many of his brethren.

A. DABNEY'S *DISCUSSIONS*

Whereas Hodge would criticize a theologian like Baur on some particular point, Dabney is more likely to get to the root of the matter and examine foundational, systemic problems with German theology.

The nineteenth century American would typically think of a theological professor as someone who was not only genuinely regenerate, but also of eminent learning. The Americans often assumed that a theological professor would be most devout and earnest.

> '…it is hard for our people practically to feel that a man
> so trusted in the holiest things may be dealing with the

sacred text in precisely the same spirit as that in which he would criticize a Saga, or an Anacreontic[15] ode.'[16]

Dabney reminds us of the apostle Paul's verdict on such men.

> 'The carnal mind is enmity against God; it is not subject to the law of God, neither indeed can be.' (Romans 8:7)

> 'The natural man receives not the things of the Spirit of God; for they are foolishness unto him; neither can he know them, because they are spiritually discerned.' (2 Cor. 2:14) 'Their thinking became futile and their senseless hearts were darkened.' (Romans 1:21)

> 'Unless we are prepared to contradict God's Holy Spirit, we must ascribe to the unregenerate critics, however learned, this consequence, that their carnal state must cause them to dislike and misconceive true godliness and salvation by grace.'[17]

The Christian must recognize this revealed truth, even though it will not be well received by these critics. The evangelical Christian must also recognize the spiritual atmosphere of these great centers of learning as 'fearfully cold.'[18] Dabney does not merely criticize a particular doctrine of Baur, but exposes his foundational principles. The first of those principles is 'that nothing supernatural can ever have really occurred.'[19] This kind of foundational, presuppositional criticism is much more difficult to find in Hodge. Naturalism is rotten at the foundation, so our criticism must begin there rather than trying to answer the mass of detail in its false conclusions.

---

15. This refers to light lyrics as in a drinking song.

16. Robert Lewis Dabney, 'The Influence of the German University System on Theological Literature,' in *Discussions of Robert Lewis Dabney*, vol. 1 (Edinburgh: Banner of Truth, 1967), p. 444.

17. Ref. 16, p. 445.

18. Ref. 16, p. 446.

19. Ref. 16, p. 449.

Dabney warns of the dangers of academia in urging the theologian to 'do new work' which is an open invitation to heretical innovation. We learn from Scripture that God values faithfulness to the revealed Word, far above imaginative innovation. What is the verdict on most of German theology?

'It tends to unsettle everything, and settle nothing.'[20]

Dabney gave us more insights into his general philosophy of education. He saw the tendency to transfer educational responsibility away from the home and church to the State school as a secularizing trend. It would surely encourage a revolt from the Christian faith.

> 'Every line of true knowledge must find its completeness in its convergence to God, even as every beam of daylight leads the eye to the sun. If religion [by which Dabney means biblical Christianity] be excluded from our study every process of thought will be arrested before it reaches its proper goal.'[21]

God is so much the foundation and goal of every area of study that to omit His role renders such secular teaching like 'the play of Hamlet, with the part of Hamlet omitted.'[22]

Now it remains to be seen how Dabney applies these scriptural foundational principles to the topics of science and geology. Dabney wrote three lengthy articles in his *Discussions*, volume three. 'Geology and the Bible,' 'A Caution Against Anti-Christian Science', and Dabney's reply to Woodrow's criticism of his 'Caution.'

B. GEOLOGY AND THE BIBLE

Dabney begins with observation that the dispute is often carried on with few facts and to little use. He seeks to establish some principles

---

20. Ref. 16, p. 461.

21. Robert Lewis Dabney, 'Secularized Education,' in *Discussions: Secular*, vol. 4 (Harrisonburg, VA & Vallecito, CA: Sprinkle / Ross House, 1979), p. 233.

22. Ref. 21, p. 234.

of discussion, not to propose some geological theory. 'We firmly protest the arrogant and offensive spirit in which geologists have often met clerical criticisms of their reasonings.'[23] Neither a parson nor a geologist should pretend to know what he does not know. How is it that the evolutionists wish to indoctrinate our children with their theory, yet claim that well educated clergy are not qualified to offer criticism? Their theory is alternately simple enough to be understood by children and too complex to be understood by the clergy. We can be confident in the Bible, which has withstood many assaults through the ages. Every genuine discovery of science will be in perfect harmony with the Bible. Dabney deplores the hasty way in which some clergy abandoned their understanding of Scripture and accepted as truth some uncertain hypothesis.

> '[T]hey have adopted on half-evidence some new-fangled hypothesis of scientific facts, and then invented, on grounds equally insecure, some new-fangled explanations to twist God's word into seeming agreement with the hypothesis.'[24]

The nineteenth century church was too willing to sound the retreat, when their duty post remained quite secure. Churchmen have quickly come up with an ingenious new understanding (to agree with 'science') only to see the scientists give up their old theory for another. Then the churchman must scurry for another imaginative interpretation, which will probably not be his last. No wonder thinking men have been brought to doubt the authority of inspiration. As Dabney said, 'If they are to be believed, then the word of God is but a sort of clay which may be moulded into any shape required by the purposes of priestcraft.'[24]

The unity and harmony of truth prevents us from saying that something may be true in science, but false in theology. If the Bible, properly understood, affirms what geology denies, the difference is

23. Robert Dabney, *Discussions of Robert Lewis Dabney*, Vol. 3, p. 128.
24. Ref. 23, p. 130.

irreconcilable. We may not take liberties with the text of Scripture. There are both scientific and biblical distinctions between the geocentrism versus Galileo controversy and the modern controversy of Scripture versus uniformitarian geology. We could represent the issues in this way:

The creation record is not merely a theological statement, but an historical and physical reality. Because it is true, it is scientifically, historically and theologically true.

Most geologists proceed as though the Bible is totally irrelevant to their study. If the Scripture speaks at all, it is permitted to say nothing more than their deductions will permit. The Bible is treated as a handmaid dependent upon their permission.

Dabney acknowledges that there have been faulty interpretations of the Bible, just as there have been many errors of science in its tentative advance.

> 'But still, the Bible must be held to have its own ascertainable and valid laws of exposition; and its teachings, when duly ascertained, must be absolutely authoritative in all their parts, without waiting on or deferring to any conclusions of human science whatsoever; otherwise, it is practically no Bible; it is no 'rule of faith' for a human soul.'[25]

Controversy	Science	Scripture
Galileo	Observational evidence	Poetic descriptions
Bible vs uniformitarian geology	Presupposing naturalism	Presenting the Creator's own account

It is a preposterous idea that the 'real meaning' of Genesis is something that would have been impossible for the original writer to have intended and impossible for the intended audience to understand. Can we really believe the passage could not be understood until

---

25. Dabney, 'Geology and the Bible' in *Discussions of Robert Lewis Dabney*, Vol. 3, p. 134.

(the deists/atheists) Cuvier and Lyell presented their 'infallible' cosmologies? Must we hold back on trusting the word of God, because hundreds of years from now, a scientific theory may be proposed that contradicts it? Who can then guess where in Scripture these pits of quicksand may be? The objectivity of Scripture must not be sacrificed for the pressures of expediency. To hold the authority of Scripture only in a tentative sense is to remain '…but a rationalist in spirit, whatever may be his Christian or his clerical profession.'[26]

It is appropriate to have the glory of Scripture illustrated by the light of science. But science must be the servant, not the master. The Scripture may have its meaning 'illustrated, *but not created*, by all the discoveries of true science.'[27]

Dabney considers the authority of Scripture to have been established by its own independent evidences (literary, historical, moral, internal, and prophetic). Therefore the burden of proof is upon those who differ with the Mosaic record. His firm conviction is expressed as follows:

> 'We are not bound to retreat until he has constructed an absolutely exclusive demonstration of his hypothesis; until he has shown, by strict scientific proofs, not only that his hypothesis *may be* the true one, but that *it alone can be* the true one; that it is impossible any other can exclude it.'[27]

Is the opponent's hypothesis uncertain, his demonstration incomplete? If so we successfully maintain our position. The miraculous event of Creation does not and cannot fit into a preconceived strait of naturalism and gradualism. How can the flurry of harmonizing expedients have any other effect than the undermining of confidence in Scripture? Dabney cites the contrary schemes of the gap theory and the day-age theory. He also exposes the faulty procedure followed by the ungodly. In the case of Niagara Falls and River, Lyell had

---

26. Dabney, Ref. 25, p. 135.
27. Dabney, Ref. 25, p. 136.

made speculative assumptions about both the cause and rate of the receding edge of the Falls. His assumptions appear to be calculated to give an older date than necessary to the gorge. His presuppositions are controlling his interpretation and theorization. The same kind of uniformitarian assumptions are at work in estimating the time it took to form the Mississippi delta. Selecting from the array of estimates offered, and assuming a constant rate, Lyell may 'prove' that the Mississippi River has been running one hundred thousand years.

Dabney points out that the fossil record shows distinct genera of life, not transitionary forms. We should also remember that creation involves an appearance of age, as seen in newly created adult Adam and fully grown trees, etc.[28]

Because Creation was supernatural, the imposition of naturalism often leads to false conclusions. But it is not only miraculous events that can affect the rate of changes, even 'natural' disasters such as volcanoes and floods can suddenly bring about geologic changes that would take years to produce by gradual processes. Science can also err by assuming that if B follows A, A was the cause of B. But while the cause is necessarily antecedent, the antecedent is not necessarily the cause.

What motivates the obsession to push the creative act back into remote ages before man? Why this minimizing the role of God to the fewest possible forms? Why would nominal Christianity adopt the unbelieving Laplace's nebular hypothesis, without demonstration? Whence come 'laws of nature' if not from the God of Creation? Something other than purely scientific observation is obviously at work.

> 'If therefore, there is any authentic testimony that God did, from the first, create such an earth, no sound inference drawn from natural analogies is of any force to rebut that testimony.'[29]

---

28. Such *inevitable* appearances of age can involve no charge of deceptive intent on the Creator's part, as could be leveled at arguments such as fossils created in rocks 'readymade', or isotope ratios created in young rocks to make them appear old.

29. Dabney, Ref. 25, p. 151.

C. A CAUTION AGAINST ANTI-CHRISTIAN SCIENCE

NAS Colossians 2:8: See to it that no one takes you captive through philosophy and empty deception, according to the tradition of men, according to the elementary principles of the world, rather than according to Christ.

It may seem surprising that Dabney can recognize the possibility and reality of anti-Christian science, since he shares Princeton's interest in Natural Theology and the traditional proofs for the existence of God. This track usually led its proponents to conclude that the 'book of nature' established an independent area of authority for science, to which the Bible would have to yield since the truth found in Scripture could not contradict the truth found in Nature. Dabney stated, 'Not that religious ideas are innate: but the capacity to establish some such ideas, from natural data, is innate.'[30] The Bible speaks of natural revelation, in which God confronts people in such a way as to make them inexcusable. Nineteenth century theologians, even the orthodox ones, preferred to speak of natural theology, in which fallen man deduces by his reason from the facts of nature that God (or a 'god') exists. This trail historically led to the triumph of 'science' and reason over 'religion' and revelation, as it did increasingly even at Princeton. That Dabney so steadfastly opposed evolution is either a happy inconsistency, or it is evidence of his insight that the evolutionary worldview was not arrived at on the basis of provable objective science.

The total depravity of man means that his mind as well as his heart is impaired by sin. The Christian has no warrant to expect that scientists will not or cannot be plagued by the universal depravity of the human nature. Even though man devises ideal principles for scientific investigation, there remains a problem of the application of the true data discovered. 'Fallen minds must always ensure in the

---

30. Dabney, *Lectures in Systematic Theology*, p. 6.

results more or less of error'.[31] But we have in Christ an infallible guide, in whom are all the treasures of wisdom and knowledge. How can we be enticed to leave our unerring guide to follow after the philosophies of confused uncertainties? What is this but following the 'traditions of men' of which the Scriptures often warn us?

What explains the tendency of the physical sciences to become anti-theological? There are two facts that explain it: First, man is a depraved creature, naturally at enmity against God; he does not like to retain God in his knowledge. Secondly, when man has some success in finding out natural causes, he wants to refer everything to these causes. These natural processes become a substitute for the infinite personal God of Scripture.

Dabney gives several examples, which he believes demonstrate that many Christians are being taken captive by empty and deceptive philosophies. These are:

1. We are being required by physicists to admit that the six days' work of God was not done in six days, but in six vast tracts of time.

2. That the deluge did not cover 'all the high hills which were under the whole heavens,' but only a portion of Central Asia.

3. That mankind has been living upon the globe for more than twenty thousand years; not limited to the five thousand nine hundred years assigned it by the Mosaic chronology.

4. Man is not a special creation direct from the dust of the ground, but a development from the lowest type of animal life.[32]

Note here that as far as Dabney is concerned, the Christian who denies the six-day creation, the worldwide flood, and the chronologies of Genesis has been deceived by vain philosophy. Notice that he goes

---

31. Robert Lewis Dabney, 'A Caution Against Anti-Christian Science', in *Discussions of Robert Lewis Dabney*. Vol. 3, Edinburgh: Banner of Truth, 1967, p. 152.

32. Dabney, Ref. 31, p. 154ff.

beyond Hodge by not throwing aside biblical chronology. This was wise, since a purported history without a chronology will soon be dismissed as mythology. Of those so willing to compromise, we might say they have been evolutionized. It is still true today, that in almost every case, whoever adopts the first misinterpretation will adopt all three. Since it is an absurd supposition to think that the original intent of the author or the understanding of the original audience was anything but a straightforward view (calendar days, worldwide flood, accurate chronology) we should look for a common denominator. The common thread is that the Christians who misinterpret all three plainspoken passages have been evolutionized, or in Dabney's terms, deceived by empty philosophies. Dabney asks, 'Can the Scriptures, my brethren, be shown plastic enough to be remoulded, without total fracture of their authority, into agreement with all these views?'[33] Dabney rejects such an attitude because it presupposes that human speculation in the area of science is more certain than the revelation of the Creator in Scripture. These evolutionary philosophers would never dream of submitting their vain speculations to the Bible's contradiction of them. This misplaced priority may be axiomatic for evolutionary science, but it is an abomination for Christianity. At one pole are those who will not have God in their knowledge, at the other pole are those who will test all things in the light of God's own word.

We hear much of how the Christian must concede certain truths to avoid giving offense to the worldly. Should the Christian be requiring the world to concede certain truths to avoid giving offense to the church? For what cause can Christians so quickly concede the biblical testimony because some scientists have come up with another empty speculation? The Bible is infallible; science is fallible. Dabney understands that a basic foundational, non-negotiable issue is at stake. He says:

> 'But I ask, can any exegesis make our Bible speak all the propositions which I enumerated above [regarding the

---

33. Dabney, Ref. 31, p. 155.

six days, the flood, and biblical chronology], and all the rest which it may please the adventurous innovators to announce, without damaging its authority as a sure rule of faith? The common sense of most men will conclude that such a book is only a lump of clay in the hand of priestcraft, to be moulded into such shape as may suit its impostures.'[34]

Words like these should have been heard at Princeton, but alas, were not!

Dabney protests that textbooks were including these speculations as though they were well-established scientific truths, even in professedly Christian colleges. More than one hundred years later, this has not changed. Dabney predicted disastrous results would follow such compromises and he was more correct than he knew. To Dabney, this is an issue where 'the friendship of the world is enmity to God.' You must take sides 'for or against your God.'[35]

He believed the Christian pastor must stand on this position. Dabney points out that no naturalistic arguments from presently observed effects can rule out a supernatural origin, except upon atheistic premises. Even the mere possibility of creation and catastrophe makes it impossible to have any certainty in speculations of origins or in supposed vast eons of pre-human history. If God created anything at all, if there really was a worldwide flood, then to force a naturalistic uniformitarian explanation upon the data is a serious error. Modern creationists would say that among the rocks there are created rocks and flood-formed rocks, neither of which have their origin in naturalistic sources or uniform processes. But the theory of vast ages of time depends on assuming that only naturalistic causes and uniform, presently observed, processes can be considered.

Using the example of the adult Adam, an examination of his long bones would, like those of a modern adult, suggest that they

---

34. Dabney, Ref. 31, p. 157.
35. Dabney, Ref. 31, p. 159.

commenced in cartilage form when he was still an embryo, which was gradually replaced by bone growing out from centers, finally fusing in early adulthood. But this seeming history would be wrong, since he was created as an adult. To exclude this truth of creation is to necessarily err in an overestimate of his age. Trying to push God back into the remote past (or eliminate God altogether) seems to be a symptom of not wanting to have God in our knowledge. Are not men 'reaching after atheism'?[36]

> 'Neither have we any need to force a strained exegesis upon God's record of his own omnipotence in order to conciliate uncertain and fluctuating human sciences.'

'Naturalism is virtual atheism, and *atheism is despair.*'[37]

To adopt the naturalistic premises of certain scientists is to destroy the authority of Scripture, the governing providence of God, and all hope of salvation. We must prefer God's own eyewitness testimony to the speculations of men.

In contrast to the timid Princeton approach (concede before entering into battle), Dabney predicts that the assured ultimate triumph of the Bible will be the outcome of this battle. His view was farsighted and remains justified by the horrendous fruit brought forth by the evolutionary worldview in the twentieth, and now the twenty-first centuries. Lord, ever grant us such faithful men.

---

36. Dabney, Ref. 31, p. 169.
37. Dabney, Ref. 31, p. 170ff.

CHAPTER   8

BENJAMIN B. WARFIELD

Warfield carried on the Reformed orthodoxy of Charles Hodge. Warfield was an outstanding New Testament scholar and systematic theologian. The passing of decades has not diminished the value of his work. It is a travesty that a typical text on the history of doctrine will pass over Benjamin Warfield without a mention. For example, Justo Gonzalez in his history of Christianity does not even mention Hodge or Warfield in his 840 page work, although he has plenty of space for those whose claim to being 'Christian' or 'theologians' is dubious on both counts.[1]

Bromiley's *Historical Theology* also passes over the Princeton theologians without mention. Olson's account mentions Hodge and Warfield, but not in a way that would leave us indebted to them. Their conservative theology is said to have only hardened 'traditional categories' and served as precursor to Fundamentalism. Real progress, according to Olson, awaited the arrival of neo-orthodoxy to triumphantly bridge the gap between the old liberal and fundamentalist theologies.[2]

It must be kept in mind that the weaknesses critiqued in this work represent only a small part of the total treasury of Princeton theology. Their errors herein presented, though serious in their

---

1. Justo L. Gonzalez, *The Story of Christianity*, Prince Press edition (Peabody, Massachusetts: Prince Press, 1999).

2. Roger E. Olson, 'Conservative Theology Hardens Traditional Categories,' in *The Story of Christian Theology, Twenty Centuries of Tradition & Reform* (Downers Grove, Illinois: InterVarsity Press, 1999), pp. 554–569.

consequences, are like a bit of tarnish on sterling silver in comparison to most modern theology, which tends to be more like a thoroughly rusted old tin can.

Though Warfield retained Hodge's position that 'Darwinism is atheism', he went further than Hodge by affirming an openness to non-atheistic views of evolution. In the one hundred years from 1820–1921 Princeton had either Hodge or Warfield as their champion of orthodoxy for all but eight of those years. Warfield is best known as a defender of biblical inerrancy and Reformed theology. His collected writings are mostly made up of essays and reviews on a wide range of subjects. Hodge and Warfield were the outstanding editors of Princeton's theological quarterlies. Warfield defended Scripture and the doctrines of the Westminster Confession against the attacks of his day.

Warfield believed in a concurrence theory of inspiration, which held that all parts of Scripture are both human and divine. As we learn more about the person and style of the human author, we increase our understanding of the human character of Scripture without diminishing its plenary divine character. But with all that, Warfield was willing to make concessions to evolutionary theory. It was conceivable to him that the human body evolved from a primitive ancestor, so long as God is credited with creating the soul of man.

In 1888 Warfield published an essay review in response to the three-volume *Life and Letters of Charles Darwin,* edited by Darwin's son Francis.[3] Warfield presented Darwin's departure from the Christian faith, natural theology, and finally from the uniqueness of human moral consciousness. Warfield believed such decline was both tragic and unnecessary. Even acceptance of evolutionary natural selection would not inevitably lead us away from Christianity. His treatment of the subject is clouded by his sympathy with theistic evolution. He did not see the great problem with theistic evolution: the claim to know something about God that is contrary to what God Himself has revealed to us about the details of creation.

---

3. Benjamin B Warfield, 'Charles Darwin's Religious Life: A Sketch in Spiritual Biography,' *Presbyterian Review*, (October 1888) Vol. 9: pp. 569–601.

Darwin wrote of his early days in his *Life and Letters*, '...as I did not then in the least doubt the strict and literal truth of every word in the Bible, I soon persuaded myself that our Creed must be fully accepted.'[4] Thus, according to Darwin's understanding at the time, the Creed is an accurate representation of the Bible's teaching. Later events would prove how little he understood the Bible and how shaky was his reluctant acceptance of the Creed. As pointed out in chapter five, by the time Darwin sailed on the *Beagle* he thought the Old Testament of no more value than the book of the Hindus. This was his private opinion, not necessarily meant for publication.

His time at Cambridge was largely wasted, though he did get his divinity degree—the only degree he ever earned. While attracted to the respectable life of a country parson, he was distracted from this interest. Immediately after graduation, he signed on as naturalist and companion to the captain on the *Beagle* expedition. He had given up the clerical office and his faith would soon begin to erode away.

Warfield said of Darwin's doctrine of evolution that it '...directly expelled his Christian belief...Darwin was persuaded that Genesis teaches creation by immediate, separate, and sudden fiats of God for each distinct species.'[5]

Since the authority of Christianity is inseparably bound up with the authority of Genesis and the Old Testament, gradually the whole of Christianity had to be cast off.

We have already noted the problems that arise when we equate the biblical 'kinds' with species, and then allow evolutionists to define 'species.' This made the Bible look like it was mistaken. But if we carefully define 'species' and the biblical 'kinds,' we find that the Bible's distinctions were not violated at all. Furthermore, the various special breeds represent a loss of genetic information compared to the originally created pair. Evolution demands an increase in genetic information to move the animal 'up' into another category. The very

---

4. Benjamin B. Warfield, 'Charles Darwin's Religious Life,' in *Evolution, Science, and Scripture. Selected Writings*, ed. Noll, Mark A. & Livingstone, David N. (Grand Rapids, Michigan: Baker Books, 2000), p. 73.

5. Ref. 4, p. 78.

idea of 'fixity of species' is an example of trying to force the Bible into the mold of current scientific theory. Nothing but trouble awaits the Christian world as long as we impoverish ourselves by forsaking the infinite riches of Christ for the pottage of the world. Wanting to fit the Bible into their scientific mold, they ended up undermining its credibility. Thinking themselves wise…. and we know the result of that path.

Warfield observes that it was not long before Darwin could not imagine any evidence that would convince him of the reliability of the gospels. Darwin's theism was more or less of the deistic type. God may have created one or a few forms, but natural selection takes over from there. Like Lucretius of old, he felt that whatever gods there may be would not be involved in the mundane life cycles on Earth. Darwin felt he could not believe in a beneficent and omnipotent God, with so much misery in the world. Would God create parasites, or cats to play with mice? Not believing this, Darwin felt free to also reject the eye as a product of design. Darwin thinks there may have been designed laws, which work themselves out by chance, for good or bad. But the subject, he professes, is too deep for the human intellect. So shall it ever be with those bereft of divine revelation, they have no ultimate answers. In Darwin's own words to Asa Gray: 'I am, and ever shall remain, in a hopeless muddle.'[6]

But Darwin does know how to use a typical tactic of agnostics. He professes himself not to know these mysteries about God. Yet he asserts many times what he knows God would not do! For example, God would not ordain a variation in the pigeon that was of no benefit to the bird. He never seems to have gotten beyond this type of argument. Knowing nothing of what God has done, he professes to know everything of what God simply would not do. Perhaps we could invent a new oxymoronic category of the all-knowing agnostic.

In 1860 Darwin wrote 'I cannot think that the world as we see it is the result of chance'[7] By 1876 he has changed his mind. He speaks

---

6. Ref. 4, p. 90.

7. Francis Darwin (ed.), *Life and Letters of Charles Darwin*, rev. ed. 2 (London: John Murray, 1888), p. 353. Cited by Warfield in 'Charles Darwin's Religious Life,' p. 102.

of 'the extreme difficulty or rather impossibility of conceiving this immense and wonderful universe, including man ...as the result of blind chance or necessity' Yet immediately he adds, 'But then arises the doubt, can the mind of man, which has, as I fully believe, been developed from a mind as low as that possessed by the lowest animals, be trusted when it draws such grand conclusions?'[8]

Darwin cannot accept evidence of design because his mind is just an evolved form of that possessed by lower animals. Yet his up-from-the-slime mind can confidently assert evolutionary tenets and freely pontificate on theology.

Wanting to salvage some type of morality, Darwin wrote, 'The safest conclusion seems to be that the whole subject [of God] is beyond the scope of man's intellect, but man can do his duty.' But as Warfield rightly observed, 'But when there is no one to show us any truth, who is there to show us duty?'[9]

Warfield concludes his essay on this topic by the comparison and contrast of Charles Hodge and Charles Darwin. Both of them thought back on their childhood prayers with a smile. For Darwin it was almost a sneer. Hodge's smile is the pleasant smile of one who looks back on small beginnings from a well-won height. Darwin's praying childhood was his highest religious attainment; Hodge's praying childhood was but the inconsiderable seed out of which were marvelously to unfold all the graces of a truly devout life.

A. EVOLUTION OR DEVELOPMENT 1888

Warfield's views on Darwinism went from early enthusiasm, later caution, finally settling on a few accommodations to evolution he felt were safe. Warfield consistently rejected both the atheistic versions of Darwinism and the conception of Darwinism as a total philosophy of life. But he did not always see clearly that Darwinism is designedly atheistic and claims to explain all of life. Politics,

---

8. Ref. 7, p. 312–13.

9. Benjamin B. Warfield, *Evolution, Science, and Scripture*, p. 108.

economics, morality, law, education, even the Bible itself were to be viewed through the lens of evolution. Warfield should have noticed these consequences, even if Hodge can be partially excused because the consequences of evolutionary thought were not as far progressed in his time. But a strong and naively held view of science as a value-free endeavor prevented the Princetonians from making the connections unless they could see that core issues of the faith were at stake. Thinking they had to preserve at least the 'scientific' part of Darwinism, they failed to realize that Darwinism, root and branch, was not on about science.[10]

Warfield agreed with Hodge that Darwinism *as a worldview* is atheistic. This is also shown in Darwin's own drift away from theism. But Warfield speculates that evolution might be a possible scientific explanation of God's second causes. He wants to see evolution, not as something antithetical to Christianity (which it is and was designed to be), but as a working hypothesis on probation. It is still on trial to see if it were fact or fiction. Is it probable or improbable?

On the positive side Warfield says, 'We shall not adjust our theology to what is as yet a more or less doubtful conjecture.' A theory becomes more probable in proportion to:

1. The number of facts it can explain.

2. The clearness of its explanations.

3. The ability to show the connections: deductions and predictions.

We cannot say that any theory that accounts for the facts observed is the correct explanation, but we can be confident that a theory that does not account for the facts is not the correct explanation. The point is, there is more than one theory to account for the observed facts. This leads Warfield to say, 'When Dr. McCosh says that we have

---

10. Repeatable observation and experiment can be carried out to demonstrate the fact of natural selection, for example, but Darwinism extrapolates this (originally creationist) observation to being a creative force throughout the planet's history, far out of the realms of observable evidence.

the same proof for it [theory of evolution] that we have for Newton's theory of gravitation, he has allowed his enthusiasm to run away with his judgment.'[11]

This is cautious, and far better than many of his contemporary Christians; but it is also far less than what God has given us. We can know, and Warfield could have known, that the evolutionary theory is most certainly false. All that was needed was to take God at His word, as revealed in the Scripture. Warfield gives the example: the horse evolution theory. Just because someone can line up various varieties of horses (and non-horses) and explain the series by evolution, does not demonstrate evolution to be correct.

Warfield raises some issues of geology. The trilobites do not appear to be adequately explained by evolution. In fact Darwin had to defend himself against the geologic record rather than appeal to it. Warfield also raises the question of embryology. This is Haeckel's theory, though he is not mentioned by name. Warfield rightly thinks the theory not only unproven, but also false. Due to the paucity of any real proof, evolutionists continue to hold on to parts of Haeckel's theory by calling the developing fetal spinal column a remnant of 'our evolutionary past.' If mere assertion constituted proof, evolution would thus be proven.

Warfield raises the issue of the enormous amounts of time demanded by evolutionists. He feels that the indications of contemporary science have reduced the beginning of life on Earth from a virtual eternity to at most hundreds of thousands of years. Also a problem for evolution is how much alike are the earliest humans and the modern. 'The matter of time that was a menace to Darwinism at the beginning thus bids fair to become its Waterloo.'[12] We may appreciate Warfield's optimism, but since he rejected the Genesis chronology, it is quite unfounded. What was really happening was an increasing concession to evolutionary thought. Hodge was willing to discard biblical chronology and insert a few thousand

11. Warfield, Ref. 9, p. 119.
12. Warfield, Ref. 9, p. 124.

extra years. By the time Warfield taught, inserting hundreds of thousands of years was thought a trivial concession. Having destroyed the Genesis chronology, he claims a victory because he has stopped short of granting the evolutionists millions of years. But once the Genesis genealogies are discarded, there is no basis for stopping the concession of millions of years. One concession demands another because evolutionists are never satisfied with anything less than evolution as a total worldview. We cannot fight something (the millions of years) with nothing, but 'nothing' is all we have left if we reject the biblical genealogical chronology. Events would prove that Warfield's apologetic, conceding so much to fallen man's reason, was too weak to stand against the downward slide of compromises.

Warfield notes that there appear to be limits to an organism's potential for variation. He points out that all the variations of pigeons are still pigeons. Here he hits at one of Darwin's favorite supports for his theory. All cows, however divergent, remain cows. 'It is in the highest degree improbable that the line that separates them [i.e. the kinds] is passable.'[12] Strangely, Warfield the defender of inerrancy cannot rise above the level of probability. Why would it not be *certain* that the kinds cannot be violated, given the inerrancy of Scripture? This is faint praise for the very words of God.

Warfield has the habit of starting with a fairly good (though imperfect) statement, followed by another statement that ruins everything:

> 'On these and similar grounds, I should therefore venture to say that any form of evolution which rests ultimately on the Darwinian idea is very improbable as an account of how God has wrought in producing species...'We may even hold to practically the same theory of the working of the evolutionary process and yet be theists, believing in an everywhere present and active God who nevertheless acts only according to law. So far as theism is concerned, therefore, there is no necessary conflict with evolution in any of its forms.'[13]

---

13. Warfield, Ref. 9, p. 125.

Warfield is overly concessive and tentative here. While Darwinian evolution has an atheistic tendency that must be rejected, he likes to think there may be other forms of evolution that are not atheistic. There is no necessary conflict with theism, in Warfield's view. But he correctly observes that to be a theist is a different thing than to be a Christian. Christianity demands and must demand the direct supernatural interference and immediate production of new things. Christianity recognizes second causes, but cannot agree to exclude God Himself working in this world. On this there can be no compromise. The soul of man is an example of something that could not arise by natural processes. The miracle of the Resurrection would certainly qualify here, though Warfield does not mention it at this point. For the unique origin of man the Scripture must be cited, 'God breathed into his nostrils the breath of life.'

Here is a point where Warfield realizes that empiricism alone is not enough; he must appeal to the Word of God regarding a *detail* of creation. Here is a description regarding God's *method* of the creation of man. Though the compromised position on creation likes to say there is nothing of the method of creation in Scripture, when it comes to something believed 'essential' to the faith, details about the method must be maintained. The danger here is that in conceding the visible and insisting only on the invisible, we introduce an unbiblical dualism. Those who cede to evolution the creation of man's body, and reserve only the invisible addition of a soul to the supernatural, are undermining the total worldview of Scripture. This also introduces an unbiblical view of man. When God breathed into man the breath of life, man *became* a living soul. Man does not *have* a soul as an optional accessory; man *is* a soul. Here again the message is communicated to the unbelieving world: whenever we discuss the material world, science is more reliable than Scripture. Only when we discuss the spiritual (invisible) world is the Bible supreme. This results in a sub-Christian view of God and His Word. The Sovereign of the universe controls not only the destiny of 'souls,' but also the falling of a sparrow (an extremely material being). If the Bible tells us earthly things, which we cannot believe, how shall we believe when it tells us heavenly things? (John 3:12).

Despite all this, Warfield stills fears that there may be something to this evolution theory. He is therefore unwilling to present the biblical account as a total antithesis to evolution. This kind of apologetic tactic assures that the word of God is duller than any two-edged sword, for it cannot slice through even the flimsiest of man-made anti-Christian theories. Warfield pauses over the creation of Eve, which seems to be a bar to the idea of 'creation by evolution.' But the empirical evidentialist method cannot produce a confident boldness. Instead we get this:

> 'The upshot of the whole matter is that there is no *necessary* antagonism of Christianity to evolution, *provided that* we do not hold to too extreme a form of evolution... if we condition the theory by allowing the constant oversight of God in the whole process, and his occasional supernatural interference... we may hold to the modified theory of evolution and be Christians in the ordinary orthodox sense.'[14]

Warfield holds back from saying we ought to accept evolution, simply that we may. Once again, the value-free view of science allows Warfield to consider a modified evolutionary theory to be acceptable. That the very Word of God may need to be modified by an atheist 'designer' theory (a theory designed specifically to exclude the God of Scripture) is an astounding concession. An apologetic that purposes to defend only the 'essentials' ends up forfeiting more and more. An apologetic that thinks a 'textbook' is the highest authority is bound to fail. The path of compromise ends only in agreement with the evolutionist. For just one example, Nathaniel Taylor's (1786–1858) attempts to compromise orthodoxy in order to win over the Unitarians ended only with moving the 'New Haven' theology that much further away from historic orthodoxy.[15] As far as is known, no Unitarians

---

14. Warfield, Ref. 9, p. 130ff.

15. Iain Murray, in his *Revival and Revivalism*, observes that when in 1831 Finney preached a sermon 'Make Yourself a New Heart,' 'The voice was Finney's, the thinking Taylor's' (p. 261).

were drawn closer to orthodoxy by the proffered compromise. In like manner, no compromise is ever enough for the evolutionist because both evolution and Christianity demand to govern every aspect of life and thought. A theory that was specifically designed to exclude the God of the Bible will not easily readmit Him. Evolution is surely compatible with 'theism' only as long as the deity is silent. Most theism could have as its motto, 'a god may be there, but he is silent' but, as Francis Schaeffer said of God, 'He is there and He is not silent.'[16] In the Christian worldview, neither science nor any other area of life and thought may be conducted outside the Lordship of Christ and governance of His word. Christians should not rush to embrace ideas rooted in evolution, just because some proponent is a theist.

Warfield is concerned about Darwin's arguments against Christianity. He keeps hoping there can be an evolutionary theory that will not lead to atheism or agnosticism. How a theory rooted in and driven by atheism can avoid atheistic conclusions he does not say. He sees the first stage in Darwin's declining belief as being at age forty when Darwin renounced Christianity. Actually he was attending the Unitarian 'church' of his wife's family. A compromised Anglican Church and a heretical Unitarian cult did not give Darwin a foundation built on the Rock. The death of Darwin's favorite daughter and the general evil in nature turned Darwin toward a vague theism, then to agnosticism and practical atheism. From this point on he struggles to maintain any sort of theism. Notice how impossible it is to live out the evolutionary worldview. Later Darwinists would see clearly that an event like Darwin's daughter's death is a good thing for humanity. As the weaker specimens die, the stronger survive and the genetic quality of the race is improved. Somehow the theory proves unthinkable when death comes to one's own family. The evolutionary worldview bears bitter fruit; its falsity is seen in that fruit.

---

16. *The Complete Works of Francis A. Schaeffer*, Vol. 1, Book 3 *He is There and He is Not Silent* [1972] (Westchester, IL: Crossway Books, 1982).

Warfield continues to review Darwin's arguments against Christianity. Darwin seems to have assumed, in line with the deistic trends of his day, that Genesis teaches a fixity of species. God was said to have created each individual species more or less as we find them today, unchanged. Where a species was beautifully suited to its environment, this was only to be expected; God had created it that way *in its present habitat*. So seeing that science had found evidence that species change, and that some new species had likely become adapted to a new habitat, he claimed that Genesis was in error. But of course Genesis teaches no such thing. It refers to a creation of original 'kinds', leaving ample scope for variation within the limits of those kinds.[17] Furthermore, by describing a global Flood, Genesis actually proclaims that creatures could *not* have been created in their current habitat. The sort of adaptive variation/radiation that Darwin's finches exhibited is an example of what should be expected if we take Genesis history as written.

Nonetheless, by setting up such a straw man argument of what Genesis allegedly taught, it could then be claimed that it was in error. And if Genesis is in error, the Old Testament is not reliable. And since Christianity is founded on the OT, it could not be true either.

Darwin felt that our knowledge of the laws of nature prevents us from believing in the miracles reported in the Bible. He does not deny that miracles are possible, but suggests that there is not enough evidence for them. As Darwin himself admitted, 'But I found it more and more difficult, with free scope given to my imagination, to invent evidence that would suffice to convince me.' As Warfield says 'Nothing short of a miracle would, then, have convinced him; and nothing short of a miracle could have convinced him of a miracle.'[18]

---

17. The Genesis kind does not have to correlate to a fixed category in today's manmade, and somewhat arbitrary, nomenclature. It probably equates most often to the genus level, sometimes the family, and occasionally the species. Creatures that can hybridize, whether the offspring are fertile or not, are most likely the offspring of the same original kind. This includes dolphins and false killer whales, which are classified as different genera. See also C. Wieland, 'Variation, Information and the Created Kind', <creation.com/kind>.

18. Benjamin B. Warfield, 'Darwin's Arguments Against Christianity,' in Selected Shorter Writings of Benjamin B. Warfield, ed. John E. Meeter, 2 (Nutley, New Jersey: Presbyterian and Reformed Publishing Company, 1973), p. 137.

Darwin attempted to counter Paley's argument from design by explaining *apparent* design as the result of natural selection acting on inherited variations. He opposed the popular nineteenth century argument from the general beneficence of nature with the observation that there is much misery and suffering in the world. Therefore random changes seemed more appropriate to him. He felt his theory was rescued by Natural Selection that could bring apparent order out of randomness. But Darwin still has some doubts about dismissing the arguments from design. As Warfield reminds us, these doubts were dismissed on the basis of his belief that the mind of man evolved from lower life forms. Concerning his own doubts, Darwin wrote, 'Would anyone trust in the convictions of a monkey's mind, if there are any convictions in such a mind?'[19]

When Darwin wants to impress us with his theory of evolution through natural selection, he approaches the issue from the vantage point of having great knowledge. When he wants to show that we must be agnostic regarding God, he dismisses his own doubts about blind chance being sufficient to create all things as the musings of a mutated monkey brain. Why wouldn't his own theory be suspect, having been thought up by a brute-bred brain?

But there is a lesson to be learned. Darwin's prior commitment to naturalistic evolution brought him into conflict with Scripture and led to his rejection of Christianity. Those advocating that we 'reinterpret' Scripture to accommodate evolution are setting a course of failure. The effect of their approach, even if sincere, is not the Christianizing of evolutionists, but the evolutionizing of Christians.

B. ON BEING OVERLY IMPRESSED WITH 'EXPERT' TESTIMONY

John Dawson was a Canadian geologist specializing in fossil plants. Both Hodge and President McCosh wanted to recruit him for Princeton College and seminary. Warfield was quite impressed with his work, expressing the hope that Dawson could be our new

---

19. Ref. 18, p. 139.

Paley. Dawson's main points are that the Bible is not committed to any theory of the mode of creation, but the evolutionary theory is not 'fortified by the evidence of facts…the testimony of paleontology is, on the whole, adverse to it.'[20]

Warfield is happy to see a genuine expert in geology raise these doubts about evolution. His happiness would be understandable if it were simply having Dawson as an ally to help confirm what is known to be true from the God-breathed testimony of Scripture. However, it rather reflects his belief that the question of the correct interpretation of Genesis must be settled by professional paleontologists.

What if Dr. Dawson later accepts the evolutionary theory? Is the assertion from Dawson that the Bible is silent on the mode of creation a credible assertion? Why should any Christian get excited that Dawson makes this small nod of acceptance of the Bible, just so long as Scripture does not try to inform him on the method of creation? Dawson will inform us as to what the Bible does not teach. He does this not through careful exegesis, for which he was unqualified, but through mere assertion. Why should we expect that his expertise in geology gives him the right to impose certain limitations on the interpretation of Scripture? This is another example of the piecemeal apologetic of the evidentialist. There is no consideration of the presuppositions behind Dawson's (or others') explanation of data. There is a strong tendency to see 'science' as unrelated to Scripture, along with an easy uncritical acceptance of 'scientific' opinion. That there must be a Christian explanation of the data seems to have escaped the Princeton men. Only if some central doctrine of the faith, such as the existence of God, were attacked would they be on the alert to defend the faith. But given something they considered non-essential (such as the method of creation, or the chronology of Scripture) Warfield was content to let the scientists call the tune. Instead of confronting Dawson's unbiblical worldview, Warfield is grateful to receive his few doubts on evolution. This is like forsaking the infallible worldview given to us by our omniscient Creator, and

---

20. Benjamin B. Warfield, *Evolution, Science, and Scripture: Selected Writings*, p. 143.

hunting for scraps in alien worldviews. Scripture gives us the standard by which to judge all truth claims, whether the alleged 'facts' come from paleontology or any other source outside Scripture.

As a Presbyterian theologian of the old school, Warfield would heartily agree with the Westminster Confession's statement:

> 'The infallible rule of interpretation of the Scripture is the Scripture itself: and therefore, when there is a question about the true and full sense of any Scripture (which is not manifold, but one) it must be searched and known by other places that speak more clearly.' (WCF I.9)

If Warfield had been dealing with the deity of Christ, he would strictly and brilliantly follow this Westminster principle of interpretation. But if an issue was a 'scientific' issue rather than a 'religious' issue, the 'scientists' must give the correct interpretation of Scripture to us. Little regard is given to the comprehensive worldview of Scripture, or the presuppositions of the 'scientist' interpreting the data of his science.

'The Bible tells us nothing about the mode of creation' is little more than a euphemism for 'I do not accept what the Bible tells us about the mode of creation.' Evolutionists and liberal theologians can honestly admit the latter statement. Only the accommodating evangelical undertakes the extremely awkward position of maintaining the first statement while denying the second.

C. HENRY CALDERWOOD:
EVOLUTION AND MAN'S PLACE IN NATURE.

Henry Calderwood (1830–97) was a Scottish philosopher and ordained Presbyterian minister. Warfield was pleased that although Calderwood maintains evolution of organic life, he allows a place for the First Cause. Warfield, even at this stage, was receptive to evolutionary views as long as they left room for teleological concerns. Evaluating this position biblically, we should keep in mind that a vague 'First Cause' deity, aloof from the world, is not significantly different from atheism. If a man moves from atheism to idolatry, he is still under the wrath of God. There is only One true and living God.

He is the Triune God revealed in Scripture. To deny the Lord God is to deny the only God there is. The feeble resistance of Warfield's apologetic regarding evolution reveals an impoverished worldview. Christians must develop a consistently biblical philosophy. Too often Christians have sold their birthright for a mess of pottage. Too often Christians have forged their philosophy of life as philosophical 'dumpster diners' who delight in finding a scrap of food in the secular dumpster. But they could have had a feast of the purest milk, honey, and meat of God's own revelation. Why should we be pleased that the Calderwoods of the world have thrown us a scrap? Why should believers (as Calderwood professed to be) discard what God has revealed, for the vain speculations of unbelievers? We already have an account of creation infinitely more valuable. It is capable of being added to by observations and deductions, in the sense of filling in some of the details, but never taking away from or contradicting the creation account.

D. PRESENT-DAY CONCEPTIONS OF EVOLUTION.

Warfield is always insistent and often eloquent in maintaining that Christianity is a supernatural religion. That is quite true, but it must be added that Christianity is also supernatural in its account of creation and its chronological structure of history, not merely when it touches on 'religious thinking.'

It shows up as an essential element of evolutionists to insist that there was no outside interference with the natural processes. In other words, they presuppose that if there is a god at all, that god had nothing to do with the process. Like Epicurus, the thought of a Creator to whom they are accountable is too disturbing of their tranquility to be entertained. This is yet another indication that evolution is not a science, but a presupposed framework into which all data must be fit. It is the already completed story that will be told about any 'fact' discovered. The story was complete long before there was 'modern science.' Once presupposed, it becomes *the* story that is told about *any* data whatsoever in any area of life and thought. This essential character of the evolutionary theory is the reason Christians cannot consistently compromise with it. To try to accommodate evolution is to abandon some parts of revealed truth. Often it leads to a total abandonment of the faith. The accommodating Christian has no answers to the questions of origins, no antithesis to present, no divine word. The accommodating Christian's worldview is like a patchwork garment comprised of rags from this or that worldly philosophy.

Of course, there is a limit to the amount of compromise with evolution Warfield will tolerate. He recognizes that (at least) LeConte[21] and Darwin hold evolution as a philosophy of the universe. They directly and emphatically exclude a higher power. 'Observed fact cuts no figure in these theories…Nor can it possibly escape the reader that evolution conceived thus as an all-inclusive philosophy leaves little room in the universe for what the Christian calls God.'[22]

Warfield acknowledges that the evolutionary philosophy may be consistent with a deistic or pantheistic conception of God, but not the God of Scripture. The problem arises when Warfield *et al.* want to borrow some parts of the God-excluding philosophy and reinterpret Scripture to accommodate these alien parts. It looks like a one-way street. It is not the designers of evolution accommodating their theory to Christian revelation; it is *always* the Christian who is urged to accommodate revelation to whatever current speculation happens to be misnamed 'science.'

After a brilliant statement recognizing evolution as a God-excluding philosophy of life, Warfield still wants to hold out for a version of evolution that makes room for God. A Christian worldview is not some agnostic-atheistic production into which we try to make a place for God somewhere. The Christian worldview presupposes that the Triune God—Father, Son and Holy Spirit—created the world *ex nihilo* by the word of His power in the space of six days, and all (at that time) very good. The thing excluded by the Christian worldview is evolutionary philosophy. We must not settle for a sterile hybrid, because Christianity and molecules-to-man evolution do not mix.

---

21. Joseph LeConte (1869–1901) was the leading US proponent of evolution in the 1800s.
22. Warfield, *Evolution, Science, and Scripture*, p. 162.

Warfield finds it possible to acknowledge a form of theistic evolution in which evolution is seen as the secondary cause of things that have come into existence. Here he names James McCosh of Princeton as an example. The other possible way is to accept a version of evolution as a working hypothesis, but remembering its tentative character. It cannot definitely be affirmed nor denied. The caution of John Laidlaw (1832–1906), professor of systematic theology at New College Edinburgh, is appropriate and approvingly quoted by Warfield:

> 'The lesson for the interpreter of Scripture is plain. For him to hasten to propound schemes of conciliation between the Mosaic account of creation and the Darwinian pedigree of the lower animals and man would be to repeat an old and, now, an unpardonable blunder.'[23]

At least in part, Warfield's ambivalent attitude toward evolution is due to Warfield's wanting to draw the line at the evolution of man, or at least of man's soul. He believes the issue should be settled by a (value-free) search for the theory that best explains the facts and has no facts standing in its way.

Laidlaw's caution should have been more consistently maintained. In one sense those Christians may be excused for not foreseeing the consequences of an accommodation of Christian revelation to anti-Christian philosophical speculations disguised as science. In the late nineteenth century, how were Christians to know what implications the twentieth century evolutionists would draw from the presupposition of evolution? If they could have foreseen it, they would not have so easily assumed that the 'mode or method' of creation was an unimportant matter. In another sense, it was inexcusable to dismiss any part of God's revelation as unimportant. Biblically, there was no excuse. Scientifically, there still was no excuse.

---

23. Warfield, Ref. 22, p. 165 (from Laidlaw's, *The Bible Doctrine of Man*).

Why did the Princeton men, so brilliant and such defenders of orthodoxy, ignore the scriptural geologists (see Chapter 9). They obviously read widely from all shades of evolutionists, frequently writing critical reviews. Yet we would be hard pressed to find any evidence of their awareness of the work of the scriptural geologists of England.[24] This group made up of biblical scholars and professional scientists had a different story to tell about the data of geology. From their perspective, a biblical one, the rocks cried out in agreement with the Christian revelation. For example, the biblical Flood had left evidence of itself all over the earth. The issue was and is, how do we explain the data of geology? The biblical Flood must *necessarily* have its impact on the geological record, since it was a real time and space historical event. The scriptural geologists had the same data, but reached antithetical conclusions. They reached correct conclusions because they loved the truth of the Word, which gave them understanding of the truths of creation. The evolutionists reached false conclusions because they were suppressing the truth in unrighteousness, exactly as the first chapter of Romans describes.

Warfield's opinions on evolution seem to vary with where he is in the development of his own thinking, and reflect his tendency to be a sympathetic reviewer if theism is not excluded. In an 1896 review Warfield asks:

> 'But is it so obvious that our ascertainment of a fact is more trustworthy than any word-statement? All statements will find their test in facts, but it does not thence follow that revelation will finds its test in science. Science is not fact, but human reading of fact; and any human reading of fact may well bow humbly before the reading given by God.'[25]

---

24. See Chapter 9, especially Section B, for details on the 'scriptural geologists'.

25. Benjamin B. Warfield, 'Review of Randolph S. Foster, Creation: God in Time and Space,' *Presbyterian and Reformed Review*, Vol. 7 (July 1896), pp. 561–62.

In 1896 Warfield proclaimed this valid principle that the Word of God in Scripture is more sure than any human interpretation of facts. In 1911 he was not as consistent in applying this principle. In his article on the 'Antiquity and Unity of the Human Race', Warfield rightly insisted that the *unity* of the human race was a vitally important doctrine that must be defended. We know the unity of the human race from the book of Genesis. Yet when this same book of Genesis gives us information on the *antiquity* of the human race, such information is declared to be unimportant and outside the purpose of the book. Did the Scripture really not mean to teach what it teaches there? Who gave human beings the right to decide what is unimportant and negotiable in the Bible?

In the background is Galileo-phobia, the irrational fear of insisting on the truth of Scripture where it infringes upon the territory of 'science.' The cure for Galileo-phobia is to let the poetry of Scripture be poetry (*e.g.* Psalms) and let the historical narratives be straightforward history (*e.g.* Genesis). And *the mistake to avoid is precisely that which the church of the seventeenth century made*: forcing the outdated science of Aristotle upon the poetic descriptions of the earth and sun, resulting in faulty conclusions.[26] They should not be blamed for maintaining some skepticism about Galileo's theory since it seemed to contradict common sense. That is, it does not feel like the earth is moving. Also most university professors taught the Aristotelian view; it was regarded as the most scientific and intellectually respectable view. The Roman church could be faulted for abandoning sound hermeneutical principles in order to force the Bible to agree with Aristotle. The modern church may be faulted for imposing the ancient philosophy of evolution upon historical narratives. Again the problem is the ignoring of sound principles of interpretation, but this time for the sake of an ancient philosophy without scientific merit. True, the Bible is not a textbook on science; it is far better. Its truth endures from generation to generation. Whenever the Bible is interpreted by outside speculations of man, error is sure to follow. The only infallible interpreter of

---

26. Russell Grigg, 'The Galileo "twist"', *Creation* **19**(4):30–32, 1997, <creation.com/gal-twist>.

Scripture is Scripture itself. There are those who insist on a 'literal' interpretation of biblical poetry, in order to ridicule it. At the same time, they insist on a 'figurative' interpretation of historical narrative in order to subvert it.

In 1897 Warfield said in a book review,

> 'When it is a question of scriptural declaration versus human conjecture dignified by any name, whether that of philosophy or that of science, the Christian man will know where his belief is due.'[27]

In an 1898 review of a Darwinist book, Warfield stated, '…if the writers did not put evolution into their premises, they would hardly find so much of it in their conclusions.'[28]

This principle, so much in harmony with this present thesis, was not consistently maintained in the twentieth century portion of Warfield's career. Even though he can recognize at times the importance of the presuppositions in shaping the conclusions, he can also revert to his concessive evidentialist apologetic with its seemingly confidence in the objectivity of fallen man when employed in the pursuit of 'scientific' knowledge.

Warfield is critical of William Elder (1899) who wanted to maintain that God originally created things with the inherent potential of developing by the process of evolution. Says Warfield: '… we see that the cloven hoof of evolutionary philosophy is not wholly eradicated from the thought of even such graceful and gracious Christian scientists as Prof. Elder.'[29]

Here is a clue toward explaining Warfield's ambivalence toward evolution. It might be accepted as a *method* of creation, but not as a philosophy of life. Yet he did not consistently maintain the distinction between observational science and man's interpretation of that data observed.

---

27. Benjamin B. Warfield, 'Review of Luther Tracy Townsend, Evolution or Creation.,' *Presbyterian and Reformed Review* 8 (January 1897), p. 157.

28. Benjamin B. Warfield, 'Review of A.A.W. Hubrecht, The Descent of the Primates,' *Presbyterian and Reformed Review* (October 1898), **9**:780–82.

29. Warfield, *Presbyterian and Reformed Review*, (July 1899), **10**:546–47.

E. WARFIELD IN THE TWENTIETH CENTURY

As the twentieth century arrives, Warfield seems more concessive toward evolution as long as it is not the extreme kind of evolution that excludes God, or the kind that becomes an atheistic view of life. There is a version of evolution that excludes all supernatural events. Christians must reject that version. God has not been silent.

He wants to insist that creation is the opposite of evolution, in one sense. Creation pertains to the origin of something, where nothing existed before. Evolution pertains to the development of an existing being. The origin of life was supernatural and instantaneous, not by gradual naturalistic process. Warfield notes that evolution from Darwin on exhibits a zeal for the exclusion of the supernatural. But evolution is not equipped to deal with the beginning of matter and life, nor with the Beginner.

Warfield brings in the subject of theistic evolution. Sometimes theistic evolution is defined as 'creation by gradualism' or as God's creating matter with the intrinsic ability to develop into other forms, or as God's method of creation. All these are rejected because they do not distinguish between the concept of creation and the concept of development.

Another distinction Warfield wanted to make is the concept of 'mediate creation' which means that God not only creates 'out of nothing' by the word of His power, but may also make pre-existing material into something it lacked any intrinsic power to produce by itself.

Consider an example not mentioned by Warfield, but illustrative of the point. The dust of the ground was an immediate direct creation by God. But the creation of Adam, out of the dust of the ground was not a 'creation out of nothing' by nothing but the Word of God. Adam's creation could be called a 'mediate creation' because pre-existing material was used. At the same time the creation of Adam is not properly called the evolution of man, because it was not a gradual development from lower life forms. Therefore, though Warfield is often called a theistic evolutionist, he objected to most of what passed for theistic evolution in the early twentieth century. Most of the 'theistic evolutionists' he cites gave credit to God only for the initial act of creation, all else must unfold by natural causes. Many of these theistic evolutionists would deny the possibility of miracles, since that would require divine 'interference' in the natural processes built into the original created substances.

Thinking Christianly, that is biblically, about the idea of 'interference' in the natural process, the idea is both absurd and blasphemous. Since God is intimately involved in every act that occurs, no matter how seemingly insignificant, there can be no rare occasional act of 'interference.' Miracles, for example, may be spoken of as God's special providence, but certainly not 'interference.' God's sustaining of His creation by his providential government is no more an interference than our heartbeat is to our body. When we look at the foundational assumptions of the theistic evolutionist, we find that the Bible is either unfamiliar to him or he does not take it seriously. Theistic evolution must remain content with a 'fuzzy' out of focus concept of 'god', for when the Bible is carefully studied the only God who exists is revealed. An imaginary deity may have created the world in any way we may imagine. However, the triune Creator God revealed in Scripture created the world exactly as He has revealed to us.

Warfield concludes by stating that evolution cannot take the place of creation because it does not explain origins. But, after rejecting theistic evolution as it was being presented, Warfield allows for another kind of theistic evolution. In his words, '...the Christian man has as such no quarrel with evolution when confined to its own sphere as a suggested account of the method of the divine providence.'[30]

Warfield wants only to insist that evolution not be substituted for creation. By 1901 his opinion is clearly that not only the theist, but also the Christian is free to make room for evolutionary thinking. He should have excluded evolution from every sphere, for all creation is under the Lordship of Jesus Christ. Therefore not one square inch can be ceded to evolutionary philosophy.

---

30. Benjamin B. Warfield, 'Creation, Evolution, and Mediate Creation,' *The Bible Student*, July 1901, p. 8.

F. THE MANNER AND TIME OF MAN'S ORIGIN

Man owes his being to a creative act of God. This conclusion is affirmed in every portion of Scripture. But by 1903, in his attempt to reach a compromise solution to the conflict between Scripture and contemporary scientific theory, Warfield makes a proposal. He says, 'Why should the biblicist assert that the creation of man by the divine fiat must have been immediate in such a sense as to exclude all process, all interaction of natural forces?'[31]

The old 'line in the sand' was the creation of man. By 1903 a new line must be drawn in Warfield's retreat. Even in the creation of man, Warfield does not object to allowing it to have taken place by natural processes—provided those processes were directed by God. While Warfield does not speak so plainly, the resultant compromise leaves the body of man as possibly arriving by natural processes, but the creation of the soul or breath of life as a special act of God the Creator. If one does not look too closely at the Scripture, all this may sound plausible. However, the proposal is totally lacking in any serious exegesis. If the Creator had not given us a revelation of creation, it might be entertaining to speculate about it. Since God has Himself spoken, let all the earth keep silence before Him!

Just to illustrate how this compromise proposal glosses over Scripture, take the phrase 'breath of life.' Is it really something unique to man, as Warfield seems to suppose? The answer is 'No' as seen in Genesis 7:15: 'And they went into the ark to Noah, two by two, of all flesh in which *is* the breath of life.' Thus all the land vertebrates have the breath of life, not man only.

What about the time of man's appearance on Earth? Warfield's proposal has an answer for this question. He asserts that the Bible gives us no precise data to estimate the age of mankind. Warfield passes over the genealogies of Genesis 5 and 11 by pointing us to William H. Green's article on biblical chronology. But Green's lack of careful exegesis has served only to move Christians to

---

31. Benjamin B. Warfield, 'The Manner and Time of Man's Origin,' *The Bible Student*, November 1903. cited by Noll & Livingstone, Ref. 4, p. 213.

accommodate more evolutionary philosophy into their worldview. This accommodating compromise serves no apologetic purpose as far as unbelievers are concerned. Warfield assures us that the genealogies have no chronological purpose, but his assurances ring hollow when one closely examines the text of Scripture. A detailed critique of this scheme has already been given in connection with William H. Green, so need not be repeated here.[32] Warfield admits an 'appearance' of chronology, but calls it illusory. His further study in 1911 is discussed below in a later section.

Incredibly, Warfield suggests that *if* chronology were in the mind of Moses, he would have merely written: 'And Adam lived 130 years and begat Seth, and Seth lived 105 years and begat Enos.' But Scripture adds the detail 'and the days of Adam after he begat Seth were 800 years and he begat sons and daughters; and all the years that Adam lived were 930 years.' He tells us that such added detail should convince us that chronology was not the purpose of the genealogy! Can we take seriously the idea that the more detailed the biblical genealogies are, the less credibility we need attach to them? The figurativists are getting desperate. Some of them said there was not enough information for a true chronology; Warfield says there is too much information for a real chronology. So a false dilemma has been thrust upon the reader. If any other purpose for the genealogy can be imagined, it must not have a chronological purpose. But even if there are other purposes for the genealogies, it says nothing against their historical chronological value. If we find theological value in the study of history, does that prove that history has no *historical* value? Since biblical history itself is *more* than a recitation of 'facts', does that mean it is *less* than factual?

On the other side of the compromise, Warfield wants evolutionists to admit that their estimates of the age of the earth are still uncertain. He also takes some comfort in seeing earlier extreme age estimates being reduced. Such widely varying estimates demonstrate their

32. See Chapter Four on 'Chronology and Genealogy'.

inherent uncertainty. Since estimates were varying between 15,000 years and 30 billion years, uncertainty was quite evident. He should not have taken any comfort in that because their estimates would soon be higher than Warfield could imagine.

Finally Warfield repeats his non-negotiable proposition. It is (only) the *atheistic* view of evolution that must be rejected. Only a theistic, God-directed, kind of evolution can be acceptable. For example, while reviewing one of James Orr's books, he says, 'If under the directing hand of God a human body is formed at a leap by propagation from brutish parents, it would be quite consonant with the fitness of things that it should be provided by his creative energy with a truly human soul.'[33]

Warfield insists that the Christian must maintain this distinction: evolution means modification, creation means origination. Therefore, Warfield would limit evolution to the modification of existing beings and exclude evolution from creating anything new.

Warfield continued to seem surprised that evolutionary theory had such a strong tendency toward naturalism. He never seems to grasp the fact that the theory was designed for the purpose of excluding the deity. The uncritical assumption persists that 'scientists' are objectively pursuing the facts. In combating certain aspects of evolution, he does not use the Sword of the Spirit, but simply refers to other scientists with differing opinions. He may point to logical or factual difficulties of a particular version of Darwinism. Scripture is seldom mentioned in his discussions, except where it must yield to the scientists. Instead of, 'Thus saith the Lord' we get something like, 'But not all scientists agree with this type of evolution.' The authority structure of his epistemology is out of order. The Word of God must be the supreme authority by which all opinions of men ('scientific' or not) must be judged.

Warfield notes the surprising zeal with which speculative theories are maintained. Yet it is up to the scientists to decide these

---

33. Benjamin B. Warfield, 'Review of James Orr: God's Image in Man and Its Defacement in the Light of Modern Denials,' *Princeton Theological Review*, no. 4 (October 1906).

issues according to the facts. He cautions against basing our 'facts' on theory rather than basing our theory on the facts. The Bible is kept out of the discussion as if it were irrelevant to these kinds of issues. Thus the Christian's most powerful weapon is kept out of the battle and our defeat is assured.

There are, of course, many valid scientific objections to the theory of evolution. The lack of fossil evidence, so lamented by Darwin, was still a problem. Warfield himself rightly asks, 'How is it that the record is free from these intermediate types? How have the rocks selected for our inspection only a few fit for preservation in their remains and destroyed all trace of the immensely more numerous unfit?'[34]

It is right to bring up the scientific considerations weighing against Darwinism; but it is unwarranted to lay the Scripture aside for 'scientific' issues. This is because the real argument is not as much about the observed phenomena, but how to account for the data obtained by observation, measurement, and experimentation. The thoroughly Christian worldview cannot leave the Bible out of any issue because Scripture relates to and governs our every thought and action.

In a 1909 review of Rudolph Otto, Warfield appreciates the fact that Otto can believe in a theory of descent without denying teleology. Otto also says that because something is caused, does not mean it is unintended. Purpose still plays its vital role. Even a person of faulty theology and philosophy, as Warfield views Otto, can sometimes speak something true and useful. But if we desire to build a consistently Christian philosophy, we will have to reply to Otto and the like as Zerubbabel answered his adversaries:

> KJV 'Ezra 4:1-3: Now when the adversaries of Judah and Benjamin heard that the descendants of the captivity were building the temple of the LORD God of Israel, they came

---

34. Benjamin B. Warfield, 'Review of George Paulin, No Struggle for Existence: No Natural Selection. A Critical Examination of the Fundamental Principles of the Darwinian Theory,' *Princeton Theological Review*, no. 6 (October 1908).

> to Zerubbabel … and said …, 'Let us build with you,
> for we seek your God as you *do;* … But Zerubbabel and
> Jeshua and the rest of the heads of the fathers' *houses*
> of Israel said to them, 'You may do nothing with us to
> build a house for our God; but we alone will build to the
> LORD God of Israel, as King Cyrus the king of Persia has
> commanded us.'

We cannot build a Christian philosophy out of scraps from atheistic and pagan philosophies. We are not forced to choose between Aristotle, Plato, Kant or Hume for they all build on sand.

In another 1909 review, Warfield continued to cite only empirical or logical objections to evolution. One particularly illogical feature of evolutionary thought was holding both abiogenesis and adaptation. Abiogenesis is spontaneous generation. But since the concept of spontaneous generation was discredited, evolutionists use a new term abiogenesis. The logical objection is if the environment produces a certain life form by abiogenesis, why would it need further adaptation? Being produced by the environment, it would already be compatible with it.[35] Once again Warfield obeys the Baconian dictum, keeping the Bible out of the discussion. Warfield's evidentialist apologetic allows him, even requires him, to fracture the field of knowledge into small pieces. In many of these pieces, such as science, the Bible is by unwritten agreement to be kept out.

In 1911, Warfield wrote on the unity and antiquity of the human race. He repeats his contentions of the 1903 article: it is important to maintain the unity of the human race, but the question of the antiquity is less important. Both the effects of the Fall in Adam and the redemption in Christ are based on the unity of the human race. He sees no theological significance to the question of the antiquity of man. It is regarded as a matter of indifference. Warfield says there is an apparent conflict over the span of human existence, between the

---

35. Benjamin B. Warfield, 'Review of James Hastings, ed., *Encyclopaedia of Religion and Ethics,* vol. 1, A-Art,' *Princeton Theological Review,* no. 7 (April 1909).

Bible and scientific professionals. This conflict he attributes on the one hand to a particular interpretation of the Bible that makes the antiquity of man unnecessarily short; and the speculations of a certain school would make the period of time unnecessarily long. He who seeks to meet the evolutionist 'in the middle' will soon find himself standing in the middle—all alone. Evolutionists never respond to such offers, but see them only as a sign of weakness.

On the face of it, the biblical record gives the impression that the human race is relatively recent. But Warfield asserts that the genealogical tables have no chronological value. He believes that our data before Abraham is not complete enough to draw the conclusions of Ussher. He relies on the 1890 article by William H. Green as an adequate explanation of why the genealogies have no chronological value. According to Warfield, 'There is no reason why a genealogy of ten links…may not represent an actual descent of a hundred or a thousand or ten thousand links.'[36] It has already been shown that such a meaning cannot be derived from careful attention to the text itself. This seems to be an eisegesis of desperation of a warrior grown weary of combating issues he felt were unimportant. This 'apology' would not challenge the foundations of the unbeliever's worldview, it would only encourage him to continue in unbelief.

The intellectual pressures to accept evolution were very great in the early twentieth century. Scholars scrambled to reinterpret the Bible, so as to salvage the essential core of Christianity. This resulted in a narrowing of the scope of Scripture; it was written merely for spiritual and theological purposes. Only the basics of Christianity must be defended and chronology is not one of the basics. Such was the cry of the rapidly retreating Church. Instead of the whole counsel of God, it is enough to save the essentials. In this view, it is up to man to decide what the essentials are.

Although Warfield was capable of excellent exegetical work (of which there are many examples) his treatment of Genesis is not

---

36. Benjamin B. Warfield, 'Antiquity and Unity of the Human Race,' in *Studies in Theology*, The Works of Benjamin B. Warfield, vol. 9, no. 7 (Grand Rapids, Michigan: Baker Books, 2003).

a typical example. He admits, 'It is quite true that, when brought together in sequence, name after name, these notes assume the appearance of a concatenated chronological scheme. But this is pure illusion...'[37]

Ironically, 'pure illusion' is a perfect description of Warfield's eisegetical desperation. He actually asserts that to connect these patriarchs into a chronology is to do violence to the text. But to assert is not to demonstrate, so we may safely take the data as presented. An interpretation so far-fetched could never have arisen without the intellectual pressure to accept (at least some of) the conclusions of the consensus of scholars on the age of humanity. Even with a vivid imagination, it is difficult to imagine how much more information needs to be revealed by God for us to draw some chronological conclusions. It is difficult to imagine a family genealogy that is *kept* (not lost) in the family, but additions are made only every ten thousand or every hundred thousand years. If we try to imagine what Genesis 5 and 11 would look like if there were a chronological purpose, how would they differ? It has already been shown (in Chapter 4, Section B) that most of the names in the genealogy have been identified elsewhere as the direct father of the son mentioned.

Warfield would have us believe that there could be hundreds of thousands of years between the patriarch who 'begat' and the one he is said to have 'begotten.' How can it be that one patriarch in the genealogy does not even know the next named son? Nor can we believe that the next named son lived thousands of years later. This is an absurdity since we read that the particular patriarch lived so many years *after* begetting his son. Yet here is the key to Warfield's position. 'The question of the antiquity of man is accordingly a purely scientific one, in which the theologian as such has no concern.'[38]

Again the Bible must be kept out of the discussion, even reinterpreted to fit current scientific consensus. When the consensus changes, we may reactivate our imagination, and come up with

---

37. Ref. 36, p. 243.
38. Ref. 36, p. 245.

another new interpretation. We can get the Bible to say whatever we need it to say, as long as the issue is not central to the theological purpose of Scripture. Soon the Bible will be rendered meaningless and useless.

Warfield recognizes that the idea of millions of years was instigated by Hutton's geology and picked up by Darwin. He considers the extremely long estimates to be speculative. He *prefers* the speculation of one hundred million years to those wanting four hundred million years, although from his professed position on the issue it should make no difference to him. Yet he would more prefer estimates of only ten or twenty thousand years. This seems to be an indication that he realized the genealogies of Genesis were already being stretched to the breaking point.

The feeble appeal to Matthew 1 as the interpretative standard governing Genesis is not sufficient for the task. Because an occasional name in Matthew 1 is a grandson or great grandson of the previously named progenitor, it gives us no warrant to make that grandson a remote descendant born centuries later and not personally known to his 'father.' Even if we wrongly forced the nature of the mere list of names onto the detailed genealogy of Genesis, the analogy would not justify the insertion of millions of years. Neither would it justify the assumption that the named 'son' was a very distant descendant totally unknown to his 'father.'

Having dismissed the historical value of the Genesis genealogies, Warfield now turns to his defense of the unity of the human race. Having preferred evolutionary chronology to biblical, he must now defend the historical statements of Scripture regarding the unity of the human race. But here he believes evolution is his ally:

> 'The prevalence of the evolutionary hypothesis has removed all motive for denying a common origin to the human race, and rendered it natural to look upon the differences which exist among the various types of man as differentiations of a common stock.'[39]

---

39. Ref. 36, p. 252.

As a matter of fact many evolutionists tried to give scientific respectability to their racism by declaring that the various 'races' had different origins and/or that certain races were less evolved. The evidentialist apologetical approach often underestimates the effects of original sin on the reason of man. Warfield allowed for areas of neutrality, especially in science. Parts of the Scripture had to be interpreted in pencil, waiting for the next theory to come along and completely change our understanding. Princeton's confidence in the old arguments and apologetic of Aquinas was misplaced. Aquinas states the exemption of reason from the effects of sin:

> '...the infection of original sin is most apparent in the movements of the members of generation, which are not subject to reason. Now those members serve the generative power in the mingling of sexes, wherein there is the delectation of touch, which is the most powerful incentive to concupiscence. Therefore the infection of original sin regards these three chiefly, viz. the generative power, the concupiscible faculty and the sense of touch.'[40]

Thus the noetic effect [on the mind] of sin is not seen as very serious. Original sin is, in Platonic fashion, attributed to the physical side of man, especially those sins relating to sexual feelings and actions.

The piecemeal evidentialist apologetic of Princeton allowed the ever-ratcheting effect of compromise to continue until Princeton's demise shortly after the death of Warfield. If ever we needed a tragic example of where the path of compromise leads, the sad history of Princeton Seminary provides that example.[41] Again we see that nothing less than an uncompromised stand on the plain Word of God is our only sure defense. The Scripture has its own objective meaning;

---

40. Thomas Aquinas, 'Of the Subject of Original Sin,' in *Summa Theologica*, vol. 2 (Books for the Ages, ver. 1.0; Albany, Oregon: Ages Software, 1997), p. 925. Part 2 Q83 A4.

41. Princeton Seminary opened in 1812 as a strong defender of biblical Christianity. As successive generations compromised 'just a little more' the seminary declined. After the death of Warfield in 1921, it would not be long before the school ceased to be a center of Bible-believing Christianity. The road to demise is paved with compromise.

it does not wait for us to bring our many arbitrary and subjective meanings to it. The National Institute of Standards and Technology could not operate if every person coming by insisted that the standard one-yard measure must be adjusted to his personal opinion of how long a 'yard' should be. We must not let our interpretation of Scripture be dictated by evolutionary speculation. The God-breathed Scripture is our standard of measure. We must learn to evaluate all truth claims by the God-given infallible standard of His Word

CHAPTER 9

COULD PRINCETON HAVE AVOIDED COMPROMISE?

Yes, it could have—biblically, apologetically, and scientifically.

A. BIBLICAL AND APOLOGETIC CONSIDERATIONS

The very first verse of the Bible, Genesis 1:1, excludes evolutionary naturalism, 'In the beginning God created the heaven and the earth.' The biblical chronologies give us a comprehensive history of mankind from the very first human being. The millions of years, the lifeline of evolutionary speculation, are excluded at the outset. The Bible slams the door on the possibility of evolution by excluding the millions of years. Yet many Christians seem not to realize that by rejecting the chronological-historical framework of Scripture, they are forced to accept a portion of evolutionary mythology. Christians, having disregarded Genesis, speak of prehistoric times. But this is the evolutionary story, not the inspired biblical-historical account. Since Genesis describes the very beginning in an historical account, there is no *pre*historic time. By rejecting the detailed chronology of Genesis, Princeton was saying to the church and to the world, 'It does not matter *when* these events took place.' That guaranteed that a couple of generations later, some of their 'heirs' at Westminster East and elsewhere would be saying, 'It does not matter *if* these events took place.' In other words, a purported history that has no chronology will soon be thought of as mythology. One characteristic feature of mythology is the lack of historical context, something simply long ago and far away. One characteristic of biblical revelation is its being rooted in time and space history. Thus, what is uninteresting and unessential to twenty-first century westerners is essential in the unfolding drama of redemption.

Hodge and others were on the alert when evolutionary theory appeared in its openly atheistic form. But by ignoring the chronology of the Bible as if it were unimportant, they opened the door to the acceptance of more and more of an evolutionary worldview. But the consequences of accepting evolution were vastly more serious than Hodge and Warfield realized. In one sense it is understandable that Hodge could not see the devastating consequences of evolutionary thought—the fatal fruit of evolution had not ripened until the twentieth century. In a greater sense, though, it is never right to reject the biblical account. The consequences of such a rejection may not be visible at the time, but they will surely follow. To depart from Scripture at any point is neither safe nor right.

One area that must be investigated is the origin of the idea of millions of years. Of course the ancient Greek philosophy regarding the random collision of atoms required vast ages of time for the random collisions to produce something of apparent order and design. But the Christian faith had largely overcome this pagan cosmology. What we have in the nineteenth century is the resurgence of the ancient anti-Christian worldview, this time with a scientific veneer. In an age caught up in the possibilities of science and technology, the veneer was mistaken for solid wood. It was an age of almost limitless optimism, founded on technology and science.

Where did the idea of millions of years originate in modern times?[1] Terry Mortensen has extensively researched the geological controversies of nineteenth century England in his *The Great Turning Point*. There were a group of men (already alluded to earlier in this work) known as 'scriptural geologists' who opposed the evolutionary notion of millions of years. Some objected primarily from their knowledge of geology, some from their knowledge of Scripture, some competent in both areas. They believed in the chronological

---

1. The Appendix shows how faulty the so-called scientific dating methods can be. See also the *Creation* magazine articles at <creation.com/earth_how_old>, <creation.com/rate and <creation.com/dating_reality>.

framework supplied by Scripture. They believed that Genesis was written by Moses under divine inspiration. They believed that the worldwide flood in the days of Noah catastrophically altered the face of the earth, and that it was responsible for the formation of most fossils.

The scriptural geologists opposed both the uniformitarianism of James Hutton and Charles Lyell and the 'catastrophist' theories of Cuvier, Buckland, and Sedgwick. The latter were more subtle, perhaps even more effective in undermining the authority of Scripture. The catastrophists were popularly understood to be more in agreement with the Bible, some of them being clergymen. But they would see the Flood of Noah as only one catastrophe in an imagined series of them. These catastrophists had actually accommodated the millions of years by 're-interpreting' the Scripture via the gap theory, the day-age theory, the tranquil flood theory, and the mythical account theory. Scriptural geologists opposed these views as compromises of Scripture and founded on unproven old-earth theories of geology.[2] Such unfortunate compromises are always the result when Christians feel compelled to choose from among various secular theories instead of constructing a Christian worldview.

The new popularity of the millions of years concept was not the result of any new scientific evidence, but the resurgence of an anti-Christian worldview. The new presuppositional foundation had a different story to tell about the same data that had always been available. In addition, new fossil discoveries were interpreted according to the new model. It gave the popular impression that somehow the fossil findings were 'proof' of evolution. The obvious indication that well-preserved fossils indicate sudden burial by water-laid sediments was too often ignored.

Thinking biblically on this issue requires us to examine the presuppositions of those geologists who began advocating millions of years of earth history. An important insight into their bias may be seen in Charles Lyell's remark about scriptural geologists.

---

2. Terry Mortenson, 'Introduction,' in The Great Turning Point, *The Church's Catastrophic Mistake on Geology—Before Darwin*. (Green Forest, Arkansas: Master Books, 2004), p. 12.

'...they are wholly destitute of geological knowledge...
incapable of appreciating the force of objections, or
of discerning the weight of inductions from numerous
physical facts....They endeavor to point out the accordance
of the Mosaic history with phenomena which they have
never studied.'[3]

So spoke the atheist/deist lawyer whose formal training was neither
in geology nor theology. From whence comes this assumption that
his own word should be accepted without question, but the Word of
God can and should be questioned? Many evolutionists have made
similar rants. William Williamson described the work of George
Young, one of the most geologically competent scriptural geologists,
as 'prejudiced rubbish.'[4]

Such a barrage of insults is supposed to relieve the evolutionists
of the necessity of actually answering the case made by the scriptural
geologists. Apparently if one is short of evidence, there remains an
inexhaustible supply of insults. Evolutionists are of course outraged if
some 'fundamentalist' Christian resorts to ridicule in order to dismiss
evolution. While these rantings tell us nothing about geology, they
do reveal the presuppositions of those making them.

To illustrate how far some evolutionists will go to reinterpret
damaging evidence, consider the problem of how life could arise
from non-living matter. Some evolutionists have acknowledged that
this is 'impossible.' Who can believe the old theory of spontaneous
generation in the 21st century? Here is how Harvard biochemist
George Wald thinks he can get around this problem:

'One has only to contemplate the magnitude of this task
to concede that the spontaneous generation of a living
organism is impossible. Yet here we are—as a result, I
believe of spontaneous generation. It will help to digress

---

3. Charles Lyell, 'Review of *Memoir on the Geology of Central France,' Quarterly Review* XXXVI,
no. 72:482, 1827. Cited by Mortenson in *The Great Turning Point*.

4. Williamson, William C, *Reminiscences of a Yorkshire Naturalist* (n.p., 1896), 56. Cited by
Mortenson, Ref. 2, p. 13.

for a moment to ask what one means by "impossible." ... the spontaneous origin of a living organism, this is not an event that need happen again and again. It is perhaps enough for it to happen once. ...However improbable the event in a single trial, it becomes increasingly probable as the trials are multiplied. Eventually the event becomes virtually inevitable....Time is the hero of the plot. ...of the order of two billion years....Given so much time, the "impossible" becomes possible, the possible probable, and the probable virtually certain. One has only to wait: time itself performs the miracles.'[5]

So the evidence must be made to fit. Of course, the evolutionists reject the old discredited theory of spontaneous generation, but can affirm it under the new name abiogenesis (aka chemical evolution). They would say that spontaneous generation is impossible now, under present conditions. But given millions or billions of years ago, under different conditions, abiogenesis could have happened at least once. Given these billions of years, a seemingly impossible event is virtually certain to happen. The belief that time is the hero who performs the necessary miracles sounds more like a confession of faith than an established scientific fact. It seems nothing is too difficult for Time. An evolutionist might say that abiogenesis is kind of like rolling a '12' on a pair of dice, 100 times in a row— theoretically it will eventually happen if given enough time to try again and again.[6] However, that argument falls down in the real world of mathematics and logic. There are only so many events that can possibly happen in this universe—limited by the number of particles in it, for one thing. And the amount of time available, even if one were to grant the evolutionist his desired 15 billion years, is also not limitless. The numbers become so astronomical as to be for all practical purposes

5. George Wald, 'The Origin of Life,' *Scientific American* (vol. 191), pp. 44–53.

6. In reality, the odds are astronomically worse. So much so that even given all the atoms in the universe as 'dice-throwing tables', and all the seconds in the evolutionists' imagined 15 billion years since the universe began, the self-assembly by time and chance alone of even the simplest conceivable living thing has been conceded by several secularists themselves to have a probability of effectively zero. See <creation.com/probabilities>.

like rolling a '13' just once on that pair of dice—impossible.[7] The late astrophysicist Sir Fred Hoyle (not a Christian) famously said that to get by chance just one single one of the many biomolecules upon which life depends is like expecting enough blind men to cram the solar system shoulder to shoulder and randomly shuffling Rubik's cubes to all hit upon the solution simultaneously![8]

Christians need to take heed to biblical chronology. When we take the trouble to examine these matters, we will find that the evolutionists' 'Hero' Time is a fantasy of their imagination.

Knowing from Romans 1 and other passages that unbelievers will not have God in their knowledge, we should note the religious beliefs of those who revived the millions of years theory. We should also note the minimal difference between a deist (with his vague theism) and an open atheist. In the nineteenth century it was more culturally acceptable to be a theist than an atheist. It should be recalled that a non-offensive deity, created in the image of man, is an attractive option for those who want to reject the biblical God (the only God there is) without being tagged an atheist. Recall also that even Lucretius could tolerate a god or gods indifferent to human events. In some cases we cannot tell whether various men were deists or atheists, but from a biblical view there is little difference.

Uniformitarian Naturalism and Old-Earth Views

Who	When	Proposed age of Earth (years)	Proposed age of Earth (years)
Buffon	1779	75,000-3 million	Deist/atheist
Werner	1786	1 million	Deist/atheist
Hutton	1795	Perhaps eternal	Deist/atheist
Laplace	1796	Long ages	Atheist
Lamarck	1809	Long ages	Deist/atheist
W. Smith	1836	Long ages	Deist/vague theist[9]
Cuvier	1812	Long ages	Deist
Lyell	1830–33	Millions	Deist/Unitarian

7. See Jonathan Sarfati, *By Design: Evidence for nature's Intelligent Designer—the God of the Bible*, ch. 11, Creation Book Publishers, GA, USA, 2008.

8. Fred Hoyle, 'The Big Bang in Astronomy', *New Scientist* **92**(1280):527, November 19, 1981.

- All these men had a bias against the biblical creation account that shaped their interpretation of geology.

- All postulated their estimates before Darwin's *Origin of Species*, 1859.

- None of them could claim that they had 'scientific proof' for the departure from biblical chronology and Flood geology.

- Those who said 'long ages' often privately held to millions of years, but publicly issued more reserved statements that would move readers away from the biblical chronology without provoking a strong reaction.

Avid evolutionist Stephen Jay Gould admits the subjectivity of Charles Lyell in this severe criticism:

'Charles Lyell was a lawyer by profession, and his book is one of the most brilliant briefs published by an advocate. … Lyell relied upon true bits of cunning to establish his uniformitarian views as the only true geology. First, he set up a straw man to demolish. In fact, the catastrophists were much more empirically minded than Lyell. The geologic record does seem to require catastrophes: rocks are fractured and contorted; whole faunas are wiped out. To circumvent this literal appearance, Lyell imposed his imagination upon the evidence. The geologic record, he argued, is extremely imperfect and we must interpolate into it what we can reasonably infer but cannot see. The catastrophists were the hard-nosed empiricists of their day, not the blinded theological apologists.'[10]

---

9. Constructed from information in two articles by Terry Mortenson, Ph.D.

1. 'Philosophical naturalism and the age of the earth: are they related?' *The Master's Seminary Journal* **15**(1):71–92, Spring 2004, available <creation.com/naturalism-church>.

2. 'The origin of old-earth geology and its ramifications for life in the 21st century' *Journal of Creation* **18**(1):22–26, April 2004, available <creation.com/oldearth>.

10. S. J. Gould, *Natural History* (February 1975), p. 16.

Evolutionary scientists like to define science in such a way as to deliberately exclude the Creator. Another example among many is Richard Dickerson:

> 'Science, fundamentally, is a game. It is a game with one overriding and defining rule. Rule No.1: Let us see how far and to what extent we can explain the behavior of the physical and material universe in terms of purely physical and material causes, without invoking the supernatural.'[11]

Evolutionists show the same attitude toward a reasonable discussion of differences as did the Spanish Inquisition. '*Scientific American* fired the science writer Forrest Mims as soon as they appointed him, simply because they discovered he was "a non-believer in evolution.'"[12] This kind of example could be repeated many times over for teachers, professors, museum directors, and others who lost jobs or opportunities simply for having another point of view. Evolutionary theory survives best under compulsion and in the darkness.

Here then are three reasons why Hodge and Princeton should have been skeptical of Darwinian thought:

1. The presuppositions of the anti-Christians who first proposed the millions of years led them to purposely construct a system that would exclude the God of the Bible. (Whether they allowed for a lesser man-created deity varied with cultural expectations, but was always irrelevant for their purposes.) The God of the Bible is the One who holds man accountable, and hell awaits His enemies. To have the Epicurean tranquility of soul, there must be no god at all or a remote unconcerned deity who will not judge.

---

11. Richard E. Dickerson, 'The Game of Science,' *Perspectives on Science and Faith*, no. 44 (June 1992): 137. Cited by D. A. Carson, *The Gagging of God*, (Grand Rapids, Michigan: Zondervan, 1996) p. 195.

12. D.A. Carson, 'What God Has Spoken: Opening Moves in the Bible's Plot-Line,' in *The Gagging of God* p. 195.

2. The 'proofs' they cited for evolution were nothing more than data that could have been explained by the Christian worldview as well or better than by the evolutionary worldview. But since evolution was their worldview, every 'fact' they came across was claimed as evidence of evolution. The evolutionary story is the story they had already predetermined to tell about any data they discovered. For example, fossils must be buried suddenly in order to be preserved. Therefore a catastrophic flood is a superior explanation of fossils than some very drawn-out gradual uniformitarian process. But the Flood disturbs the tranquility of the unbeliever's soul/mind. Not only is the Flood catastrophic, but also it was an act of judgment. No wonder unbelievers are in denial regardless of evidence presented.

3. The scriptural geologists had written extensively enough that Hodge could have made use of their insight to resist evolutionary philosophy. He gives no evidence of having read any of them. Evolutionary geologists did not refute them; they used ridicule and insults to intimidate people to accept the uniformitarian millions of years.

If ridicule and insults can make the case, the task of the creationist has been made quite simple. However, we are expected to do better.

The British uniformitarians of the nineteenth century formed their own elite circle. They considered themselves immune from criticism from anyone outside their circle. Many of them had only the same theology or law degrees as their opposition. But there were scriptural geologists who were quite competent in geology. The difference between them was not how much education they had, or what data they were aware of, but the worldview by which they interpreted the data. As seen in their religious affiliation (or mostly lack thereof) the uniformitarian naturalists had a definite bias against biblical Christianity.

This bias continues to the present time. Princeton's assumption of value-free science did not search out the presuppositions of those proposing scientific theories. With all the technological advances and scientific discoveries of the nineteenth century, the 'scientist' was accorded authority even where he had no special competence. How could scientists who predicted and then discovered the planet Neptune be as biased as ordinary human beings? But alas, they are ordinary human beings. Ardent evolutionist Aldous Huxley wrote in 1932:

> 'For myself, as, no doubt, for most of my contemporaries, the philosophy of meaningless was essentially an instrument of liberation. The liberation we desired was simultaneously liberation from a certain political and economic system and liberation from a certain system of morality. We objected to the morality because it interfered with our sexual freedom; we objected to the political and economic system because it was unjust. The supporters of these systems claimed that in some way they embodied the meaning (a Christian meaning, they insisted) of the world. There was one admirably simple method of confuting these people and at the same time justifying ourselves in our political and erotical revolt: we could deny that the world had any meaning whatsoever.'[13]

Julian Huxley, brother of Aldous, also had a 'religious' preference for evolution:

> 'A religion is essentially an attitude to the world as a whole. Thus evolution, for example, may prove as powerful a principle to coordinate men's beliefs and hopes as God was in the past. Such ideas underlie the various forms of Rationalism, the Ethical movement and scientific Humanism.'[14]

---

13. Aldous Huxley, *Ends and Means: An Inquiry into the Nature of Ideals and into the Methods Employed for Their Realization*, Fifth ed. (New York: Harper, 1937), pp. 316-17 as it appears at <www.edwardbabinski.us>.

14. Huxley, Barry, Bronowski and Fisher, *Growth of Ideas. The evolution of thought and knowledge*, ed. Huxley, Julian (London: MacDonald, 1965), p. 99.

Now we can see how the seemingly trivial issue of a certain biological theory served as a Trojan horse to bring in the whole evolutionary religious worldview. The church, for the most part, quickly and quietly welcomed the Greeks bearing gifts; little suspecting hostile forces would soon overwhelm them. At first it seemed to pose no danger to the central themes of Christianity, eventually it was seen to be hostile at every point. It was in fact an attempt to devise a comprehensive worldview antithetical to Christianity. As Julian Huxley entitled one of his books, this alternate worldview was *Religion Without Revelation*.

B. SCIENTIFIC CONSIDERATIONS: THE SCRIPTURAL GEOLOGISTS

Christians should not ignore the scriptural geologists, nor should they ignore the present-day creation scientists and theologians. Typical of the way scriptural geologists were dismissed is a reference in the *Dictionary of National Biography* article on Granville Penn (1761–1844). There the criticism is made that his work was 'an unscientific attempt to treat the Book of Genesis as a manual of geology.'[15]

This common charge is both false and irrelevant. Neither Granville Penn, nor any other scriptural geologist ever claimed that Genesis was a manual of geology. (The Scripture is far better than a typical error-laden textbook or manual of geology, but that is beside the point here.) The weakness of the evolutionary case is shown in their unwillingness to accurately state the position of creationists. They do not even begin to refute the case Penn has made. They in fact show no awareness of what his case actually was. Mere slander is deemed a sufficient cause for dismissing him from serious consideration. Penn had dealt respectfully with various noted uniformitarian geologists, disputing not the established data of geology, but the interpretation of that data. Penn would not agree that we should separate revelation from our study of geology because the God of nature is the God of Scripture. The revelation in

15. Mortenson, *The Great Turning Point*, p. 62.

Scripture includes not only the history of mankind, but of the sun, moon, stars, plants and animals—all before the history of mankind begins. The real issue is whether or not we will receive the basic principles of the biblical worldview as absolute truth, regardless of what area of life and thought is addressed. The Bible is not a manual on geology, but it reveals the true foundation on which all our thinking (even about geology) is to be founded and directed. What could possibly be more valuable to our search for origins than the testimony of the One who created all things? Perhaps creationists could say of evolutionists that they made an unscientific attempt to treat *On the Nature of Things*, by Lucretius, as a manual on geology. What we believe about origins or destiny is not a result of observation, measurement and experimentation. Since Darwin's *Origin of Species* is not a textbook on Systematic Theology, will the evolutionist agree that anything Darwin says about God or theological issues must be rejected? The real question is why did the Christians of the nineteenth century not listen more carefully to the Scriptures, let alone the scriptural geologists?

Penn opposed and refuted both the gap theory and the day-age theory as being highly unlikely interpretations made under pressure from uniformitarianism. Scriptural geologists whose training was in theology and biblical studies were particularly critical of the so-called 'catastrophic' views of clergymen-geologists Sedgwick and Buckland, as well as geologist Cuvier. People in the church may be drawn to these theories because they give superficial support to the biblical account of the Flood. In reality, these uniformitarians undermined the Scripture, counted the Flood as only local and one of many catastrophes over millions of years.

George Fairholme (1789–1846) was well trained in geology and authored several articles for scientific journals. It was his study of geology that moved him to see the accuracy of the Genesis record. He wrote two large books on the topic: *Geology of Scripture* and *Mosaic Deluge*. In the latter book he decided to restrict himself to scientific arguments although making plain his confidence in Scripture.

'I would by no means have it inferred that I undervalue, or set aside, the conclusive testimony of Revelation, on this point. On the contrary, I should myself be content to rest, with the fullest confidence, on the unerring truth of revealed testimony ...'[16]

Fairholme was convinced that the rock layers in sedimentary rock were laid down in the year of Noah's flood. The layers were in perfect conformity, with no signs of erosion between one layer and the next. If a layer had been exposed to the elements a long time, signs of erosion would be evident.[17]

Through his study of Geology he came to a greater confidence in the Genesis record. How did evolutionists receive his carefully documented and detailed scientific observations? As usual they were unable to answer his case, but had plenty of insults designed to excuse them from answering. Critics could only make false and insulting remarks claiming Fairholme knew 'scarcely an atom of geology as now taught' with 'little real knowledge of geology' or having a brain with an opening like 'a diluvial chaotic pit.'[18] Critics could always reinforce their lies and misrepresentations with an impressive vocabulary. The critics also followed their usual practice of failing to show even one example that demonstrated his alleged ignorance. Fairholme in his turn treated his opponents with far greater respect, actually taking time to show where and why their arguments were weak. He was still looking for 'a simple and consistent refutation of the subject of this paper.'[18] He made a reasonable offer to reconsider his views if the critics could present some solid evidence. For some reason they passed on the offer. Probably the biggest problem for the scriptural geologists was that the real issue was not about the evidence, but about conflicting worldviews.

---

16. George Fairholme, *New and Conclusive Physical Demonstrations Both of the Fact and Period of the Mosaic Deluge, and of Its Having Been the Only Event of the Kind That Has Ever Occurred upon the Earth* (n.p., 1837), 423. Cited by Mortenson, *The Great Turning Point*, p. 123.

17. Mortenson, *The Great Turning Point*, p. 119.

18. Ref. 17, p. 120.

John Murray (1786?–1851) was another geologically competent scientist who upheld *The Truth of Revelation*, the title of one of his books. With all his scientific knowledge he was increasingly convinced that:

> 'There is only ONE authentic record of the primordial history of the globe, and of its tenants; that ancient book may be safely referred to, and in the question of geology, is the only legitimate standard of appeal. The facts of our science corroborate its evidence...Hypotheses have indeed warred with, and may continue to assail the solemn and sublime dicta of Revelation, but it may fearlessly be asserted, that its INTEGRITY will "flourish in immortal youth."'[19]

Murray wrote numerous articles on a wide range of scientific interests. He had an in-depth knowledge of conchology (the study of shells) that has such importance in the study of rock layers. It is indeed tragic that Charles Hodge neglected to read his scientific articles. And how much more did Hodge need to read these words of John Murray:

> 'There cannot be a position more fixed and determinate than this—namely, that the right meaning of a Hebrew word is to be determined by the canons of philology, and not by the elements of geology. If scripture is to be determined by such ... an ever-changing reference, there can be no standard whatever, and the pillar of our security is shaken to its foundation.'[20]

---

19. John Murray, 'Preface,' in *A Portrait of Geology* (London: Relfe and Fletcher, 1838), pp. v–vi.

20. John Murray, T*he Truth of Revelation, Demonstrated by an Appeal to Existing Monuments and Sculptures, Gems, Coins and Medals.* (London: Longman, Rees, Orme, Brown and Green, 1831), pp. 137–139. Cited by Terry Mortenson, 'British scriptural geologists in the first half of the nineteenth century: part 11. John Murray (1786?–1851)' *TJ* (now *Journal of Creation*), **18**(2):74–82, August 2004. Available at <creation.com>, accessed 20 October 2008.

It is ironic that we have Hodge, the great theologian, ready to resort to highly doubtful 'interpretations' of the Bible out of a fear of what uniformitarian 'science' might find. On the other hand we have the well-informed scientist, Murray, expressing a firm confidence in the plain meaning of Scripture. How Hodge could have profited from the scriptural geologists, both as to their scientific work and their confidence in Scripture!

The reader may find more detailed information in Mortenson's *The Great Turning Point*, but one more scriptural geologist deserves mention. George Young (1777–1848) had both scientific and theological training and saw his extensive geological experience as an aid, not a threat, to his faith. His thorough study of the Yorkshire coast was instrumental in his refutation of John Pye Smith's local flood theory regarding the Genesis flood. Young's geological work received positive reviews, even from opponents like Adam Sedgwick of Cambridge. Young's respectful demeanor is in sharp contrast to the insulting behavior of most uniformitarian geologists. He pleaded in his *Scriptural Geology*, 'It is not by hard names, but by strong arguments, that the cause of truth is to be established.'[21]

In addition to rejecting the local flood theory, Young also made his scientific case against the tranquil flood theory, and the uniformitarianism of Lyell. Young's own study of rock strata showed that they did not follow the neat textbook pattern of the so-called 'geologic column.' His scientific arguments included the polystrate fossil phenomenon. For example, fossilized trees were found going up through many strata of sedimentary rock. These strata were alleged by uniformitarians to be of vastly different ages. The evidence suggests that such trees were first transported to the site, then suddenly buried by layer after layer of rock. The evolutionized geologists had to assume that the tree grew on that spot, and though dead, somehow did not decay during the mythical millions of years it took to form the strata in which we find it buried. To the tranquil flood theory, he pointed out the specifically destructive judgmental

---

21. George Young, *Scriptural Geology*, Second ed. (London: Simpkin, Marshall and Co., 1840), p. iv.

purpose of the biblical Flood. He also noted that even local floods cannot be described as 'tranquil'. Young also presented the evidence of flatly crushed and flatly preserved fish, which naturally decay in hours, yet frequently were found fossilized in laminated strata. This is clear proof of rapid formation of sedimentary layers. A dead fish cannot lie around for even a week, let alone long ages waiting to be slowly fossilized. The layers had to be formed in a matter of minutes and hours.[22] Young also answered critics of Noah's ark. They vastly underestimate the huge size of the ark and overestimate the number of animals needing to be on the ark.[23] It would not be necessary to bring aboard the vast numbers of species of insects and sea life. Not to mention the fact that it was two of every 'kind,' with land mammals as the main focus.

The main points to be observed are:

1. The philosophies of evolutionary thought originated in ancient times, when no pretext could be made of 'scientific' evidence to sustain them.

2. The shift from six-thousand-year chronology to millions of years took place without any new evidence. The same observed phenomena were simply reinterpreted in a naturalistic uniformitarian way.

C. ROBERT L. DABNEY, A CONTEMPORARY AND BETTER APOLOGETIC

The closed circle elite had managed to fairly well silence the propagation of the scriptural geologists' views in their control of the major scientific publications. They were obsessive about promoting only those who conformed to their anti-Christian agenda. They had some success in promoting their religious-philosophical worldview

---

22. For a modern confirmation of Young's thesis see Andrew Snelling, 'Sedimentation Experiments: Nature finally catches up!' *TJ* (now *Journal of Creation*) 11(2):125–26 available <creation.com>, accessed 20 September 2008. Mount Saint Helens provided confirmation in 1980 with 25 feet of sedimentary layers being formed in one afternoon and the Little Toutle River Canyon system formed within a week.

23. Mortenson, Ref. 2, pp. 172–78.

as 'science' while tagging the biblical worldview as merely 'religion.' They were of course in denial as to the religious-philosophical roots of their own system of thought. The academic world shows little tolerance toward those who challenge their dogmas.

But even if we could excuse Hodge for not finding the books and articles of the scriptural geologists, to seem oblivious to his contemporary R. L. Dabney is not excusable. Dabney and others in the Southern Presbyterian Church were much stronger in their resistance and opposition to evolutionary thought. We find the thoughts of Dabney most accessible in his *Systematic Theology* and the volumes of collected articles published as *Discussions*. This has already been discussed in chapter seven. How could Hodge have repeatedly invited Dabney to teach at Princeton, without even reading his works?

CHAPTER 10

CREATION WITHOUT COMPROMISE: AN EXEGETICAL STUDY OF GENESIS

Evidentialist apologists usually have a piecemeal approach to Christianity and an unwarranted confidence in the objectivity of man's reason. It is seen in the attempt to 'prove' Christianity to an unbeliever a piece at a time. It is also seen in the assumption that some parts of the Bible are unimportant and may be conceded to critics. If something said in Scripture is beside their idea of the main purpose of Scripture it is thought expendable. If that 'unimportant' passage happens to contradict the consensus of contemporary scientists, the Bible must yield. The Bible must then be re-interpreted to fit the new scientific consensus, regardless of how highly improbable the new accommodating interpretation may be. Regardless of how violently the rules of hermeneutics are violated, the Bible must be made to speak in harmony with the contemporary scientific consensus.

We may be surprised to find that the major opposition to evolution in the nineteenth century was not from the Christian church, but from the specialists in fossils. Many of these scientists could not agree that the fossils they observed needed to be explained by Darwinian theory. But the Church, by and large, was content to hastily devise new 'interpretations' of the Bible that would bring Scripture into harmony with the new scientific theory. They compartmentalized life into 'religious' and 'scientific.' In the 'religious' realm, the Bible was the authority. In the 'scientific' realm, naturalistic uniformitarian theory was supreme. Since the Bible was 'not written to tell us how the heavens go, but how to go to heaven,' we need not concern ourselves with relatively trivial scientific issues. At least, so they thought.

This proved to be a foolhardy decision for several reasons.

- The Bible was not taken seriously when it spoke to the real world. Christianity was truncated from a comprehensive biblical worldview for all life and thought to a simple plan of salvation and a guide to morality. As Douglas Kelly put it:

    'To assume that the early chapters of Genesis are just "religious" (and thus take the viewpoint of the origins of the world from unbelieving varieties of philosophy) is to relegate the Bible and "religion" to the realm of the unimportant and the unreal, and eventually to empty the churches since they are no longer thought to deal with actual truth.'[1]

- Evolution is itself a faith or dogma, not an observational science. Its foundation is philosophical, not empirical. Evolution is not some proven fact to which we must adjust; it is an alien faith that we must not mix with the purity of revealed truth. Not only have evolutionists specifically spoken in terms of 'faith', but intelligent design scholars have also shown the faith basis of evolution. The controversy is not between 'faith' and 'science', but between two different kinds of faith. In the words of Michael Denton regarding evolution:

    '...there can be no doubt that after a century of intensive effort biologists have failed to validate it in any significant

---

1. Douglas F. Kelly, 'Creation: Why it Matters,' in *Creation and Change* (Scotland: Mentor, 2004), p. 18.

sense. The fact remains that nature has not been reduced to the continuum that the Darwinian model demands, nor has the credibility of chance as the creative agency of life been secured.'[2]

• Evolution is a contrary worldview, designed to be a substitute for the biblical worldview. As Michael Denton has also said,

'The entire scientific ethos and philosophy of modern western man is based to a large extent upon the central claim of Darwinian theory that humanity was not born by the creative intentions of a deity, but by a completely mindless trial and error selection of random molecular patterns. The cultural importance of evolution theory is therefore immeasurable, forming as it does the centerpiece, the crowning achievement, of the naturalistic view of the world, the final triumph of the secular thesis which since the end of the middle ages has displaced the old naïve cosmology of Genesis from the western mind.'[3]

Who could have seen the horrific consequences brought on by the acceptance of evolution? We can never fully imagine the consequences of tampering with the Word of God, but we may be sure there will be very serious consequences.

A. INTERPRETATION AND OUTLINE OF GENESIS 1–3

Since the idea of millions of years was reintroduced, interpreters have struggled to avoid the obvious conflict between the straightforward reading of Genesis and the evolutionary theory. They may say that Genesis 1–3 or 1–11 is poetry rather than historical narrative.

---

2. Michael Denton, *Evolution: A Theory in Crisis* (Bethesda, Maryland: Adler & Adler, 1986), p. 357, cited by Douglas Kelly, ref. 1.

3. Michael Denton, op. cit., p. 66. cited by Douglas Kelly, ref. 1.

E.J. Young, noted twentieth century Hebrew scholar, has said plainly,

> 'Genesis is not poetry. There are poetical accounts of creation in the Bible—Psalm 104, and certain chapters in Job—and they differ completely from the first chapter of Genesis...The man who says, 'I believe that Genesis purports to be a historical account, but I do not believe that account', is a far better interpreter of the Bible than the man who says, 'I believe that Genesis is profoundly true, but it is poetry.'[4]

The less one knows about Genesis 1, the easier it is to be taken in by the claim that it is poetry. There is no indication of Hebrew parallelism, imagery, or figurative language. The way the New Testament refers to the early chapters of Genesis further demonstrates its non-poetic, historical nature.

Often those 'evangelical' interpreters who scramble to find a culturally agreeable 'interpretation' of Genesis will claim they are doing so for apologetic reasons. This claim seems foolhardy on the surface of it, since we are permitted to salvage only so much of the Christian faith as the unbelieving world will find agreeable. The Roman Catholic Church resisted the scientific theories of Galileo because of the opposition of most university professors and the respected authority of Aristotle. Today's compromising apologists urge the church to resist creation science, because of the opposition of most university professors and the respected authority of Darwin. Just how impressed are liberal theologians by this type of apologetic? Nineteenth century liberal expositor Marcus Dods wrote concerning these strained interpretations of Genesis 1 and 2:

> '...all attempts to force its statements into such accord are futile and mischievous...And above all, they are to be

---

4. Edward J. Young, *In the Beginning: Genesis 1–3 and the Authority of Scripture* (Edinburgh: Banner of Truth Trust, 1976), pp. 18–19.

condemned because they do violence to Scripture, foster a style of interpretation by which the text is forced to say whatever the interpreter desires, and prevent us from recognizing the real nature of these sacred writings…If, for example, the word 'day' in these chapters does not mean a period of twenty-four hours, the interpretation of Scripture is hopeless.'[5]

Many Christians have thought what Dods plainly implied: that the variety of attempts to evade the plain meaning of Genesis seems like so much sophistry. If the compromises are meant to have apologetic value by gaining the respect of secular intellectuals, they are definitely not working. Neither Marcus Dods nor James Barr believes what Genesis says, but they know well enough what it actually says. In the late twentieth century, James Barr of Oxford, referring to professors of Hebrew/Old Testament at all world-class universities, wrote,

'…the apologetic arguments which suppose the 'days' of creation to be long eras of time, the figures of years not to be chronological, and the flood to be a merely local Mesopotamian flood, are not taken seriously by any such professor, as far as I know.'[6]

Thus the compromising apologist surrenders the infallible Word of God for the passing hypotheses of men and gains only contempt for his mishandling of Scripture. The result is indulging in faulty eisegesis for the sake of harmony with faulty 'scientific' theories. Christians must learn to think Christianly, that is, to build biblically from the foundation upward. It is a shameful and totally unnecessary act for Christians to pick out of the dumpster the discarded speculations of scientists. For example, Hugh Ross eagerly embraces the 'Big Bang'

---

5. Marcus Dods, *Expositor's Bible* (Edinburgh: T. & T. Clark, 1888), 4. cited by Douglas Kelly, ref. 1.

6. James Barr, *a personal communication to David C. C. Watson* (n.p., 1984). Cited by Douglas Kelly, ref. 1, p. 51.

theory, even though the very scientist who named it 'Big Bang' did so only to ridicule it (Fred Hoyle). Furthermore, the theory is atheistic, *designed* to be antithetical to Christianity.

Now consider the gap theory. Thomas Chalmers' eisegesis of desperation no longer has the support it first enjoyed. It does not take the Hebrew grammatical structure seriously and creates as many problems as it purports to solve. As mentioned elsewhere, the *vav* disjunctive of Gen. 1:2 forms a kind of parenthetical statement. The time of the condition stated in verse 2 is connected to the same time at which God spoke light into existence on day one. In addition, it is special pleading to force the translation 'became' in place of 'was.' But there are lessons to be learned by evangelicals, and Kelly expresses them well:

> 'It teaches us first, the futility of reading into Scripture what is not there in order to force a hasty compromise with anti-theistic thought. Secondly…it teaches us to put the same kind of skeptical, foundational questions to the dogmas of humanistic authorities that they have long put to the authority of Scripture. Unfortunately, many well-intentioned evangelicals were too ready to adjust the teachings of Scripture to authority-claims of naturalistic science without taking the time and effort to examine radically the presuppositions, evidences and procedures of those highly vaunted authorities.'[7]

B. THE DAYS OF CREATION: THEIR BIBLICAL MEANING

The Bible immediately confronts us with the absolute creation (out of nothing) of the universe by an infinite, personal God. In order for evolutionists to imagine how everything could come from mindless random change, they must postulate vast ages of time. Somehow what cannot possibly occur in a lifetime, must inevitably take place in vast

---

7. Douglas F. Kelly, ref. 1, p. 98.

millions of years. They imagine that life began with some 'simple' form that could easily have been haphazardly thrown together. Research in microbiology has shown us the staggering complexity of even the 'simplest' organisms.[8] A great number of complex parts must function together. There is irreducible complexity evidencing design, not chance. It was quite easy for Darwin and others to think of small organisms as being very simple, like a blob of jelly. That kind of imagination is no longer possible. Kelly also reminds us of the fossil record, which still lacks the plethora of missing links Darwin was so confident would be found. The best explanation is that there are no links at all, just perfectly designed kinds of life.

What about the meaning of the word 'day'? While some figurative uses exist, when day is modified by a number (such as 'day one' or the 'first day') it always means a calendar day. Figurative uses of day, usually involve the plural as in Genesis 30:14 (NKJ) 'Now Reuben went **in the days of wheat harvest** and found mandrakes in the field...' Here 'in the days of' means simply 'at the time of.' Even this figurative usage would be rendered absurd if we assumed that the 'days' of harvest were long ages of time. Also note that this passage does not have a number modifying 'day', neither does it have the phrase 'evening and morning' as Genesis one does. No one has found an example in the historical narratives of Scripture where such accompanying words as 'the third day' and 'evening and morning' could be anything but a calendar day.

Hugh Ross is quite knowledgeable about current theories of astrophysics, and very likely a sincere Christian. However, when he tries to get into the Hebrew text to prove a point, we should not readily accept his opinion. He has made many errors trying to use Hebrew to support his speculations. He points to Hosea 6:2 as a figurative usage of 'day' even with a number. Hosea 6:2 'After two days He will revive us; On the third day He will raise us up, That we may live in His sight.' Does this prove anything about the use of 'day' in Genesis one?

---

8. Michael J. Behe, *Darwin's Black Box* (Touchstone edition, 1998; New York: Touchstone: Simon & Schuster, 1996).

The answer is 'No' for several reasons. There is not a single case of a number with day in historical narratives that means anything other than a calendar day. Finding something in the prophetic literature, where figure and symbolism are common, does not count against the universal usage of the historical narratives. Hosea may have signs of poetic structure as these parallels indicate:

> AFTER TWO DAYS HE WILL REVIVE US

> ON THE THIRD DAY HE WILL RAISE US UP

The fundamental unsoundness of this procedure should be obvious to all. A reliable interpreter of Scripture does not proceed by first searching for a rare usage found in a different genre of literature, and then insisting that this very unusual usage be imposed upon the historical narrative of Genesis. Too many compromising Christians have proceeded with the assumption that one can just list every possible meaning listed in the lexicon, then choose whichever one suits their agenda without regard to the contextual usage in the text in question. And all this merely to fit in with still popular nineteenth century (as well as ancient) philosophical theories. Nothing arising from the *context* of Genesis 1 could suggest such sophistry.

If there were a figurative use of day to be found, it would most likely be in the poetic books or the prophetic books where imagery abounds. We will look further at Hosea 6:2: 'After two days He will revive us; On *the third day* He will raise us up, That we may live in His sight.' Although this is prophetic imagery instead of straight historical narrative, and although there is no mention of evening and morning, the verse is still claimed to determine for us the meaning of 'day' in Genesis 1. The 'two' days and the 'third day' appear to be used in a non-literal way to speak of the restoration of Israel from their captivity, something like the dry bones of Ezekiel 37. This literary device of a number followed by the next larger number is found throughout poetic and prophetic literature of Scripture and requires no novel spinning of the text.

> Job 5:19: He shall deliver you in **six** troubles, Yes, in **seven** no evil shall touch you.

Proverbs 6:16: These **six** *things* the LORD hates, Yes, **seven** *are* an abomination to Him:

Amos 1:3: Thus says the LORD: 'For **three** transgressions of Damascus, and for **four**, I will not turn away its *punishment*, Because they have threshed Gilead with implements of iron.'

However there may be another reason the quickness of deliverance is stated in this language. The New Testament picks up the phrase 'on the third day' and gives it a new significance. The restoration of Israel typifies or points to the resurrection of Jesus Christ from the dead. The New Testament twice refers to Christ's resurrection on the third day as 'according to Scripture.'

Luke 24:46: Then He said to them, 'Thus it is written, and thus it was necessary for the Christ to suffer and to rise from the dead the third day.'

1 Corinthians 15:4: and that He was buried, and that He rose again the third day according to the Scriptures.'

There are approximately fifteen references to the 'third day' resurrection of Christ in the New Testament. Two of them specifically refer to what is 'written' or 'the Scriptures.' It is hard to imagine any other verse in the Old Testament that uses this phrase in connection with being raised up. The next closest thing would be the book of Jonah, which gave rise to the phrase 'three days and three nights.' (See Matthew 12:40.) E.B. Pusey goes further than most when he says of Hosea 6:2, 'The Resurrection of Christ and our resurrection in Him and in His Resurrection could not be more plainly foretold.'[9]

Many who do not go so far as Pusey still see an application to the resurrection of Christ. Israel's experiences serve to point to Christ. For example, Matthew 2:15 applies the words 'out of Egypt

---

9. E. B. Pusey, 'Notes on Hosea 6', *Barnes' Notes on the Bible, Hosea–Jonah.* Vol. 10. (Rio, WI: Ages Software, 2000), p. 105.

I called My Son' to the Christ child returning to Palestine after Herod's death. This is also a quotation from Hosea (11:1): 'When Israel was a child, I loved him, and out of Egypt I called My son.' We can see that the original Old Testament text referred to Israel's exodus from Egypt. This is taken by Matthew to be true ultimately of Christ Himself. In the Old Testament we have literary imagery regarding Israel's Exodus and Israel's return from captivity. But the exact words were such that the apostles, under the inspiration of the Holy Spirit, could see a further application of these words to Christ's return to the Land or to His resurrection from the dead.

Nevertheless, finding an exceptional usage of 'day' in prophetic language convention, cannot determine the meaning of 'day' in the totally different context and different genre of literature of Genesis 1. Remember, even in figurative uses, 'day' cannot be equated with millions of years.

C. ATTEMPTS TO EVADE THE LITERAL MEANING OF 'DAY' IN GENESIS 1

The calendar day is emphatically presented in Genesis and reinforced by the Fourth Commandment. Exodus 20:11 'For *in* six days the LORD made the heavens and the earth, the sea, and all that *is* in them, and rested the seventh day. Therefore the LORD blessed the Sabbath day and hallowed it.' We work six days, and rest one day because the LORD did so in the Creation Week. But the attempts to evade this meaning continue because there is greater confidence in man's theories of evolution than in the authority of the Word of God.

Another suggested way of avoiding the obvious literal meaning is used by Hugh Ross and Meredith Kline. The phrase, 'So the evening and the morning were the [ordinal number] day' is not used in the description of the seventh day. This argument from silence can hardly bear the weight placed upon it. How can the paucity of information about the seventh day be made to overrule the specific information given about the other six days? Would not any normal person assume that the seventh day is the same kind of calendar day as the rest? Would not the Exodus 20:11 commandment tell us that the seventh day occurs every week? Do we work for six literal days, and then rest forever?

D. EXEGESIS OF GENESIS 2

The 'Framework Hypothesis' uses Genesis 2 to interpret Genesis 1 in a topical, rather than chronological manner. First they present a 'problem' in the chronological reading of Genesis 2, and then propose the Framework Hypothesis as the 'solution.' For example, Gen 2.19 could be understood to say that Adam was already created, *then* God created the 'beasts of the field' and brought them to Adam to be named. But, of course, Genesis 1 has told us that the animals were created *before* man, on days five and six.

According to Dr. Kline's interpretation of Gen. 2.5–7 there could not be any plant life until two things happened. First there had to be rain, and then there had to be man to cultivate the ground. From the viewpoint of one who accepts the biblical chronology of Genesis 1, this scheme imposes a chronological order where it does not exist (Gen. 2) in order to deny a chronological order where it does exist (Gen. 1).

The consistently biblical approach sees Gen. 1 as the detailed, day-by-day account of the work of creation in six days. Gen. 2 then gives a brief overview before focusing on the situation of man in the Garden. Take for example Gen. 2:19:

> Now the LORD God had formed out of the ground all the beasts of the field and all the birds of the air. He brought them to the man to see what he would name them; and whatever the man called each living creature, that was its name.

Even 'Framework' advocate Futato agrees that the NIV's '...the LORD God **had formed**...' is syntactically correct, although he prefers to reject it because Moses *could have* used a different construction to show the priority of the animal creation to that of man.[10]

---

10. Mark Futato, 'Because It Had Rained: A Study of Gen. 2:5–7 with Implications for Gen.2:4–25 and Gen. 1:1—2:3', *Westminster Theological Journal* 60 (1998). Cited by Joseph A.Pipa, Jr. & David W. Hall, *Did God Create in 6 Days?* p. 155. Note that Futato's 'Because It Had Rained' attempts to maintain the same basic position as Kline's 'Because It Had Not Rained' despite the seemingly opposing titles.

In the Mosaic books, there is a style of writing history that uses what we would call a 'flashback' technique. The *waw* (or *vav*) consecutive [a *vav* or 'and' prefixed to a verb in historical narrative] does have a primary function of indicating sequence, but can also function as a pluperfect (English past perfect) [the LORD God had *formed*...], a kind of flashback in the midst of a narrative. Another example of this style is Exodus 11:1: 'Now the LORD said to Moses...'. But what the LORD had said to Moses was *previously* given, not given to Moses *during* the interview with Pharaoh. This is another example of a pluperfect ('flashback') usage. This is once again reflected in the NIV's translation of Exodus 11:1:

> Now the LORD had said to Moses, 'I will bring one more plague on Pharaoh and on Egypt. After that, he will let you go from here, and when he does, he will drive you out completely.'

Still another example of the pluperfect usage, like Gen. 2:19, is when Moses went to Jethro his father-in-law to ask to go back to Egypt. As an explanatory flashback Exodus 4:19 says, as most accurately translated, 'Now the LORD **had** said to Moses in Midian, "Go back to Egypt"'. In the midst of an historical narrative such explanatory notes may be included in the telling of an event, even though the flashback event took place *before* the particular events currently being narrated. So in Gen. 2:19 we have no need of an elaborate and imaginative theory to account for this common writing technique.

Several other examples of this construction with a pluperfect usage are given by Gesenius including Gen. 28:7 (Jacob *had obeyed* his father...)[11]

Bruce Waltke concludes, 'Moreover, *wayyqtl* in the received text, the object of our investigation, must be understood to represent the pluperfect.'[12]

---

11. W. Gesenius, and E. Kautzsch, 'The Parts of Speech,' in *Gesenius' Hebrew Grammar*, ed. A.E Cowley (Second English Edition; Oxford: Clarendon Press, 1910), p. 328.

12. Bruce Walke, and M. O'Conner, 'Waw + Prefix Conjugation,' in *An Introduction to Biblical Hebrew Syntax* (Winona Lake, Indiana: Eisenbrauns, 1990), p. 552. *Wayyqtl* (or *weyyqtl*) is a kind of template for a third person singular past or past perfect verb; *wa*='and'; *yy*= subject of the verb (third person singular); and the letters, '*qtl*' represent the verb of the sentence.

Another passage that has nothing to do with the length of the days in Genesis 1 is Genesis 2:5–6:

> Before any plant of the field was in the earth and before any herb of the field had grown. For the LORD God had not caused it to rain on the earth, and *there was* no man to till the ground; but a mist went up from the earth and watered the whole face of the ground.

Kline paraphrases the highlighted phrase as 'It had not rained.' It is not clear why he prefers the impersonal language to the personal language of Scripture, 'The LORD God had not caused it to rain.' In any case, says Kline, this shows that since plants can't grow without rain, it must have rained before the plants appeared. This proves that ordinary providence was in operation during the creation week. God was working by normal natural processes, such as are consistent with long periods of time. As Kline says, 'The unargued presupposition of Genesis 2:5 is clearly that the divine providence was operating during the creation period through processes which any reader would recognize as normal in the natural world of his day.'[13] He further states, 'Embedded in Gen. 2:5 ff. is the principle that the *modus operandi* of the divine providence was the same during the creation period as that of ordinary providence at the present time.'[14]

This is truly strange; this is the eisegesis of desperation. Dr. Kline calls his presupposition an *unargued* presupposition of the text. Supposedly it is clear enough for *any reader* to see. The unanswerable *problem* of the unargued presupposition is that no reader saw any such thing in the text until the twentieth century. We saw from other statements that Dr. Kline also presupposes that there is much truth in evolutionary theory and its chronology. In the height of the evolutionary frenzy in academia, the Framework Hypothesis was devised to 'rescue' the Bible from contradicting the

---

13. Meredith Kline, 'Because It Had Not Rained,' *Westminster Theological Journal* **20** (1958), p. 150.

14. Ref 13., p. 151.

culturally accepted, although false, theory of evolution.[15] The Bible is not only separated from history by this arbitrary and subjective eisegesis, but it becomes an impossible task to discern the meaning of the text. Did God speak plainly, or give us a cryptic puzzle? Does the biblical text have an intrinsic meaning, or must every interpreter impose his own meaning on the text? Does the Bible have to do with real life history, or is it merely stories and poetry meant only to teach some *spiritual* or moral lesson? By this eisegesis, Christians are led to believe that the Bible offers no antithetical worldview, but must be harmonized with the standard of modern science. It is time for Christians to realize that God has provided real historical 'true truth' that answers many of our real-world questions.

By extracting Gen. 2:5 from its context, one gets the impression that the ground was dry as dust. But reading the very next verse, we see a different *'modus operandi'* at work. Verse six turns Kline's imaginative interpretation on its head. Instead of the same natural processes, we see a special providence of God in providing a 'mist' or 'springs' to water the earth. Calvin, along with almost every other commentator prior to the modern evolutionary revival, sees Gen. 2:5[16] in a quite straightforward way. His conclusion (emphases mine) is directly opposite to that of Dr. Kline:

> 'But although he has before related that the herbs were created on the third day, yet it is not without reason that here again mention is made of them, in order that we may know that they were then produced, preserved, and propagated, *in a manner different from that which we perceive at the present day.* For herbs and trees are produced from seed; or grafts are taken from another root or they grow by putting forth shoots: in all this the industry and the hand of man are engaged. But, at that time, the method was different: God clothed the earth, not in the

---

15. Arie Noordzij of Utrecht first suggested the 'Framework' hypothesis in 1924 in a Dutch article.

16. See also Michael Kruger, 'An Understanding of Genesis 2:5', *CENTJ* (now *Journal of Creation*) **11**(1):106–110, 1997.

same manner as now, (for there was no seed, no root, no plant, which might germinate,) but each suddenly sprung into existence at the command of God, and by the power of his word. They possessed durable vigor, so that they might stand by the force of their own nature, and not by that quickening influence which is now perceived, *not by the help of rain*, not by the irrigation or culture of man; *but by the vapor with which God watered the earth.* For he excludes these two things, the rain whence the earth derives moisture, that it may retain its native sap; and human culture, which is the assistant of nature. When he says, that God had 'not yet caused it to rain,' he at the same time intimates that it is God who opens and shuts the cataracts of heaven, and that rain and drought are in his hand.'[17]

Notice there is no problem of a contradiction between Genesis 1 and 2. The 'contradiction' is a modern invention for the purpose of introducing novel theories that *really are* contradictory to the biblical text.

The second chapter of Genesis not only refers back to the events chronologically narrated in Chapter 1, but the review also serves as background for the Fall of man narrated in Chapter 3. In order to understand the conditions surrounding the Fall into sin, we need the background information of Chapter 2. The focus of the second and third chapters will be man and the Garden. The Genesis accounts of Creation and the Fall describe one-time events, not ordinary natural processes.

Although it is clear that certain kinds of vegetation appeared on day three before the LORD God sent rain, there were at least two important changes after the appearance and subsequent fall of man. Before man, on day three, we do have grasses and fruit trees and some self seeding plants good for food. Cassuto has a helpful explanation of the situation in Genesis 2:5.

---

17. John Calvin, 'Chapter II,' in *Commentary Upon the Book of Genesis*, vol. 1 (Grand Rapids, Michigan: Baker Books, 2003), p. 110ff (emphasis mine).

The narrative begins with a description of the conditions existing prior to the creation of man. There was no *siach* (חיש) of the field yet, and the *'esebh* (בשע) of the field had not yet sprung up; the word *terem* means: 'not yet'... What is meant by the *siach of the field* and the *'esebh of the field* mentioned here? Modern commentators usually consider the terms to connote *the vegetable kingdom as a whole*; hence it follows that our section contradicts the preceding chapter, according to which vegetation came into being on the third day... All interpretations of this kind introduce something into the text that is not there, in order to create the inconsistency. ...If we wish to understand the significance of the *siach of the field* and the *'esebh of the field* in the context of our narrative, we must take a glance at the end of the story. It is stated there, in the words addressed by the Lord God to Adam after he had sinned: THORNS AND THISTLES *it shall bring forth to you; and you shall eat the 'esebh* [e.g. grain] *of the field* (iii 18). The words *'esebh of the field* are identical with the expression in our verse; whilst *thorns and thistles*, which are synonymous with the *siach of the field*, are a particularization of the general concept conveyed by the latter...These species did not exist, or were not found in the form known to us, until after Adam's transgression, and it was in consequence of his fall that they came into the world or received their present form. Man, who was no longer able to enjoy the fruits of the garden of Eden, was compelled *to till the ground* (iii 23—the same phrase as in our verse here) in order to *eat bread*; and the clause quoted above, *and you shall eat the 'esebh of the field* (iii 18), corresponds to the words immediately following: *In the sweat of your face* YOU SHALL EAT BREAD (iii 19). Thus the term *'esebh of the field* comprises wheat and barley and other kinds of grain from which *bread* is made; and it is obvious that fields of wheat and barley and the like did not exist in the world until man began *to till the ground*. In the areas, however, that were not tilled, the earth brought forth of its own accord, as a punishment to man, *thorns and thistles*—that *siach of the field* that we see growing to this day in the Land of Israel, *after the rains*...Here we must point out that the two reasons given in our verse [for the absence of thorns and grain] follow the same order as the two preceding clauses that they come to explain: no thorns of the field were yet in the earth, because the Lord God *had not caused it to rain* upon the earth, and the grain of the field had not yet sprung up, because *there was no man to till the ground...* Scripture stressed again and again that the world of vegetation, as it was formed on the third day, was composed of those trees and herbs that naturally reproduce themselves by seed alone. Those plants that needed something else, in addition to seed, were excluded: to this category belonged...all species of corn, which even though isolated specimens might have existed here and there from the very beginning, were not found in the form of grain until man began to till the ground...thorn *and thistles*, or *siach of the field*, whose seeds are unable to propagate and grow fresh plants until it rains. After man's fall and expulsion form the garden of Eden, when he was compelled to till the ground and the rains began to come down, there spread through the earth thorns and thistles and fields of wheat—the *siach of the field* and the *'esebh of the field.*[18]

An additional illustration of the use of *siach* is in Job.

Job 30:7 Among the bushes they brayed,

Under the nettles they nestled.

Here the *'siach'* (bushes) are in parallel with 'nettles.' This agrees with the interpretation Cassuto has given of Genesis 2. In summary: grasses and fruit trees existed on Day three, but thorns and thistles awaited the rains following the fall of man. The cultivated fields of grain awaited the arrival of man the cultivator. Before the first rainfall, mists or streams from the ground watered vegetation.

Gordon Wenham translates Gen. 2:5 in much the same way as Cassuto. Like almost every other (non-liberal) commentator he finds no contradiction between Genesis 1 and 2, even though his interpretation is not identical to Cassuto's.[19]

---

18. Umberto Cassuto, *A Commentary on the Book of Genesis: Part I From Adam to Noah* (Jerusalem: The Magnes Press, The Hebrew University, 1961), p. 90. Cited in Kelly, ref. 1, p. 124.

19. Gordon J. Wenham, 'The Garden of Eden (2:4–3:24),' in *Word Biblical Commentary, Genesis 1–15*, vol. 1 (Dallas, Texas: Word Books, 1987).

Also finding no contradiction are Calvin, Gill, Leupold, Sailhamer, Keil & Delitzsch, Morris, and many other commentators. Among non-liberal commentaries, Kline's on Genesis may be the only one which creates a contradiction in order to solve the imaginary problem with his namesake theory that helps him be at peace with evolutionary thought. This is also demonstrated in his evasion of the plain meaning of the genealogies, and his unwillingness to affirm the worldwide universal Flood. (He can't be sure of the date of the Flood because he has rejected the biblical chronology.) But we ought *not* be at peace with a worldview antithetical (on purpose) to Christianity.

The only argument drawn from Genesis 1 itself is an attempt to make the account to be poetry. Then it is not to be taken literally, but merely to teach us certain basic lessons. But Genesis 1, even if it may contain poetic elements, is not Hebrew poetry. To repeat what E.J. Young, the great Westminster Hebrew and Old Testament scholar said,

> 'Hebrew poetry had certain characteristics, and they are not found in the first chapter of Genesis. So the claim that Genesis one is poetry is no solution to the question. The man who says, 'I believe that Genesis purports to be a historical account, but I do not believe that account', is a far better interpreter of the Bible than the man who says, 'I believe that Genesis is profoundly true, but it is poetry.' That latter has nothing to commend it at all. I disagree with the first man, but he is a better exegete, he is a better interpreter, because he is facing up to the facts.'[20]

The allegation of poetic character in Genesis 1 comes from the fact that it is possible to draw some parallels between the Days One through Three and Days Four through Six. Christians have noted this fact for centuries without the slightest idea that the days were anything other than calendar days.

---

20. E.J. *Young, In the Beginning: Genesis Chapters 1 to 3 and the Authority of Scripture* (Edinburgh: Banner of Truth Trust, 1976), pp. 18–19. Cited by Grover Gunn, *Six Day Creation*, <d.dominodeveloper.net/gsmythe/home.nsf>.

We could chart the first six days like this:

1. Light	4. Sun, moon, stars
2. Sky and sea	5. Birds and fish
3. Land and initial vegetation	6. Land animals and man.

To call the first three 'realms' and the next three 'rulers' is quite a stretch of the imagination. The parallels are far from exact. For example, birds and fish do not 'rule' anything, they are under the dominion of man, who is in turn under the dominion of God. Further, birds do not *live* in the sky; they merely travel through the sky, as do many insects. Birds nest and feed on the ground, in trees, or on rocky heights. In other words, their nests and ordinary life functions must touch the ground. It would be appropriate for our interpretation of Scripture to 'touch the ground' by being rooted in real time-space history, instead of floating in hot air. In Genesis 1:22, God commands that birds 'multiply upon the *earth*' (emphasis added). So we already have birds paralleling features of Day Three [the land] as well as Day Two [the sky]. Our dream of a perfect poetic parallel is ruined.

If we try to make the first set of days 'days of forming' and the last three 'days of filling', there are at least three problems with making the scheme fit.

1. Genesis 1 is concerned with three problems, not two. The problems introduced in Genesis 1:2 are not just 'shapeless and empty' but also 'darkness.'

2. On the second half of the *third* day, the earth is *filled* with plants, but that breaks out of the imposed pattern of forming and filling.

3. Birds (Day Five) do not fill the firmament, or even live in it. They merely travel across the face of it. Birds multiply on the *land* (Day Three) but the pattern imagined insists that birds must parallel Day Two.[21]

---

21. James B. Jordan, 'Appendix B: Chiasm and Structure,' in *Creation in Six Days, A Defense of the Traditional Reading of Genesis One* (Moscow, Idaho: Canon Press, 1999), p. 218.

James Jordan does show how it is possible to discover several chiastic literary structures without rejecting the historical narrative of six calendar days. Even if it were much more poetic than it actually is, we could still ask with Berthoud,

> 'What difficulty would it be for [the Author of the Universe] to cause the most complex, refined literary form to coincide with the very way in which He Himself created all things in six days? Artistic form is in no sense opposed to an actual relation of facts, especially since the Author of the account is none less than the actual Creator of the facts which are described in that account…'[22]

One very objectionable feature of the Framework hypothesis is the assumption that literary style and literal historical truth are mutually exclusive. Yet if this extreme statement is rejected, as it should be rejected, what is left of the argument? One is left wondering whether any of the events described in Genesis 1 actually happened! Is the Bible again being 'rescued' from critics by being transported into the realm of the higher register? Is the 'higher register' anything like the Barthian *'Heilsgeschichte'* or 'salvation history', which is not real earthly history? How would Kline know there is such a thing as upper register time, or that it differs from earth time? Kline asserts what needs to be demonstrated:

> 'The six evening-mornings days then do not mark the passage of time in the lower register sphere. They are not identifiable in terms of solar days, but relate to the history of creation at the upper [invisible register] of the cosmos.'[23]

He gives no examples of such a usage of 'evening and morning.' This is probably because there are no such examples. It is totally out

---

22. Jean-Marc Berthoud, *Positions Creationnistes*, no. 12 (May 1990): 7f. Cited and translated by Kelly, ref. 1, p. 115.

23. Meredith G. Kline, 'Space and Time in the *Genesis Cosmogony,'* *Perspectives on Science and Christian Faith*, no. 48 (1966).

of character in biblical theology to think of heavenly days having evening and morning. This is especially true as the heavenly days are pictured as having 'no night there.' Revelation 22:5: 'There shall be no night there: They need no lamp nor light of the sun, for the Lord God gives them light. And they shall reign forever and ever.' As a bonus, the above verse also shows allegorizers how one can have light without the sun. That answers the rather weak objection that says we can't have twenty-four hour days without the sun, yet supposes we can have millions of years without the sun! If any insist that we identify that light of the first three days of creation, let us suggest the *Shekinah* glory of God Himself. We do not have to be certain about questions the Bible does not address. It is certainly illegitimate to use such silence to overturn what God has revealed, namely six calendar days. It really pays to take the Scripture more seriously, and the current evolutionary worldview less seriously.

Genesis 1 'clearly presents God as working over the course of a week of seven days, days that have regular evenings and mornings. Either this is just a poem, a literary figure, or else it is a description of what God actually did.'[24]

This non-historical approach to biblical theology creates far worse problems than it solves. Where will the 'demythologizing' stop? As James Jordan says of taking this non-historical approach:

> '...this kind of thing goes back long before the Reformation—the narratives of the Bible are usually taken as moral tales rather than as stages in God's development of the human race. Jacob's story is the story of a bad man who was punished by God until he became a good one. The story of David and Bathsheba shows us that God does not like adultery. So does the story of Samson and Delilah. Note that such moral messages would be valid whether the stories ever really happened or not. It is no accident that after centuries of this kind of reading of the

24. Grover Gunn, 'Six Day Creation,' March 26, 1998,<capo.org/cpc/sixdays.htm>, accessed April 24, 2007.

historical parts of the Bible, liberalism arose to claim that these stories never really did happen.[25]

The biblical theology is rooted in history, real space-time human history. It is of a different character than Aesop's Fables, which are designed simply to teach 'the moral of the story' with no intention of affirming their historical reality. The problem with views like the Framework hypothesis is opposing a theological interpretation to a literal one. For another example, does the literary structure of Philippians 2:5–11 mean that the humiliation and exultation of Christ did not take place literally? Of course not. Neither does any literary structure, real nor imagined, in Genesis 1 compel us to take the historical narrative as anything but a normal chronological account.

> 'The theological dimension of creation in six days lies precisely in its being a temporal sequence...God had no reason to make the world in six days, except as a pattern for His image, man, to follow.[26]

Gleason Archer echoes the almost puerile objection that on Day Six there was just too much to do. 'Who can imagine that all of these transactions could possibly have taken place in 120 [*sic*] minutes of the sixth day (or even within twenty-four hours, for that matter)?'[27] This may be the only instance of a figurativist having difficulty using his imagination. Usually figurativists demand that Adam name every species known to us. Often the number of species they give includes categories of insects and marine life, not included in the Genesis narrative. All Adam had to name were 'kinds' of mammals ('beasts of the field', including the domesticatable varieties—'cattle') and birds

25. James B. Jordan, 'Gnosticism vs. History,' in *Creation in Six Days, A Defense of the Traditional Reading of Genesis One* (Moscow, Idaho: Canon Press, 1999), p. 79.

26. James B. Jordan, *Through New Eyes: Developing a Biblical View of the World* (Brentwood, Tennessee: Wolgemuth & Hyatt, 1988), 11. As cited by Kelly, ref. 1, p. 116.

27. Gleason L. Archer Jr., 'Genesis (I),' in *A Survey of Old Testament Introduction* (Chicago: Moody Press, 1964), p. 176. Archer probably meant '720 minutes.'

('fowl of the air') the Lord brought to him. Adam did not have to go hunting for them. For those still having trouble trying to 'imagine' how all this could be done, Jordan has provided a hypothetical schedule which allows Adam eight hours to name the various kinds of beasts of the field, with a half-hour for lunch and time to spare.[28] Grigg shows how, if pressured, an hour or so would have sufficed for Adam to name all the required creatures.[29]

Finally, consider the arbitrary naming of the days as 'anthropomorphic' days. Of this E. J. Young writes:

> 'What then, shall we say about the representation of the first chapter of Genesis that God created the heaven and earth in six days? Is this anthropomorphic language? We would answer this question in the negative, for the word anthropomorphic, if it is a legitimate word at all, can be applied to God alone and cannot properly be used of the six days…Hence, we do not believe that it is accurate to speak of the six days as an anthropomorphic mode of expression.[30]

Marvin Lubenow is one of many creation scientists who give expert scientific evidence against evolution. But here it is our purpose to show that he has more than scientific expertise on human fossils; he has a foundational biblical worldview. Speaking of the human fossil charts he has compiled he says,

> 'Although the dates on these charts speak in terms of millions of years, I do not accept those dates. I march to the tune of a different drummer based upon the data set forth in the early chapters of Genesis.'[31]

---

28. James B. Jordan, *Creation in Six Days, A Defense of the Traditional Reading of Genesis One*, p. 47.

29. See Russell Grigg's 'Naming the animals: all in a day's work for Adam', *Creation* **18**(4):46–49, September–November 1996; <creation.com/animalnames>; and Andrew Kulikovsky, How could Adam have named all the animals in a single day? *Creation* **27**(3):27, 2005 <creation.com /naming_animal>.

30. E.J. Young, *In the Beginning: Genesis Chapters 1 to 3 and the Authority of Scripture* (Edinburgh: Banner of Truth Trust, 1976), pp. 57–58. Cited by Pipa, p. 164.

31. Marvin L. Lubenow, 'Preface,' in *Bones of Contention, A Creationist Assessment of Human Fossils* (Grand Rapids, Michigan: Baker Books, 1992), p. 7ff.

And of the radiometric dating methods as applied to the fossil KNM-ER 1470, he says,

> 'This case study clearly reveals that the radiometric dating methods are not independent confirmations of evolution and an old earth, nor are the various dating methods independent of each other. These dating methods are, instead, "faithful and obedient servants" of evolution.'[32]

It is the recognition of the basic foundational presuppositional issues that must be an apologetical priority in order for Christians to accept the straightforward biblical account and resist all attempts at compromise with the anti-Christian worldview. No one has, ever has had, or ever will have more accurate scientific knowledge than the Creator of all things. No one is better able to communicate those realities to mankind than the Lord God who created man in His own image. A scientific theory does well to last a few decades; the Word of our God endures forever.

E. THE *TOLEDOTH* OF GENESIS

While undue emphasis has been put upon the word 'day' in Gen. 2:4, evolutionized thinking has ignored the significance of '*toledoth.*' The word '*toledoth*' (often translated 'generations') is a key organizing principle of the entire book of Genesis. The usual divisions are introduced by 'these are the *toledoth* of' ten times in Genesis.

Standard reference works such as TDOT[33] help us understand what the '*toledoth*' are, but they are often so obsessed with the documentary hypothesis that they miss the profound implications. One of the best brief summaries of the '*toledoth*' is found in a NET Bible note on Genesis 2:4.

The Hebrew phrase אלה תודלות (*'elle tol^edot*) is traditionally translated as 'these are the generations of' because the noun was

---

32. Ref.31. p. 9.

33. Schreiner, 's.v. toledoth,' in *Theological Dictionary of the Old Testament*, ed. G. Johannes Botterweck & Helmer Ringgren, trans. David Green, vol. 15 (Grand Rapids, Michigan: William B. Eerdmans Publishing Company, 2006), p. 582ff.

derived from the verb 'beget.' Its usage, however, shows that it introduces more than genealogies; it begins a narrative that traces what became of the entity or individual mentioned in the heading. In fact, a good paraphrase of this heading would be: 'This is what became of the heavens and the earth,' for what follows is not another account of creation but a tracing of events from creation through the fall and judgment

The expression *this is the account of* is an important title used throughout the Book of Genesis, serving as the organizing principle of the work. It is always a heading, introducing the subject matter that is to come. From the starting point of the title, the narrative traces the genealogy or the records or the particulars involved. Although some would make the heading in 2:4 a summary of creation (1:1–2:3), that goes against the usage in the book. As a heading it introduces the theme of the next section, the particulars about this creation that God made. Genesis 2 is not a simple parallel account of creation; rather, beginning with the account of the creation of man and woman, the narrative tells what became of that creation. As a beginning, the construction of 2:4–7 forms a fine parallel to the construction of 1:1–3. The subject matter of each toledoth (*tolᵉdot*, 'this is the account of') section of the book traces a decline or deterioration through to the next beginning point, and each is thereby a microcosm of the book which begins with divine blessing in the garden, and ends with a coffin in Egypt. So, what became of the creation?

> Gen 2:4–4:26 will explain that sin entered the world and all but destroyed God's perfect creation.[34]

> Genesis 5:1 provides a remarkable clue to the nature of the *toledoth*.

> 'This is the <u>record</u> of the family line of Adam.' (NET Bible)

---

34. 'Genesis 2,' in *Net Bible*, ed. W. Hall Harris III, first ed. (n.p.: Biblical Studies Press, L.L.C., 2005), pp. 6–7. Also available <www.Bible.org>.

The word translated 'record' is ספר (*sepher*) meaning 'book' or 'written record.' The word translated 'family line' is *toledoth*. The records, which Moses could use in composing the Pentateuch, were *written* records, not the long generations of oral tradition imagined by our evolutionized culture. Adam himself may have written Genesis 2–4, since he was created in the Image of God and quite conversant in language skills. Noah, Abraham, and other patriarchs likely left written records as well.

F. THINKING BIBLICALLY

Thinking biblically, the Genesis record is not some 'cleaned up' pagan mythology; it is the inspired inerrant original historical account. The pagan myths represent a distorted memory of the actual events. Pagans suppressed the knowledge of the true and living God, attributing all events to the gods they invented. Also, because the pagans relied so much on oral tradition and because of the confusion of languages at Babel, their accounts became both confused and deliberately distorted. For example, many nations have preserved an account of the Flood, but only the Bible preserved the account with perfect accuracy. This is based, not on the Bible's borrowing from and cleaning up the pagan myths, but the pagan's distorted memory of events.

On a related topic we may consider the genealogies of Genesis 5 and 11. In our modern American culture where few people can name their great-grandparents, it seems incredible to us that the genealogies of Genesis are important. They are regarded as boring and irrelevant, thus easily dismissed. But the long lives of Adam and Noah are particularly important in the preserving of God's revelation. The genealogical chart on page 227 shows that the gap between Adam and Abraham can be spanned in as few as three individuals.

The genealogies assume an importance for at least two reasons: The promise of the Seed in Gen. 3:15, and, later, the promise of the Land by which each tribe received their family inheritance to be preserved through the generations. So we are amazed at how different a history the Bible presents, in sharp contrast to the humanistic education most Americans have received.

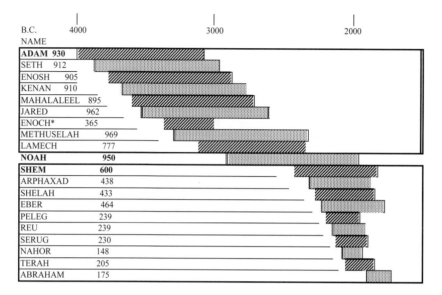

GENEALOGIES OF GENESIS 5 & 11

Adam-Lamech: All alive during the lifespan of Adam

Shem-Abraham: All alive during the lifespan of Shem

Charts compiled from Ussher's Annals of the World and F.N. Jones The Chronology of the Old Testament

Enoch taken up (translated) without dying

Long lives and few generations eliminate the evolutionary idea of many thousands of years of oral tradition story telling before being written down

Instead of the grunting savage, we see Adam as image bearer of God, who can name the animals, communicate in language, and (quite possibly) make written records.

To reject the biblical chronology leaves us with nothing but the corrupted stories of paganism. Why any Christian would want to make this Esau-like trade is a mystery indeed. Giving up our birthright (a solidly founded Christian worldview) for a mess of pottage (intellectual respectability from the humanists) is a foolish trade. Letting the culture 'fill in the blanks' in our worldview, instead of studying to show ourselves workmen approved of God, is a disastrous trade-off.

CHAPTER 11

THE CONSEQUENCES OF THE EVOLUTIONARY WORLDVIEW

A significant factor in the weak response of the Church to evolutionary thought was the lack of thinking in terms of worldview. A worldview may be defined as 'A comprehensive and integrated understanding of reality in all of its aspects.'[1] The nineteenth century Christian response was faulty in two respects. First, they did not see the Christian faith as a worldview through which all things were to be understood. Second, they failed to see evolutionary thought as a worldview, thinking it only a theory about relatively unimportant issues.

Evolutionists from ancient times to the present are very much aware that their evolutionary thought is a comprehensive worldview. This has been true at least from the time of Epicurus and Lucretius who wanted to rid themselves of troubling thoughts like having to give an account after death to a personal yet infinite God. Their solution was to deny the existence of the soul, the afterlife, and the kind of God revealed in Scripture. A god or gods of serene indifference were, of course, no threat to them. Evolution has long been, from its beginning, an attempt to substitute a more man-pleasing explanation for life than that offered by biblical testimony. Evolutionists serve as living illustrations of the truth of the scripture which says, Romans 1:28 'And even as they did not like to retain God in *their*

---

1. John K. Reed, *Natural History in The Christian Worldview* (St. Joseph, MO: Creation Research Society Books, 2001), p. 102.

knowledge, God gave them over to a debased mind, to do those things which are not fitting;' This is the truth about evolutionists whether they know it or not, whether they admit it or not. The Bible says they did not **approve of** having God in their knowledge, so God gave them over to an **unapproved** mind.

The worldview nature of evolutionary thought should not be a surprise to Christians; it was designed that way. Sir Julian Huxley (1887–1975) offered a typical expression of evolutionary thought when he wrote:

'The concept of evolution was soon extended into other than biological fields. Inorganic subjects such as the life-history of stars and the formation of the chemical elements on the one hand, and on the other hand subjects like linguistics, social anthropology, and comparative law and religion, began to be studied from an evolutionary angle, until today we are enabled to see evolution as a universal and all-pervading process.'[2]

The only ones who refused to see the worldview religious nature of evolutionists were those evangelical Christians scrambling to make the Bible fit the latest theories of secular scientists. Even though he was a Roman Catholic priest, Pièrre Teilhard de Chardin[3] was an avid evolutionist and enthusiastic supporter of the 'Piltdown Man' discovery, which turned out to be a hoax. He spoke of the comprehensive nature of evolution:

'[Evolution] is a general postulate to which all theories, all hypotheses, all systems must henceforth bow and which illuminates all facts, a trajectory which all lines of thought must follow.'[4]

---

2. Julian Huxley, 'Evolution and Genetics,' in *What Is Science* (New York: Simon and Schuster, 1955), p. 272.

3. David Lane, *The Phenomenon of Teilhard: Prophet for a New Age*, Mercer University Press, Macon, Georgia, 1996.

4. Francisco Ayala, 'Nothing in Biology Makes Sense Except in the Light of Evolution: Theodosius Dobzhansky, 1900–1975,' *Journal of Heredity* 68, no. 3:3. Cited by *Morris, Long War Against God*, p. 22.

Instead of standing boldly and faithfully on the Word of the living God, evangelicals talked to themselves, trying to convince themselves that some absurd interpretation of the Bible could bring it into line with the current cultural consensus. The predictable result was a constant compromising on the part of the evangelicals and an increasing contempt for a Bible that could be made to say whatever anyone wanted it to say.

Aldous Huxley, Julian's brother, was not shy about telling why he and his comrades so readily accepted evolution: it promised them liberation from the restraints of biblical (especially sexual) morality. The modern motives for accepting evolution have not changed much since ancient evolutionary philosophy sought to escape the thought of God and the afterlife. Faith is an essential part of the acceptance of evolution. The uncertainty of the evidence is made up for by the confident confession of faith as in Richard Goldschmidt,

> 'Evolution of the animal and plant world is considered by all those entitled to judgment to be a fact for which no further proof is needed. But in spite of nearly a century of work and discussion there is still not unanimity in regard to the details of the means of evolution.'[5]

A confident confession of faith is asserted as a fact. Anyone who disagrees is not entitled to make a judgment on the question. Evolution is not subject to questioning, according to its true believers. Naturalistic presuppositions are the ultimate standard from which there is no appeal. Evolutionists keep their faith in naturalism in a way parallel to the Christian's appeal to God's revelation as the highest and ultimate standard. No one can 'verify' his ultimate standard by some *other* criterion, or else that other criterion would be his ultimate standard. The faith statement of Goldschmidt saves him the need to produce evidence supporting his theory. Since evolution is a foundational presupposition of all his thinking, every piece of data

---

5. Richard Goldschmidt, 'Evolution as Viewed by One Geneticist,' *American Scientist* 40 (January 1952): 84. Cited by Morris, *The Long War Against God*, p. 34.

he finds serves as 'evidence' for evolution. By contrast, everything a Christian sees is evidence of the Creator and the truth of Scripture. Neither worldview is a result of observational experimental science. The evolutionary worldview is antithetical to, not compatible with, the Christian biblical worldview. The evolutionary creed was specifically designed to be antithetical and no evolutionist is open to synthesis.

The atheistic nature of the evolutionary philosophy would become more evident over time as they became more consistent with their foundational presuppositions of naturalism. Only naïve compromising Christians were concerned with salvaging merely the moral core of Christianity. Only the evangelicals were interested in accommodation, and one accommodation always led to several more in due time. Sooner or later we must either be consistently biblical or continue down the slippery slope of compromise. The hastily assembled compromises never quite fit the biblical record and never quite satisfy the demands of the naturalist's philosophy. Most modern Christians have been educated in government schools—not trained in critical thinking, but indoctrinated toward cultural conformity. Most professors in nominally Christian colleges have degrees from evolution-approved institutions. It never enters their minds to develop a consistently biblical worldview when it is so effortless to be a cultural conformist. Evolutionists like Edmund O. Wilson are no longer hindered by the nineteenth century reticence to openly criticize Christianity. He stated, 'Bitter experience has taught us that fundamental religion ... in its aggressive form is one of the unmitigated evils of the world.'[6]

Wilson, like most evolutionists, would consider most evangelical and Reformed Christians as 'fundamentalists', not merely those who identify themselves that way. It is interesting to note that Wilson sagely recommends liberal theology as a transition from Christianity to atheism. He recognized what liberals themselves often deny: Christianity and liberalism are two different religions. That was the

---

6. Edmund Wilson, 'Toward a Humanistic Biology,' *The Humanist* 42:56, September/October 1982. Cited by Morris, *The Long War Against God*, p. 34.

thesis of J. Gresham Machen's book *Christianity and Liberalism* (1923). The evolutionists see it clearly; the compromising Christians pretend it is not so.

Christianity is rightly applied to every area of life and thought. Its antithesis, evolution, was likewise applied to every aspect of thought. Evolution requires that the early chapters of Genesis not be historical, and liberal theology, along with compromising evangelicalism, has agreed. Any subject from literature and art to economics and morality must be viewed through the evolutionary lens. Literature courses are obviously selective in what is presented and the selection is clearly influenced by the worldview of the selectors. History likewise is selective and interpretive, determined by the worldview preferences of the author. Theistic evolution did great harm to the general confidence in the Bible as the Bible was progressively removed from the 'real' world and relegated to the upper story 'spiritual' realm. Professing Christians determined to hold on to a theistic evolution found themselves having to abandon (through yet another 'reinterpretation') more and more of Scripture.

A most distressing aspect of the Christian compromise is to see some kind of 'theistic evolution' being taught at ostensibly Christian colleges and seminaries. The fact that theistic evolution looks to a non-existent 'god' is usually overlooked. The only God who exists has spoken in Scripture so that we need not be ignorant of the truth. The antithesis is plain; evolution demands that all things must be accounted for by random natural processes. Biblical Christianity demands that all things be accounted for according to the word of God the Creator. The fact that the biblical revelation is of one piece means that in order to hang on to even a 'theistic' evolution, with its unknown deity, more and more biblical revelation must be 'figuratized' away. Passages clearly understood by universal Christendom for centuries are now said to need the expertise of evolutionized experts. Once these experts have worked the Bible over, the once clearly antithetical passage will come out in agreement with whatever the cultural consensus calls for. By this means the Church loses the conviction that the omniscient Creator has clearly revealed vital knowledge of how He created. No human being is even close to omniscience. No human being has the right to reject currently unpopular portions of Scripture, however loudly we might hear the antithesis called 'science.' There is a vast difference between the idolatry of a vague 'theism' and a trust in the sovereign and omniscient Creator revealed in Scripture. Probably the best excuse we can offer for the compromising Christians is that they could not yet see the horrible consequences evolution would bring.

A. LIFE ISSUES: ABORTION, EUTHANASIA AND EUGENICS

In the biblical worldview man has special value as uniquely created in the image of God. The image of God has been well defined:

> 'After God had made all other creatures, He created man, male and female, with reasonable and immortal souls, endued with knowledge, righteousness, and true holiness, after His own image, having the law of God written in their hearts, and power to fulfill it; and yet under a possibility of transgressing, being left to the liberty of their own will, which was subject unto change.'[7]

As should be expected, evolution's denial of divine creation led to a devaluation of human life. Evolution postulated a continuum of life from the one-celled animal to the human being. Humans were lowered to the level of animals. The well-known and influential evolutionist Ernst Haeckel wrote to his Christian father about how Darwinism had changed his thinking about the value of life.

> 'I share your view of life, dear father, only I value human life and humans themselves much less than you...The individual with his personal existence appears to me only a temporary member in this large chain, as a rapidly vanishing vapor...Personal individual existence appears to me so horribly miserable, petty, and worthless, that I see it as intended for nothing but destruction.'[8]

---

7. Chapter 4: 'Of Creation,' in *The Westminster Confession of Faith* (Glasgow, Scotland: Free Presbyterian Publications, 1994), p. 32 (4.2).

8. Heinrich Schmidt, *Ernst Haeckel. Leben Und Werke* (Berlin: Gemeinschaft, Deutsche Buch, 1926), pp. 203–204. Cited by Weikart, p. 76. Weikart's translation.

Before the mid-nineteenth century it would have been hard to find anyone who did not uphold the sanctity of human life. But Darwinism paved the way for the acceptance of all sorts of once forbidden and unthinkable practices. Without the development of evolutionary thinking we would not have a country where killing an unborn eagle is punished with a $5,000 fine, while the killing of an unborn human baby may be rewarded with a $5,000 provider's fee. This lower estimate of the value of life was not confined to Germany on its way to Hitler. The common connection from one country to the next is not Hitler, but the evolutionary worldview. The United States' own Margaret Sanger, celebrated late founder of Planned Parenthood expressed her opinion in a way that would have made Haeckel proud: 'The most merciful thing a large family can do for one of its infant members is to kill it.'[9] Obviously the passing of Hitler did not rid the world of this cheapening of life. Even Beverly Harrison, professor of Christian Ethics at Union Theological Seminary, has not drawn her 'ethics' from Scripture but from an evolutionary worldview. She said,

> '*Infanticide is not a great wrong.* I do not want to be construed as condemning women who, under certain circumstances, quietly put their infants to death.' (emphasis in the original).[10]

A culmination of the evolutionization of American culture has been the election of the first pro-infanticide president, Barack Obama, who naturally is an ardent evolutionist and supporter of abortion.[11] His support by many ostensibly evangelical churchians shows the depth of penetration of evolutionary ethics in once-biblical churches.

---

9. Margaret Sanger, *Women and The New Race* (New York: Brentano's, 1920), p. 63.

10. Francis J. Beckwith, *Politically Correct Death: Answering The Arguments for Abortion Rights* (Grand Rapids, MI: Baker Books, 1993), p. 174. Beckwith quotes from *Policy Review* (Spring 1985) p. 15.

11. See for example Lita Cosner, 'Bioethicists' and Obama agree: infanticide should be legal, <creation.com/obama>, 2 July 2008.

Psalm 139 illustrates the sharply contrasting biblical worldview:

Psalm 139:13–16 For you formed my inward parts; you knitted me together in my mother's womb. I praise you, for I am fearfully and wonderfully made. Wonderful are your works; my soul knows it very well. My frame was not hidden from you, when I was being made in secret, intricately woven in the depths of the earth. Your eyes saw my unformed substance; in your book were written, every one of them, the days that were formed for me, when as yet there were none of them. (ESV)

What part of 'Killing innocent human beings' is hard to understand? Once again a false starting point (the evolutionary faith) leads to a false and deadly conclusion. Even though many people can believe in evolution without going to this extreme, the fact remains that the evolutionary faith provides a scientific veneer to justify the cheapening of human life. In addition, the evolutionary worldview offers no solid basis from which to criticize those like Hitler who believed they were merely being more consistent in their application of evolution. Evolutionists are left in the awkward position of wanting to say there are no absolutes, yet affecting horror when someone takes them seriously.

In addition to abortion and infanticide, evolution helped prepare the way for euthanasia. The term literally means 'good death' and may often be presented as 'mercy killing' by its partisans. In biblical thought death is the 'last enemy' and is slated for destruction in the total triumph of the Lord Jesus Christ. In evolutionary thought death is good because it leaves the human race younger and/or stronger as the old and unfit die off.

Darwin's cousin Francis Galton developed a theory that might be considered a 'cousin' to the theory of evolution—eugenics. Galton felt himself liberated from the church upon reading *Origin*. This was another case, not of faith seeking understanding, but of unbelief seeking an excuse to continue. Galton had made several significant contributions to the knowledge of South African geography, meteorology, and the use of fingerprints for unique identification.

But he saw in Darwin's book that, 'Its effect was to demolish a multitude of dogmatic barriers by a single stroke and to arouse a spirit of rebellion against all ancient authorities whose positive and unauthenticated statements were contradicted by modern science.'[12] Typically Galton attacks Christianity, without calling it by name, as dogmatic, ancient, and unauthenticated. Darwin's theory is called modern science, which certainly sounds preferable. It is ironic how frequently the words of the evolutionists apply so well to their own thinking. The phrase 'positive and unauthenticated' describes the evolutionary faith precisely. Even the words 'ancient' and 'dogmatic' are fitting for this revival of ancient Greek philosophy so dogmatically asserted. Darwin's book helped Galton to justify his rebellion against the God of the Bible, and to erect 'dogmatic barriers' of his own against Christianity. For the evolutionary faithful the catchphrase 'modern science' serves as a dogmatic barrier that hinders them from accepting the gospel of Christ.

Galton is also known for unleashing the horror of eugenics. The evil of evolution was unmasked in the late nineteenth and early twentieth centuries when fallen man got the idea of directing and hastening evolutionary progress by force of civil government. Galton believed that superior, beautiful people, like himself, should be encouraged to have society's children. Non-superior, non-beautiful people should be forbidden to have children as it dilutes the quality of the human stock. In his own words,

> 'Consequently, as it is easy…to obtain by careful selection a permanent breed of dogs or horses gifted with peculiar powers of running, or of doing anything else, so it would be quite practicable to produce a highly gifted race of men by judicious marriages during several consecutive generations.'[13]

---

12. Francis Galton, 'Chapter XX. Heredity,' in *Memories of My Life* [book on-line] (n.p., n.d., accessed 4 May 2007 at <www/galton.org/books/memories/chapter-XX.html>).

13. Francis Galton, 'Introductory Chapter,' in *Hereditary Genius: An Inquiry Into Its Laws and Consequences* [book on-line], 2d ed. (London: Macmillan & Co., 1892, p. 31. Accessed 18 October 2007 at <www/galton.renoster.com/books/hereditary-genius/text/pdf/galton-1869-genius-v3.pdf>).

Evolutionist Niles Eldredge acknowledges that social Darwinism and eugenics lent scientific support for the Nazi program of the Holocaust. But he claims that these are illegitimate offspring of Darwin.[14] Again we should ask by what standard can Eldredge know that the Nazi Holocaust was an 'illegitimate' offspring of Darwin? To call it illegitimate sounds like a value judgment, which the evolutionary worldview forbids us to make.

Social Darwinists and advocates of eugenics supposed that evolution had produced 'good' results slowly, blindly, and sometimes cruelly. If only superior men like themselves could direct the process of evolution, progress would be rapid, intelligently directed and for the good of humanity.

Margaret Sanger took up the cause of eugenics by establishing Planned Parenthood. This was represented as a birth control plan for the betterment of society. In order to help lower the number of those she considered inferior stock, she established abortion clinics, particularly in black neighborhoods.

B. SOCIAL DARWINISM

The idea that evolutionary science demanded new social policies gave rise to programs of state-directed Darwinism. Darwinism is not merely a false, anti-biblical theory of biological origins; it is also a false worldview that distorts everything in sight. The most devastating effects of the evolutionary worldview were unleashed as men began applying that worldview to the social sciences—economics and politics. We will illustrate the effects of Social Darwinism in the history of our own United States. In an industrial age of the late nineteenth century there were incredible new opportunities to make great wealth. The oil companies, the railroads, and the steel mills all had their wealthy industrial barons, many of whom had worked their way up through the ranks. Man's natural depravity being what it is, materialism became a widespread working philosophy. The theory of evolution seemed to fit right in because conditions were getting

---

14. Tom DeRosa, 'Darwin's Disciples,' in *Evolution's Fatal Fruit: How Darwin's Tree of Life Brought Death to Millions* (Fort Lauderdale, FL: Coral Ridge Ministries, 2006), p. 140.

better for many people. Progress was inevitable. The evolutionary worldview also spoke of the survival of the fittest, which seemed to justify exploitation of workers, monopolies, and unfair or even dishonest business practices. The goal was to survive and that justified almost any means.

Social engineers made the case for a new social order, a new economic policy, even a new theology to ensure that society would keep on making evolutionary progress. The Northern defeat of the South in the 1860s was taken as a sign that the South's political, economic, and theological conservatism must give place to the more 'progressive' ideas of the North. The evolutionary worldview must be applied to every area of life, for it was the way of progress. Even the Bible must not be allowed to remain static; as a 'living document' it could be enlisted in the inevitable wave of progress. The old established order must be overthrown in every field of endeavor.

C. EVOLUTION'S NEW THEOLOGY

Natural law was no longer understood as God's immutable law revealed in creation, but instead as a non-supernatural understanding of 'law' as obtained from nature. This understanding needed to keep changing and evolving after the Hegelian dialectic model. The natural result of this was a new challenge to the old idea that thinking should result in a synthesis or settled conclusion. Often something of value could be salvaged from the old, but it must accommodate the new challenge. Many churchmen adopted this same procedure in their response to evolution's challenges to the Bible. A downward spiral began as one accommodation demanded another. The salvageable core of Christianity became smaller and smaller, disappearing altogether in theological liberalism.

Of course, evolution is an ancient philosophy whose basic premises were decided before anything remotely 'scientific' was available for support. The early church had largely defeated the Epicurean evolutionary worldview; the nineteenth century brought a kind of evolutionary revival with a new pseudo-scientific veneer. Not surprisingly, the new 'science' happened to tell the same story as the ancient philosophy. It was not surprising because both were designed to combat biblical theism. Consider some specific ways in which the evolutionary worldview was a substitute religion. It is antithetical to biblical Christianity at every point.

1. A PRIMER ON EVOLUTIONARY THEOLOGY

GOD. If the evolutionist acknowledges any god at all, it must be like the gods tolerated by Epicurus. Their deity must be like the deist god, living in serene indifference to the potentially troubling affairs of men. A god who is permitted to exist must be a god of nature only. A god who got things started in the very distant past, and need not interfere with the working process. This was not the God who specifically reveals himself in words and propositions; this was a god fashioned as each man's intellect gathered data from nature. If fallen man comes to an atheistic conclusion or an idolatrous one, it makes little difference for the two can dwell comfortably together. The only God the evolutionists cannot tolerate is the Creator and only God that exists.

CREATION: The evolutionary worldview sought to make the Creator God both unnecessary and unwanted. Their goal was to eliminate even the need for a celestial watchmaker. Nature is not good and kind like the deists said it was supposed to be, so Christianity must be false.

PROVIDENCE. The sovereign God governs all things and all creatures for his own purpose and glory. But evolution excludes everything except a naturalistic random process, stumbling its way to an unknown god. God's sovereign control is distasteful and threatening to the evolutionary worldview and must be ignored, denied and ridiculed out of our thinking. God's providence must be replaced by man-directed (state-directed) evolutionary progress.

FALL OF MAN. The fall of man is denied by the evolutionary worldview. Some people act unacceptably because they are less evolved, or because of their ignorance. The calamities and cruelties of nature are just the way nature always has been—an all-out struggle for survival. The evolutionary worldview denies the fall of man and the resultant curse on creation. When nineteenth century churchmen spoke only of the beauty and order of creation, critics could easily counter with what they considered waste and cruelty in nature. Deistically inclined churchmen were not likely to mention the fall of man and the curse on creation. This sentimental sub-Christian religion was easily defeated on this point. Here too the biblical witness opposes evolution.

THE DEPRAVITY OF MAN. The evolutionary faith would also deny the depravity of fallen human nature. Man needs no revelation, only his senses and his reason, to discover truth. So far from being depraved, man is seen as the pinnacle of evolutionary progress. Early in the twentieth century, it was common for evolutionists to think of their own kind ('race') of human being as far superior to every other kind.

SALVATION. The evolutionary faith does not believe in salvation by grace through faith in Jesus Christ. If there is anything to be saved from, it is only those who hinder evolutionary progress. We have hope in this life only. That hope is that the state can use its force and intelligent planning to speed the evolutionary process. To achieve this end almost any means are justified.

HEAVEN AND HELL. The biblical doctrine of heaven is rejected as a mere distraction from the need to address present problems of poverty, hunger and the environment. The biblical doctrine of hell is treated in typical Epicurean style. Just the mention of the doctrine of hell is enough for the evolutionist to conclude that Christianity must be wrong. Darwin was not the first or the last to specifically mention the doctrine of hell as one major reason for rejecting Christianity. After all, he and his whole family would be doomed if Christian doctrine is truth. Therefore it just cannot be true.

2. EVOLUTION: ANTITHETICAL TO BIBLICAL CHRISTIANITY

It was not enough for evolutionists to criticize the doctrine of creation. *Every* biblical doctrine opposed their philosophy of life. Only those in the church who were naïve and held a truncated 'spiritual things only' view of Christianity would be deceived. The evolutionary faith offered a philosophy of life by which to understand all things. It could not be defeated by an already compromised view that failed to apply biblical truth to every area of life and thought. Churchmen professed to salvage Christianity by removing it from relevance to time and space history and relating it only to other-worldly matters and moral guidelines. The salvaged religion, however, was no longer biblical Christianity.

To illustrate this problem, take the example of two popular nineteenth-century English preachers. Joseph Parker and Charles Spurgeon both attracted large audiences and had their sermons published. We could not expect a consistent worldview from Parker as he held to a minimalist creed, insisting on nothing more than the broad outlines of the Apostles' Creed. Parker expressed his view of Spurgeon in a public letter of 1890. He detested Spurgeon's reformed doctrines, but could appreciate the love shown in founding an orphanage.[15] Calvinistic Christianity seems to be particularly hated by evolutionists. Calvin affirmed that Scripture teaches a supernatural creation by the spoken word of God in a period of one week, the sovereignty of God in providence and in saving grace, the depravity of man as a fallen sinner, man's need of revelation and redemption, the exclusivity of the claims of Christ, the doctrine of eternal punishment, moral absolutes, and the application of biblical truth to every area of life. All these stood in the way of evolution. Liberalism willingly gave up almost all the biblical truths; others gave up only the most offensive doctrines. Liberals surrendered completely to evolution; lesser theological compromises by evangelicals prepared their proponents to compromise with evolution. These compromises would not lead evolutionists to the church, but would lead the church toward evolution.

But even Spurgeon, being much more biblical in his worldview, never drew out the implications of the Christian worldview in the matter of evolution. Like Charles Hodge he would openly denounce atheistic evolution, but did not trouble himself about the age of the earth and other matters that he had decided were peripheral. Strange how God considered it important enough to include in

---

15. Iain Murray, 'Free Grace and the Downgrade in Perspective,' in *The Forgotten Spurgeon*, 2nd ed. (London: Banner of Truth Trust, 1973), p. 181.

His revelation, but man can inform the omniscient Creator that He has included superfluous material. Consider these excepts from Spurgeon's sermons:

> '...for it [evolution] is not only deceptive, but it threatens to be mischievous in a high degree. There is not a hair of truth upon this dog from its head to its tail, but it rends and tears the simple ones. In all its bearings upon scriptural truth the evolution theory is in direct opposition to it. If God's word be true, evolution is a lie. I will not mince the matter: this is not the time for soft speaking.'[16]

That statement is even stronger than the protests of Charles Hodge, but like Hodge, Spurgeon had opened the church door to the chronology of the evolutionary worldview. There was an uncritical acceptance of old-earth geology's postulated millions of years. It was the Trojan horse by which evolutionists largely subverted the professing church. Although Spurgeon never attempted to show how the uniformitarian, naturalistic chronology could possibly be fitted into the biblical record, he seemed to regard such matters as unknowable and of little importance. Man must live by every *really important* Word of God. Sounding like a different person, and speaking when he should have been silent, Spurgeon said,

> 'Can any man tell me when the beginning was? Years ago we thought the beginning of this world was when Adam came upon it; but we have discovered that thousands of years before that God was preparing chaotic matter to make it a fit abode for man, putting races of creatures upon it, who might die and leave behind the marks of his handiwork and marvelous skill, before he tried his hand on man.'[17]

---

16. Spurgeon, Charles H., 'Hideous Discovery,' in The Metropolitan Tabernacle Pulpit, vol. 32 (Version 1.0; Albany, Oregon: AGES Software, 1997), p. 516. Sermon of July 25 1886 on Mark 7:20–23.

17. Spurgeon, Charles H., 'Election,' in *The New Park Street Pulpit*, vol. 1 (Version 1.0, Albany, Oregon: AGES Software, 1997), pp. 558–59. Sermon of September 2, 1855 on 2 Thessalonians 2:13–14.

God speaks His word and man cannot resist being a kibitzer. The statement above shows an incredible unawareness that the evolutionary faith will not be confined to the question of the age of rocks or Earth. Spurgeon made the common mistake of the times by confusing evolutionary naturalism's interpretation of the rocks with an actual scientific *discovery*. The only observable fact is that the rocks are there, but there is no reason to reject the perfect biblical explanation for a naturalistic one. Most nineteenth- century evangelicals felt that throwing in a few thousand extra years would make the conflict go away. The evolutionary faithful responded by demanding millions, then billions of years. Evolutionists demanded a total destruction of biblical chronology and most evangelicals eventually gave them what they wanted. A perfect, infallible and inerrant, God-breathed chronology was glibly exchanged for a mess of pottage called naturalistic uniformitarianism. Notice that after rejecting biblical chronology, Spurgeon is left parroting the fantasy of pre-Adamic humanoids. Such confident assertions as he makes would be more fitting for a comedy routine than a sermon. In the biblical faith we study history by written records, but in the evolutionary faith we have to create an imaginary history by extrapolating present processes back into the distant past. The details are filled in so as to conform to the preconceived faith in evolution and illustrated by imaginative artists. But God's word is not subject to the reprobate's corrections, not even to the evangelical's professed superior knowledge.

The Anglican professors at Oxford and Cambridge were even more ready to compromise with evolution. Instead of challenging the false presuppositions of the evolutionary faith, they were ready to adjust the Bible to fit in with the intellectual and cultural consensus. Although these professors were rich in excuses for not becoming involved in the evolutionary controversy, their excuses were utterly useless in the war of worldviews. They excused themselves as not qualified in the area of science or that the Bible was not really concerned with questions in geology. Since the Bible was not a textbook on science, they would yield to the experts. They neglected their duty to proclaim the whole counsel of God, and for that there is no excuse. Slothfulness in preference to diligent study is no demonstration of piety. Ignorance is no virtue.

Gregg Singer, in *A Theological Interpretation of American History*, has written in detail of the development of Social Darwinism. For our purposes we will illustrate how Darwinism was consistently applied as a worldview antithetical to Christianity.

D. WILLIAM GRAHAM SUMNER (1840–1910)

Sumner had been an Episcopal rector, but resigned his pastorate for graduate study abroad. He returned a convinced and enthusiastic Darwinist, obtaining a faculty position in political economics at Yale. He fervently believed that Darwinism should be the determinative principle in our economic and political thinking. Survival of the fittest became the guiding principle for personal and industrial life. His abandonment of the Christian faith is clearly seen in statements like the following:

> 'Nothing but might has ever made right, and if we include in might (as we ought) elections and the doctrines of the courts, nothing but might makes right now.'[18] And he said, 'Rights can never be natural, or God-given or absolute in any sense.'[19]

The most commendable thing about Sumner is his resigning the pastorate because he was openly promoting evolution. At least he did not continue as a disgrace to the Church of Jesus Christ as did so many other preachers.

The evolutionary philosophy promised freedom, liberation from the old moral restraints and casting off 'superstitions' that hinder our pleasure and bring discomfort of mind. What evolution actually delivered was a loss of freedom. A sovereign God created man both responsible and free. Evolution pictured man as just a few mutations away from the lower animals. When applied to business practices, the 'survival of the fittest' permitted almost everything. After all, who could be in favor of the survival of the unfittest?

---

18. William Graham Sumner, *Folkways*, (Boston: Ginn and Co., 1906), p. 65. Cited by Singer, p. 104.

19. Sumner, ref. 18, p. 29.

Events would prove what we already knew: Sovereignty is an inescapable concept. When denied to the Lord God, it does not disappear, but is merely transferred elsewhere. Sumner's philosophy had a very unappealing pessimism by portraying man as controlled by blind purposeless forces.

E. LESTER FRANK WARD (1841–1913)

Lester Frank Ward devised a more appealing, but more dangerous, form of Social Darwinism. Ward sought to devise a version of Darwinism that freed man from the determinism of Sumner. Ward proposed that evolution did not have to be a blind random process. Man was able to direct the evolutionary process toward goals of his own choosing. Ward's faith was in science and education. He wrote,

> 'Science is the great iconoclast. Our civilization depends wholly upon the discovery and application of a few profound scientific and philosophical principles, thought out by a few great minds who hold the shallow babble of priests in utter contempt and have no time to dabble in theology.'[20]

Sovereignty in Ward's philosophy was transferred from God to the State. The State ruling by the scientific principles of sociology (in preference to the Constitution) could provide universal education. Education, he said, is the greatest panacea for all our doubts and dangers. Ward has been called the father of American sociology and laid the foundation for the welfare state being expected to solve all the problems of its citizens. The practical result of godless schemes like Ward's is a totalitarian regime. For if the State is to be our Savior, it must also be our Lord. Needless to say, Ward denied biblical creation in his avowed hostility to evangelical Christianity.

---

20. Lester Frank Ward, *Iconoclast*, August 1870. Cited by Singer, p. 114.

F. HITLER AND FRIENDS: A COMMON WORLDVIEW

This connection of Darwinism to Hitler is outrageous as far as most evolutionists are concerned, yet it is an undeniable connection. The devaluing of human life by the evolutionary worldview must have its consequences. There will always be those who draw out the implications of this philosophical view with ruthless consistency. It is not that everyone who accepts Darwinism comes to the same conclusions as Adolf Hitler. The point is that evolution has no absolute moral standards by which to condemn Hitler, even though as human beings created in the image of God they know they should condemn his actions. If Darwinism were true, as is widely believed, Hitler's conclusions and actions are not irrational, nor can they be called immoral.

Darwin's *Origin* was recognized at once as a force that would tend to devalue human life. Darwin's mentor at Cambridge, Adam Sedgwick, said of *Origin*:

> 'Passages in your book…greatly shocked my moral taste… There is a moral or metaphysical part of nature as well as a physical. A man who denies this is deep in the mire of folly…Were it possible (thank God, it is not) to break it [the link between the material and the moral] humanity, in my mind, would suffer a damage that might brutalize it, and sink the human race into a lower grade of degradation than any into which it has fallen since its written records tell us of its history.'[21]

This proved to be a very accurate prognosis by Sedgwick, but his increasingly compromised position with regard to the evolutionary worldview rendered his resistance ineffectual. He did not stand on the foundational rock of Holy Scripture. The worldview of evolution must be met and defeated by a consistently biblical worldview.

---

21. Charles Darwin, 'Letter of Adam Sedgwick to Darwin, November 24, 1859,' in *The Correspondence of Charles Darwin* (Cambridge: Cambridge University Press, 1991), p. 397. Cited by Weikart, *From Darwin to Hitler*, p. 1.

A feeble protest, built on sand, cannot carry the day. The synthetic patchwork—using the evolutionary worldview to explain the 'real' world, and biblical elements for 'spiritual' matters—will always fail. Sedgwick himself would drift further and further away from the biblical testimony. While Darwinism's moral implications were shocking to many, there were those who leapt at the opportunity to be liberated from moral restraints, even at the cost of devaluing human life.

Darwin had planted the seed that would later bear such deadly fruit. In his *Descent of Man* he spoke of the principles of natural selection in selective breeding:

> 'With savages, the weak in body or mind are soon eliminated; and those that survive commonly exhibit a vigorous state of health. We civilized men, on the other hand, do our utmost to check the process of elimination; we build asylums for the imbecile, the maimed, and the sick; we institute poor-laws; and our medical men exert their utmost skill to save the life of every one to the last moment. ...Thus the weak members of civilized societies propagate their kind. No one who has attended to the breeding of domestic animals will doubt that this must be highly injurious to the race of man. ...but excepting in the case of man himself, hardly any one is so ignorant as to allow his worst animals to breed.'[22]

Darwin, not as far from a Christianized culture as later followers would be, felt that we should not force these logical implications of the evolutionary worldview on the population. He held back because he believed that the instinct of sympathy was in the noblest part of our nature. Therefore, we just have to bear the bad effects of our sympathy. Later generations of evolutionists would count this sympathy as a weakness and condemn it as a hindrance to human

---

22. Charles Darwin, 'Civilised Nations' (Chapter V), *The Descent of Man and Selection in Relation to Sex*, (New York: The Modern Library, [1871]), p. 501.

advancement. After all, even ethics have to be evolving, according to the evolutionary worldview.

The seventy-five years after Darwin saw the evolutionary faith taking deep root in Germany and the bitter fruits of evolution would soon follow. The evolutionary-based eugenics and racism programs would shock the world, yet seemed perfectly logical and even virtuous solutions to Germany's woes. Many of the players are little known today, but all had their influence for evil.

As early as 1880, Robby Kossmann wrote:

'...that the Darwinian worldview must look upon the present sentimental conception of the value of the life of a human individual as an overestimate completely hindering the progress of humanity. The human state also, like every animal community of individuals, must reach an even higher level of perfection, if the possibility exists in it, through the destruction of the less well-endowed individual, or the more excellently endowed to win space for the expansion of its progeny...The state only has an interest in preserving the more excellent life at the expense of the less excellent.'[23]

Kossmann was by no means alone, and neither was Germany the only place hearing these sentiments. The American zoologist Madison Grant wrote in 1916:

'Mistaken regard for what are believed to be divine laws and a sentimental belief in the sanctity of human life tend to prevent both the elimination of defective infants and the sterilization of such adults as are themselves of no value to the community. The laws of nature require the obliteration of the unfit, and human life is valuable only when it is of use to the community or race.'[24]

---

23. Robby Kossmann, 'Die Bedeutung des Einzellebens in der Darwinistischen Weltanschauung,' *Nord und Süd* 12 (1880): 420–21. Cited by Weikart, p. 2.

24. Madison Grant, *The Passing of the Great Race* (n.p., 1916). Weikart, p. 10, citing a quote from Diane Paul, *Controlling Human Heredity*, p. 17.

Note that both Kossmann and Grant attribute the sanctity of human life to 'sentimental' causes, while their own opinions are delivered as though they were oracles. Arbitrary, subjective and unfounded as these opinions were, they were asserted with a confidence in their own authority. The Christian worldview, in sharp contrast, has an objective basis in the personal revelation from the Creator, recorded in Scripture.

Ernst Haeckel was the virtual fundamentalist preacher of Darwinism. His deliberately fraudulent drawings were eagerly received by the faithful as conclusively demonstrating their belief in evolution as the true religion. Haeckel knew very well that his evolutionary worldview was antithetical to Christianity and gloried in that fact. He dismissed any religious account of man as an 'anthropocentric fable.'[25]

Like the worst of religious charlatans, Haeckel falsified drawings of various embryos in an attempt to show that a human fetus goes through many evolutionary stages (*e.g.* the 'fish' stage) on its way to becoming human. Evolutionists eagerly accepted these drawings and continued to use them long after the fraud was exposed. Even the 2006 textbook from Prentice Hall still uses a modified form of Haeckel's drawings to show how birds and reptiles have a 'kinship of vertebrates.'[26] Many authorities today have dissociated themselves from this notion that the human embryo goes through past ancestral stages in the womb ('embryonic recapitulation') —at least in its extreme form. Haeckel's embarrassingly wrong 'gill slits' are now often called merely 'throat pouches'. More frequently, though, the term is 'branchial (= gill) pouches', demonstrating that evolutionists do not want to let go of the connection altogether. And this misleading notion is still very much alive in the popular media and imagination.[27]

---

25. Richard Weikart, *From Darwin to Hitler: Evolutionary Ethics, Eugenics, and Racism in Germany* (New York: Palgrave Macmillan, 2004), p. 12.

26. N. Campbell, B. Williamson, and R. Heyden, *Biology: Exploring Life* (Florida Teacher's Edition; Upper Saddle River, New Jersey: Pearson Prentice Hall, 2006), p. 303. Cited by Patterson, *Evolution Exposed*, p. 95.

27. See, for example, the story about the 'fish gills girl' at <creation.com/gillgirl>.

Haeckel was also so sure there must be a missing link somewhere, he had a drawing made of a totally imaginary race of ape-men he called '*Pithecanthropus alalus*' (= speechless ape-man). There was not even a bone fragment or tooth to substantiate his ape-man. Haeckel's imaginary race of pre-humans might be well described as an anthropocentric fable. His fraud would not be the last in the parade including the Piltdown Man (1912) and the Nebraska Man (1922).

The substitution of animal ancestry for the creation of man in the image of God was bound to have a deleterious effect on the value of human life. The absolutes of God's law could be 'scientifically' replaced by whatever seemed best for mankind or even the individual. As Darwin said in his *Autobiography*, one who does not believe in God or an afterlife, '…can have for his rule of life, as far as I can see, only to follow those impulses and instincts which are the strongest or which seem to him the best one.'[28]

Darwin, who at one time imagined himself as a country parson, did not go to the extremes of moral depravity himself. If fact, what he wrote in his *Autobiography* was not intended for publication and thus more openly expresses his views. Since he had no absolute standard, it was quite difficult to criticize his more radical followers. Radical Darwinists believed they were simply carrying his views to a logical conclusion. Christians who opted for a synthesis ended up trying to add 'God' to the evolutionary worldview, resulting in a heterogeneous mixture that was hard to take seriously. God was neither needed nor wanted in the evolutionary worldview. The exclusion of God is the main motive for devising the theory in the first place. Besides, the 'god' thus added was no longer really the God of Scripture, because the one and only God the Creator revealed an antithetical account of creation. Nothing could be better than that account.

The evolutionary faith is relentlessly applied to every area of life and thought. Far from being exempt, the Bible is the special target. Evolution can tolerate almost any other religion, just so long as it is

---

28. Charles Darwin, *Autobiography* (New York: Norton, 1969), p. 94. Cited by Weikart, p. 21.

not the biblical faith. David Friedrich Strauss (1808–1874) in 1872 set out to replace supernatural Christianity with a naturalistic scientific worldview. His application of the evolutionary philosophy to the study of the Bible resulted in a weakening of Christian resistance. By biblical standards unqualified for any teaching office in the Church, he nevertheless secured a position at Tübingen where he promoted a critical attitude toward the Bible, dismissed miracles as myths, and advanced modern biblical criticism. The Bible must be force-fitted into the dictates of the evolutionary faith. The Bible has something to say about myths and its description fits Strauss perfectly:

> 2 Timothy 4:4: 'And they will turn away from hearing the truth, but on the other hand they will turn aside to myths.'

German higher criticism could not have gotten far without the support of the evolutionary naturalistic dogma combined with a virulent anti-Semitism. The Old Testament, being a Jewish writing, was attacked with special ferocity. In place of the biblical account of man's being created upright and subsequently *falling* into sin, the evolutionary view imagined man *rising up* from lower forms of life. According to the research of Robert Bowie Johnson, the evolution-minded ancient Greeks perverted the historical event of the Fall, so that the serpent and the rebellious woman would be the 'heroes' of the event. Athena, from the Greek for 'deathless one' fulfilled the serpent's promise to Eve that she would not die. For Greek mythology Eve (Hera, then Athena), the serpent, Cain, and Nimrod (Hercules) were the heroes who became gods and goddesses.[29]

G. DARWINISM AND RACISM

Darwin himself was no more of a racist than was thought proper for an English gentleman. For all his talk of 'lower races' and the inevitable extermination of the inferior races as losers in the struggle

---

29. Robert Bowie Johnson, Jr., The Parthenon Code. Mankind's History in Marble (Annapolis, Maryland: Solving Light Books, 2004), p. 24

for life, he did not go so far as to advocate violence or the force of civil government to bring it about. Though less racist than many of his followers, he commended the more radical evolutionists. Thomas Huxley (1825–95) was such an avid supporter of evolution's acceptance in England that he was called 'Darwin's bulldog.' Huxley's racial view may be summarized in words from one of his 'sermons': 'No rational man, cognizant of the facts, believes that the average Negro is equal, still less the superior of the white man.'[30] Evolution's doctrine of distinct races of human beings, ranked from lowest to highest, is contrary to the biblical record of our common descent from Adam and again from Noah. All people belong to the same *human* race; there is no such thing as racial superiority or inferiority, except on evolutionary foundations.

Henry Fairfield Osborn (1857–1935) was America's most prominent anthropologist in his lifetime. He drew these deductions from his firm commitment to evolution:

> 'The Negroid stock is even more ancient than the Caucasian and Mongolian, as may be proved by an examination not only of the brain, of the hair, of bodily characters, such as the teeth, the genitalia, the sense organs, but of the instincts, the intelligence. The standard of intelligence of the average Negro is similar to that of the eleven-year-old youth of the species *Homo sapiens.*'[31]

According to Osborn, the Negro is not really human. The mention of the Mongolian 'race' is significant as a certain type of mental retardation was called 'Mongolism' in accordance with the evolutionary faith that Mongolians belonged to an inferior race. By being 'more ancient' the Negro is assumed more ape-like. These racist attitudes, with their newly acquired 'scientific' façades, caused much trouble and many deaths in the late nineteenth and into the

---

30. Huxley, Thomas H., *Lay Sermons, Addresses and Reviews* (New York: Appleton, 1871), p. 20. Cited by Morris, *The Long War Against God*, p. 60.

31. Henry Fairfield Osborn, 'The Evolution of Human Races.' *Natural History,* 89 (January/February, 1926, reprinted April 1980): 129. Cited by Morris, *The Long War Against God*, p. 62.

twentieth century in America and elsewhere. It is not difficult to find such racist quotations, because Osborn was neither an obscure figure, nor a unique one.

The New Testament continues the biblical worldview as expressed by the apostle Paul's address to the Greeks: Acts 17:26 'And He has made from one blood every nation of men to dwell on all the face of the earth, and has determined their preappointed times and the boundaries of their dwellings.'

Evolutionary faith also gave rise to the strange pseudo-science of craniometry. Craniometry assumed that character analysis of a person could be based on the physical characteristics of the skull. This was used as more 'scientific' evidence in favor of racism. Artists' drawings once again supplied the lack of real evidence. The Negro and the Australian Aborigine were frequent targets of the drawings allegedly showing how 'ape-like' they were.

H. EVOLUTIONARY 'PROGRESS' AS THE HIGHEST GOOD

As evil as it was for evolutionists to think, say, and write their racist and eugenic sentiments, the real horror awaited the use of government force to speed up the inevitable process of evolution. Lacking a standard of good, evolutionists settled on progress as the highest good. They refused to appeal to anything or anyone higher than the process itself. Thus the 'best' survive, the 'worst' perish.

Friedrich Nietzsche (1844–1900), one of Germany's most provocative and influential philosophers, rejected the typical Christian sympathy and compassion for the poor and downtrodden. Alexander Tille (1866–1912), a German Social Darwinist, approved of Nietzsche's views.

> '...even the most careful selection of the best can accomplish nothing, if it is not linked with a merciless elimination of the worst people...And the proclamation of social elimination must therefore be one of the supreme features of every ethics, which elevates as its ideal the goal that the theory of evolution has demonstrated...Out of love for the coming generations...Zarathustra preaches: Do not

spare your neighbor! For the person of today is something that must be overcome. But if it must be overcome, then the worst people, the low ones, and the superfluous ones must be sacrificed...Therefore, this means becoming hard against those who are below average, and in them to overcome one's own sympathy.'[32]

These views were becoming more common in Germany, even as early as 1895. We do not have to merely imagine what might happen if someone of this mentality came to be a dictator over Germany. It actually happened less than forty years later in the person of Adolf Hitler! Most Enlightenment thinkers had sacrificed the supernatural elements of the Bible, but sought to preserve some 'moral core,' assumed to be the real value of the Bible, if there was any value in it. This position was extremely unstable, for when the supernatural is removed, there is no special authority for the moral standards. Hitler could not have justified his program without Darwin's evolutionary philosophy and Galton's Darwin-derived eugenics. Hitler could thereby convince himself and most others that helping evolutionary progress along was actually a *good* thing. 'Good' was now going to be defined by the faith of evolution rather than the revelation of the Lord God.

Those who hated biblical ethics seized upon Darwinism as a foundation for a new 'scientific' ethic. The de-supernaturalized Bible was incapable of resistance and actually furthered naturalism and secularization. Those in rebellion against God are always seeking a way of escaping the absolutist standards of Scripture. Darwin had developed his godless 'explanation' of origins; his cousin built on that foundation a new 'science' of eugenics. The combination of these two ideas brought a new 'ethical' standard to Germany and from there to the rest of the world. Hitler had a long line of like-minded thinkers who paved the way for his accession to power. While Darwinism did not make every adherent embrace the Nazi philosophy, Hitler could

---

32. Alexander Tille, *Von Darwin bis Nietzsche. Ein Buch Entwicklungsethik*, trans. Richard Weikart (Leipzig: C. G. Naumann, 1895), pp. 232–34. Cited by Weikart, p. 45.

not have justified himself without it. He could manage to convince himself and thousands of others that helping evolutionary progress along was a *good* thing, regardless of how it was done. The modern secular American liberal faces an impossible situation. He wants to say, and does say, that Hitler was 'evil'. At the same time, he insists that there are no absolute moral standards because he shares Hitler's faith in evolution. The liberal self-contradiction goes something like this: 'There is no such thing as good and evil, but Hitler is evil.' A previous generation had sucked all the supernatural out of the Bible in order to rescue its fine moral system. The resulting naturalism freed the next generation to also discard the old moral system. Morality itself would be seen as nothing but a product of naturalistic gradual evolutionary steps. Haeckel and others worked to promote the idea that morality and ethics resulted from biological (evolutionary) causes. Nothing could be more appropriate for the new (twentieth) century than to move on to a more highly evolved, more scientific ethical standard.

In order to replace biblical Christianity with the evolutionary faith, it was not unusual to give the theory of evolution a 'religious' flavor to make the transition more palatable to the average citizen. This goes beyond Thomas Huxley's 'sermons' on evolution. Moritz von Egidy gained an enthusiastic following in the 1890s with the religious (but non-biblical) use of Christian terminology. He said,

> 'In the place of the contemporary conception of God, a personal God, God as a Spirit, God as a Being, Triune, or even a unitary God, the conception of a "holy law of evolution" will emerge…The thought of pure materialism cannot satisfy, we need something that will meet our desire for imagination and that does not contradict serious and honest thought. We have this in the conception of a "holy law of evolution," a concept, which we piously call "Providence."'[33]

Here was a 'solution' to the conflict between science and religion: a 'scientific religion.' A person could be in step with the intellectual elite (think themselves wise) without being totally devoid of religion. Note that in Egidy's view religion is to satisfy our need for imagination and feelings, but *thought* is reserved for more scientific endeavors. Even though most had not even heard of Egidy, his views became widespread.

To understand how Hitler could think of his activities as moral and ethical, we need to see what leaders for 'moral renewal' were saying in Germany. Anti-Semitic publicist Theodor Fritsch (1852–1933) said in 1914:

> *'The preservation of the health of our generation* belongs to our highest commands…We do not approve of *false humaneness.* Whoever aims at preserving the degenerate and depraved, limits the space for the healthy and strong, suppresses the life of the whole community, multiplies the sorrow and burden of existence, and helps rob happiness and sunshine from life.'[34]

A practical application of this kind of thinking meant that a German citizen who opposed Hitler's scientifically based program for the improvement of humanity should actually feel guilty for helping to 'rob happiness and sunshine from life.' Such is the dilemma of man-made ethics. As the Scripture says, Isaiah 5:20 'Woe to those who call evil good, and good evil; Who put darkness for light, and light for darkness; Who put bitter for sweet, and sweet for bitter!'

I. RACIAL INEQUALITY

There were some humanists who opposed parts of Darwinism because they believed in the equality of all persons. Darwinism demanded that we recognize superior and inferior specimens of humanity. On the Darwinian scale, Europeans were at the top, and Africans and Aboriginals were at the bottom, nearer to the ape. The American Supreme Court Dred Scott decision (1857), which declared

---

33. Moritz von Egidy, 'Weltanschauung: Pfingsten,' in *M. von Egidy. Sein Leben und Wirken*, ed. Heinrich Driesmans, 1 (Dresden: E. Pierson's, 1900), p. 110. Cited by Weikart, p. 62.

34. Theodor Fritsch, *Fundamental Principles of the Renewal Community* (Leipzig: Verlag Hammer, 1914), p. 240. Weikart's translation, quote cited on p. 69 of ref. 25.

that slaves were non-persons, was a result of this kind of thinking. In the Christian worldview, such a racist attitude is totally unjustifiable and sinful. But the Darwinist could find nothing inconsistent about having racist attitudes and practices. Those Darwinists who objected were really borrowing their objections from the Christian worldview, in which there is a basis for a critique.

Ernst Haeckel (1834—1919) gladly picked up Darwin's racial classifications and ran with them. Haeckel's own 'race' was, of course, more superior to other races than those 'lower races' were to the apes. To Haeckel a picture was worth a thousand words, even if the 'picture' was nothing but another of Haeckel's bogus drawings. The frontispiece of his *Natürliche Schöpfungsgeschichte* features (inaccurate) drawings of six human 'races' and six simian species.[35] Those spreading these ideas were highly educated people, not some illiterate peasants. Their education did not save them, it only reinforced and gave sophisticated rationale for their sinful inclinations. An 'education' built on the presupposition of the evolutionary worldview can produce only a more sophisticated and more sinister depravity.

Modern liberals would be happier if they could attribute this radical racism to some barely literate, preferably religious, conspiracy. Instead it was the leading intellectuals of Germany who held the same evolutionary views shared by modern liberals.

Hermann Klaatsch (1863–1916), anatomist, was one of the many who believed the 'lower races' (e.g. Negro) were closer to the apes than to the whites. He also opined that slavery was a great benefit for these primitive people.[36]

Darwinism and racism were instrumental in 'explaining' criminal behavior. Blaming crime on defective genetics or impure blood became a favorite activity of professional psychiatrists.

J. STATE CONTROL OF HUMAN REPRODUCTION

Speeding evolution along was seen as among the chief virtues; the biological degeneration of the race was among the chief evils.

---

35. Weikart, ref. 25, p. 107.

Evolutionists saw the need to rid the race of the inferior or unfit. The superior should reproduce more, the unfit not at all.

Once again, evolutionary thought was the presupposed worldview by which all things, including sexual morality, were to be interpreted. Evolution was accepted by many for the very reason that it justified their sexual behavior. The popular *The Sexual Question* by Swiss ant specialist and psychiatrist Auguste-Henri Forel (1848–1931) went through 16 German editions and was translated into English and French.[37] Forel felt that *ordinarily* monogamy was best, but if a superior man were married to an infertile woman or a woman with bad traits—adultery, polygamy, or concubinage could be good alternatives. The chief good was to improve the genetic superiority of the race. All that is necessary to justify immorality is for the particular man to think of himself as one of those 'superior' exceptions. This was an easy sell. Those wanting to overturn 'traditional' (by which they meant biblical) sexual morality, made specific appeal to Darwinian theory. This is not a wild accusation from a backwoods fundamentalist, but an explicit and intentional basis of their views of morality (and all else) in the 'scientific' worldview of evolution. All other views could now be dismissed as superstition. The scientific view had finally arrived.

One important implication for the eugenicists was to encourage the lower classes to use birth control and make it more easily available to them. In this way, the number of inferiors could be diminished. In their utter contempt for these people, they could pretend to be compassionate. Some eugenicists were alarmed that the superior people were having fewer children than the inferior class. The easiest side of the equation for the state to mandate was to impose more controls on the lower, poorer, and less powerful of society—the perceived 'lower races'. The rich and beautiful superior people could not be forced to have more children, so let the inferiors be forced

---

36. Hermann Klaatsch, 'Die Morphologie und Psychologie,' *Internationaler Kongress für Kriminalanthropologie (Oktober 1911)*, ed. Gustav Aschaffenburg and Dr. Partheimer (Heidelberg, 1912), 58–71.73. Article referred to by Weikart, ref. 25, p. 115.

37. Weikart, ref. 25, p. 131.

to have fewer. Education and persuasion were useful, but more was needed to stop the degeneration of the race. Criminal and mentally ill persons should be locked away to prevent the reproduction of their defective genetics. Certain categories of people such as habitual criminals, the mentally ill, and alcoholics should be subject to forced sterilization.

K. KILLING THE UNFIT

Since Darwinists were convinced that the unfit would perish anyway in the struggle for survival, it would be useful for the race if the demise of the unfit were hastened. Christian compassion for the weak was viewed as just another example of Christianity hindering progress. Haeckel was the earliest significant German advocate for killing the unfit. He praised the ancient Spartan practice of killing the weak or sick infants.[38] Thanks to his fervent faith in biological evolution, Haeckel could present infanticide and abortion as sound, rational, scientific (and therefore good) courses to take. Anyone who opposed their 'scientific' program was letting emotion or superstition get in the way of progress. Which would you prefer: being scientific and rational, or being emotional and superstitious? To Haeckel's twisted mind, the unborn child is only a life form at a lower stage of evolution, on the level of a rabbit or a fish. Even the newborn child has not yet developed into a fully human person. So even though life begins at conception, evolutionists considered it only animal life, not yet capable of benefitting society, so without real value. Hitler, coming along later, could do nothing worse than what was already widely suggested by these early evolutionists.

Darwinism's devaluation of human life had further development in the issues of euthanasia and suicide. Euthanasia, in the nineteenth century, had meant making the dying person more comfortable, perhaps with painkillers. But in the early twentieth century, it took on the additional connotation of speeding up the death of the ill person. Suicide was beginning to have more favorable press. With the high

---

38. Weikart, ref. 25, p. 146.

numbers of able-bodied men dying in World War I, who needed those 'defectives' who were doing us the favor of committing suicide?

Once euthanasia and suicide became more acceptable, the relentless logic of Darwinism marched on. (Remember only compromising Christians are satisfied with a *mixed* worldview.) Eugenicists pushed for *involuntary* euthanasia and *assisted* suicide. There were some evolutionists who balked at these implications of Darwinism, but by what standard could they condemn them? They could not effectively oppose these implications because they had already bought into the same evolutionary worldview that gave rise to these implications. Heidelberg physician Hoche, sounding terribly modern in 1920, opined: '...there are circumstances in which killing by a physician is no crime...if through the shortening of this one lost life immediate insights could be gained, which would save other better lives.'[39] Haeckel was right about one thing. Once a person has embraced the evolutionary worldview, there are no logical grounds on which to oppose these atrocities against human life.

Lest Americans think this was only a German or Nazi problem, we acknowledge with shame America's own early twentieth-century enthusiasm for using the force of civil government to promote the goals of eugenics. Eugenics was selective breeding applied to human beings, for the improvement of the race. America's selective breeding and forced sterilization programs have been thoroughly documented in Edwin Black's *War Against the Weak*.[40]

The point of mentioning this work is to dispel the notion that we can blame everything on the individual named Hitler or the group known as Nazis. The common denominator for the multinational crisis was the theory of evolution and the eagerness of fallen man to follow its implications for human life.

The Englishmen Charles Darwin and Francis Galton combined to form an evolutionary eugenics. The Germans were not alone

---

39. Karl Binding and Alfred Hoche, *Die Freigabe der Vernichtung lebensunwerten Lebens* (Leipzig, 1920), 49–62. Translated and cited by Weikart, ref. 25, p. 156.

40. Edwin Black, War Against the Weak: *Eugenics and America's Campaign to Create a Master Race* (New York: Four Walls Eight Windows, 2003).

in making the logical deductions. Furthermore, we have already shown how the movements were going strong years before Hitler came to power in Germany. The drumbeat was actually begun before Hitler was born. These ideas were picked up by Americans Charles Davenport (1866–1944), founder of the Eugenics Record Office in 1910, and the first head of the office, Harry Laughlin (1880–1943). Eugenics would eventually win the support of well known and powerful figures including President Woodrow Wilson, the Rockefeller Foundation, Margaret Sanger of the Planned Parenthood abortionist organization,[41] Chief Justice Oliver Wendell Holmes, the Carnegie Institution, and many others of wealth and influence. America did not need Hitler to suggest these ideas to us. All that was necessary was to embrace evolutionary thought and the devaluation of human life would inevitably follow. The eugenics craze resulted in laws against so-called mixed-race marriages (in twenty-seven states), human breeding programs, forced sterilization of over 60,000 United States citizens, and even euthanasia. The U.S. Supreme Court approved eugenics years before it approved abortion.[42]

A 1993 television documentary presented *The Lynchburg Story.* Beginning in the 1920s thousands of people in the U.S. were sterilized against their will and without their consent just to prevent 'undesirable breeding.' Over 8,000 of these procedures took place at a center for 'undesirables' at Lynchburg, VA. The Lynchburg doctor, who performed most of the sterilizations in his own town, looked to evolutionary biologist Harry Laughlin to provide legal cover for proposed legislation. Laughlin's law called for *compulsory* sterilization of the 'feeble-minded', the blind, drug addicts, those with tuberculosis or syphilis, epileptics, paupers, the deaf and the homeless. The manipulated test case involved a young woman targeted for sterilization because there had allegedly been three generations of feeble-mindedness in her family. Her lawyer's

---

41. See also Jerry Bergman, 'Birth control leader Margaret Sanger: Darwinist, racist and eugenicist', *Journal of Creation* **22**(3):62–67, 2008.

42. Jonathan Sarfati, 'America's evolutionists: Hitler's inspiration?' at <creation.com/weak>, accessed 20 September 2008 (review of Black, ref. 40).

primary interest was winning legitimacy for the sterilization program. Not only did the young woman have her own lawyer working against her, but also the Supreme Court's Chief Justice was the very influential Darwinist Oliver Wendell Holmes Jr. (1841–1935). He declared the law constitutional, opening the way for other states to pass similar laws.[43]

Justice Holmes' enthusiasm for forced sterilization is openly stated in this 1927 Buck v. Bell case,

> '[I]t is better for all the world, if instead of waiting to execute degenerate offspring for crime, or to let them starve for their imbecility, society can prevent those who are manifestly unfit from continuing their kind. The principle that sustains compulsory vaccination is broad enough to cover cutting the Fallopian tubes. Jacobson v. Massachusetts, 1927 U.S. 11. Three generations of imbeciles are enough.'[44]

If our nation is to recover, we must come to realize that three generations of amoral Darwinist judges, trampling the Constitution underfoot in the name of progress, are more than enough.

Vermont in 1931 became the thirty-first state to enact sterilization laws for the handicapped or feeble-minded. This law was not repealed until 1973.[45] This means that thirty-one states in the United States had these laws before Hitler came to power in 1933 and enacted his own eugenics laws.

Not only was Hitler's forced sterilization of the 'unfit' praised by U.S. eugenicists, but the Nazi law was actually modeled after

43. Carl Wieland, 'The Lies of Lynchburg. How U.S. Evolutionists Taught the Nazis,' at <creation. com/lynchburg>, accessed 20 September 2008.

44. Thomas D. Russell, 'American Legal History: Buck v. Bell, 274 U.S. 200 (1927),' March 24, 2006. University of Denver, Sturm College of Law, www.law.du.edu/russell/lh/alh/docs/buckvbell.html (accessed May 7, 2007). Oliver W. Holmes delivered the opinion of the Court.

45. *The Washington Post*, August 8, 1999, p. 21 (A) Cited by Russell Grigg, <creation.com/ eugenics>.

the law framed by Harry Laughlin. Hitler's government awarded Laughlin an honorary doctorate.[46]

The chronology of events shows us that Nazism was not the root of the atrocities, but the 'common conclusion' of evolutionary thinkers in both the U.S. and Germany. Scholars from many other countries drew the same conclusions from Darwinian premises. There is no force of moral restraint in Darwinism. First generation Darwinists, reared in a Christianized culture, usually retained some moral standards as cultural leftovers. Since their morality no longer had any foundation, the second generation Darwinists felt that all was permitted if it could improve the race. So it was that the miserable fruits of Darwinism did not fully ripen until the early twentieth century.

L. WAR AND PEACE

Darwinian evolution can also be credited with laying the foundation for the bloodiest war in history, World War I. This was the opinion not only of William Jennings Bryan, but also of William R. Thayer, president of the American Historical Association. In 1918 he made these remarks:

> 'I do not believe that the atrocious war into which the Germans plunged Europe in August, 1914, and which has subsequently involved all lands and all peoples, would ever have been fought, or at least would have sustained its actual gigantic proportions, had the Germans not been made mad by the theory of the survival of the fittest.'[47]

Most evolutionists recognized that Germany's militarism was a result of, or at least justified by, the Darwinian theory of the survival of the fittest. They held out the hope that this was an aberration, not a necessary consequence of evolutionary thought. Once again the evolutionary worldview cannot be consistently lived out, unless a holocaust is your ideal.

---

46. Wieland, ref. 43.

47. Antonello La Vergata, 'Evolution and War, 1871–1918,' *Nuncius* 9 (1994): 148. Cited by Weikart, ref. 25, p. 163.

Even the pacifists in Germany were not opposed to war out of concern for the value of human life. Their objection was that war kills the *wrong people*. In war some of Germany's finest specimens of manhood were being killed. The government should be targeting the weak, the sickly, and the mentally disabled, not strong healthy German soldiers. The lack of moral absolutes also meant that 'pacifists' like Haeckel could almost immediately become patriotic supporters of the war once it began. If only Germany could have sent the weak and unfit to the front lines, Haeckel would have had no regrets.

There were other motives at work beside Darwinism. The intellectuals recalled the good old days of Chancellor Otto Bismarck (1815–98) from 1864 to 1871. Those were days of Germany's greatness, days worth recapturing. However, Darwinism could provide a *scientific* justification for Germany's new militarism. Militarism could sell to the people much more easily if it could be coated with a layer of modern scientific progressivism. After all, if it was 'scientific' how could it be bad? The superior race needed more room to multiply; the inferior people must make way for German expansion. This was not a hard sell if the audience is made up of Germans. Had not Malthus shown that there were too many people? War is just a part of the 'struggle for existence.' The survival of the fittest necessarily involves the death of the less fit. This kind of thinking was leading up to World War I.

In the years leading up to World War II, the issue of racial purity would be central. The quality of the human breed would be raised by eliminating the unfit peoples: the Jews, the gypsies, Poles, the Slavic peoples, and Jewish-sympathizing Christians. If all these could be replaced by pure Aryan stock, what a beautiful world it would be. At least, according to Hitler and his ilk.

Another advantage of placing war on biological grounds is the immunity from moral criticism. The war was a matter of rational scientific progress, a natural part of the struggle for survival. Moral criticisms were out of place since a scientific natural process was unstoppable. One might as well object to the morning sunrise.

It is easy for us today to think of Hitler's militarism, but the Darwinian justification for wars of aggression goes much further back. When Darwinism was relatively new, in 1860, Oscar Peschel spoke for many others when he justified Bismarck's wars as follows:

> 'Even we in Germany should view the most recent events [i.e., the war] as a lawful evolutionary process...With such magnificent events it is no longer a matter of right or blame, bur rather it is a Darwinian struggle for existence, where the modern triumphs and the obsolete descends into the paleontological graves.'[48]

They usually did not want to say out loud that Christianity was the obsolete concern for right and wrong sinking into its grave, and Darwinism was the 'modern' scientific and rational idea that was bound to triumph. Again we see that it did not take Hitler to see Darwinism as a justification of wars of aggression. Evolutionists may wish us to think that Hitler was just a lone madman who made improper use of evolution. But Hitler had many leading intellectuals, past and contemporary, on his side. He in fact drew his ideas from these others. Furthermore, the atrocities were not confined to Germany, but are easily seen in Russia, in England, and even in the United States. Darwinism led Germany of pre-World War I to use the same arguments already used to justify Bismarck's wars. It would be convenient for evolutionists to blame everything on Hitler, but the Darwinian justification had been around for sixty years before Hitler came to power. As early as the Franco-Prussian wars of the nineteenth century, the new theory of Darwinism was taken up to justify wars of aggression against the less fit peoples.

Peschel was not alone in his view, but had widespread support. Similar sentiments were heard from anthropologist Alexander Ecker, and from Rolle, Jaeger, and a host of others. Even the

---

48. Oscar Peschel, 'Ein Rückblick auf die jüngste Vergangenheit,' *Das Ausland* 39, no. 36:874, September 1866. Translated and cited by Weikart, ref. 25, p. 167.

pseudo-theologian David F. Strauss lost interest in theology to study 'science' by which he meant Darwinism. He had found the new-old religion of evolution, the age-old standard replacement for biblical faith. Strauss specified that evolution was his new faith. The title of his book was *The Old and the New Faith*, (1872). At least his honesty can be appreciated; evolution was indeed his new faith.

Although the evolutionary worldview preceded Christianity by centuries, Christianity was called the old faith, but evolution was called the new science. It was a point of dogma, religiously held, that Evolution was not religious. As for real objective evidence, it simply *must* come some day. Meanwhile we will use the story of evolution to interpret every observation we meet. Until then, Haeckel's drawings will have to do.

Friedrich Hellwald (1842–1892), editor of a leading scholarly journal, *Das Ausland*, pushed aside moral objections in the name of scientific progress. In 1875 he wrote:

> 'Just as in nature the struggle for existence is the moving principle of evolution and perfection…so also in world history the destruction of the weaker nations through the stronger is a postulate of progress.'[49]

Since 'science has proven' this principle we know that oppression, barbarism, and mass killing are not moral issues. The winner of the struggle is automatically 'right.' Warfare, even if aggressive, is not a moral issue, but a natural part of the evolutionary process. War could well be called a biological necessity in this view. Note here that on the foundation of evolutionary philosophy 'right' has no objective meaning. Only revealed biblical truth can give us such an objective foundation. Otherwise 'right' and 'wrong' become the equivalent of nonsense syllables. The only way to be 'wrong' in militarism's theory is to *lose* the war!

---

49. Friedrich Hellwald, *The History of Culture in its Natural Evolution* (Augsburg, 1875), p. 58. Cited by Weikart, ref. 25, p. 169.

M. RACIAL STRUGGLE AND EXTERMINATION

While Hitler was not in power in the days before World War I, he was an active listener absorbing the racist and militaristic rhetoric of Germany's Social Darwinists. Hitler was a soldier in the Bavarian army in World War I fighting for the greatness of the Fatherland.

Many pacifists objected to wars with fellow Europeans, but saw nothing wrong with annihilating the inferior races whose very existence posed a threat to the European, especially to the German people. Even the Anglo-American faux historian and science fiction writer H.G. Wells echoed the social Darwinist viewpoint, 'There is only one sane and logical thing to be done with a really inferior race, and that is to exterminate it.'[50–51] Darwin himself considered the extermination of inferior races to be inevitable, but did not advocate aggressive measures to bring it to pass. That was left to his followers. Thus Hitler was not necessary to the development of these policies, but Darwinism was an essential component.

Haeckel was active in promoting notions of racial superiority. Of course he had his imaginative drawings to show how ape-like those other races really were! He was always prepared to put a scientific veneer on his prejudices. Although it took most Darwinists a generation or two to get the implications of their adopted faith, some 'got it' right away. Only a year after Darwin's *Origin of Species* was published, Oscar Peschel, editor of *Das Ausland*, was justifying racial extinctions on the basis of Darwinism. Peschel, Hellwald and their ilk said that the Spanish atrocities against the American Indians really accomplished much good for the advancement of the human race. Australian Aborigines, being the lowest on the evolutionary scale might as well be exterminated. There might be an element of sadness in the extermination of such peoples, but the progress of humanity must go on.

The new 'scientific' ethic differed little from the old 'cruelty.' The very influential Büchner expressed his racial views in the 1870s:

---

50. Diane B. Paul, *Controlling Human Heredity, 1865 to the Present* (Atlantic Highlands, New Jersey: Humanities Press, 1995), p. 75. Cited by Weikart, ref. 25, p. 185.

51. See also Jerry Bergman, H.G. Wells: Darwin's disciple and eugenicist extraordinaire, *TJ (now Journal of Creation)* **18**(3): 116–120, 2004; <creation.com/wells>.

'The white or Caucasian human species is ordained to take dominion of the earth, while the lowest human races, like Americans [Indians], Australians [Aboriginals], Alfuren, Hottentots, and such others, are proceeding toward their destruction with huge steps.'[52]

Darwinism also led to a desire to expand German territory and colonized countries occupied by 'inferior' races. The colonies could be run for the benefit of the German people. This would be guaranteed by having Germans in power in the colonies. Too bad about those inferior races, but it is progress for the human race. Woltmann's views (1903) were not unusual for social Darwinists, 'The Germanic race is called to encompass the earth with its dominion, to exploit the treasure of nature and the labor forces, and to make the passive races serving members of their cultural development.'[53]

The less radical Darwinists could not effectively counter the sentiments of the radicals. First, because they had lost the foundation for moral certitude. They no longer had a worldview that permitted moral absolutes. Second, because their Darwinism convinced them that the demise of the inferior races was inevitable, even if they had a personal preference for less violent means of achieving this otherwise noble end.

Since the Germans regarded the African people as being on about the same level as baboons; they often referred to them as such. The Herero Revolt (1904–06) was put down by the German military under the command of General Trotha. The General ordered the annihilation of this Namibian tribe, explicitly using Darwinian concepts. To any who might raise objections, and there were some, he justified his 'race-war' saying, '...the philanthropic disposition will not rid the world of the above-mentioned law of Darwin's, the

52. Ludwig Büchner, *Der Mensch und seine Stellung in der Natur*, 2nd ed. (Leipzig: Theodor Thomas, 1872), p. 147. Cited by Weikart, ref. 25, p. 191.

53. Ludwig Woltmann, *Politische Anthropologie* (Jena: Eugen Diederichs, 1903), p. 267. Cited by Weikart, ref. 25, p. 196.

'struggle of the fittest.'"[54] The General may not have been the brightest Darwinist, but he understood that all those who had adopted the Darwinian worldview had no solid foundation from which to object. He could also assume that both the most and least educated would share his racial prejudices.[55]

At this stage, the Jews were not particularly singled out as inferior. There were some who suggested deportation or even assimilation, but not yet extermination. Most of the early concern was in reference to Africans and Asians.

N. HITLER'S ETHICS

It might seem surprising to many people to suggest that Hitler had any ethics at all. He is the poster child of evil for modern humanists. He is the ultimate contradiction of their worldview. They want to maintain at the same time that there is no such thing as 'evil' yet Hitler is 'evil.' The lack of any absolute standard of good and evil has reduced 'Hitler' to a name to call anyone who objects to their agenda. The code word 'right wing' has became a defamation versatile enough to apply to anyone from American Christians to Adolf himself, even though it is nearly impossible to see any similarity. Many of Hitler's policies are actually favored by those who so use his name.

Eberhard Jäckel's study of Hitler concluded that he was a principled politician with a well-defined worldview that he pursued relentlessly.[56]

What modern Americans find hard to grasp is that in Hitler's worldview, the expansionist warfare and the genocide were not only morally justifiable, but morally praiseworthy. His ideas, though pernicious, were consistent with the widely held Darwinian worldview. He was not an original thinker; his views had been around for more than sixty years. Despite the perversity, there is

---

54. Peter Schmitt-Egner, *Kolonialismus und Faschismus* (Giessen, 1975), p. 125. Cited by Weikart, ref. 25, p. 206.

55. See also Marc Ambler, 'Herero genocide', *Creation* **27**(3):52–55, 2002, <creation.com/herero>.

56. Eberhard Jäckel, Hitler's Weltanschauung: A Blueprint for Power, trans. Herbert Arnold (Middleton, CT: Wesleyan University Press, 1972). Cited by Weikart, ref. 25, p. 209.

an ethical dimension to Hitler's worldview that helped him achieve immense popularity. Hitler promised to bring prosperity, health and power to the German people, along with moral improvement. The ideal of achieving a higher and better humanity had a strong utopian appeal. His police force not only suppressed political dissidents, but tried to eliminate criminality. He was an effective rhetorician denouncing 'immorality' and promoting 'family values' (at least in public speeches). But he had decisively rejected a Christian foundation for ethics. He did not even accept the weaker Kantian concept of the 'categorical imperative'. That is, an individual's act is good only if such an act would be good if followed universally; and humans and humanity should be treated as an end, never as a means to an end.[57]

The sole criterion in Hitler's moral system was the Darwinian struggle for survival, or the survival of the fittest. It was not hard to convince the German people that the German or Aryan race is the most highly evolved people ever known. According to the Darwinian theory, nature reveals the constant struggle for survival. Why should we expect anything else among humans? The important thing is to be one of those superior surviving people. It was really a matter of 'might makes right' as seen in this 1923 speech:

> 'Decisive [in history] is the power that the peoples have within them; it turns out that the stronger before God and the world has the right to impose its will...Right alone is of no use to whomever does not have the power to impose the right. The strong has always triumphed...All of nature is a constant struggle between power and weakness, a constant triumph of the strong over the weak.'[58]

---

57. Immanuel Kant (1724–1804), *Grundlegung zur Metaphysik der Sitten (Groundwork of the Metaphysics of Morals)* 1785.

58. Adolf Hitler, 'Weltjude und Weltbörse, die Urschuldigen am Weltkriege' 13 April 1923, in Hitler, Sämtliche Aufzeichnungen, 1905–1924, ed. Eberhard Jäckel (Stuttgart: Deutsche Verlags-Anstalt, 1980), p. 887. Cited by Weikart, ref. 25, p. 210.

Hitler's ethic had no revealed absolutes, no transcendent source of authority. A thing was morally 'good' in his system if it promoted evolutionary progress and the purity of the race. Therefore expansionist warfare was moral because it made room for the numbers of superior people to increase. Exterminations were morally good provided they served to eliminate the inferior elements of the human race and thus raise the overall quality of the species.

For Hitler, the application of Darwinism demanded eugenics for those within Germany, and the subjugation or extermination of inferior races outside Germany. The Aryan race was extolled by Hitler as the most highly developed race before whom every other race must inevitably give way. The Aryan 'race' was defined by Nazis as non-Jewish Caucasians, especially those of Nordic features.

After the devastating humiliation of being defeated in World War I and having the Versailles treaty imposed upon them, Hitler inspired new hope for the German people. A scapegoat was needed and Hitler singled out the Jews. Why were Jews prospering when so many German people were struggling? Hitler said it was because of their greed, deceit, sexual deviance, and general immorality. How else could such an inferior people be doing better than the Aryan race?

Hitler's ethic was really like that spoken of in Proverbs 21:2 'Every way of a man is right in his own eyes, but the LORD weighs the hearts.

Hitler could publicly denounce abortion, but in practice he opposed it only if the mother was a healthy German woman. He favored abortion for those of inferior races or in cases of congenital illness.[59] An Aryan should be working to increase the number of the superior race. The 'right kind' of mother would be honored by the German government for having several children. The highest moral good was the advancing of the Aryan race; nothing can be allowed to stand in the way of this ultimate good. Any agreement between Hitler's ethic and traditional Christian values was purely coincidental and very superficial. Hitler could do without the Bible,

---

59. Weikart, ref. 25, *From Darwin to Hitler*, p. 213.

Christianity or Judaism, but he could not do without Darwin, Galton, and Haeckel.

Hitler, in his *Mein Kampf* (meaning My Struggle, deliberately using the Darwinian vocabulary) gives honorable mention to Georg von Schönerer, leader of the Pan-Germany Party. Hitler eagerly adopted his advocacy of German nationalism and anti-Semitism. He also mentions another anti-Semitic writer, Houston Stewart Chamberlain. The British-born Germanophile Chamberlain (1855–1927) was fondly remembered in the 1930s as the 'spiritual founder' of Nazism.[60] Several other sources were available to Hitler in the process of forming his ideas. He felt free to pick and choose ideas that suited his purposes; therefore, many popularizers of anti-Semitism and Nazism probably influenced Hitler. Hitler thought it was common currency, not particularly shocking to the people. The ideas had been in circulation long enough to filter down to the common people. Who wanted to stand against science and progress? Nazis used propaganda films to spread their ideas among the people. Films include *I Accuse* (1941), *Hereditary Illness* (1936), and *All Life is Struggle* (1937). This line from *Victim of the Past* (1937) is illustrative:

> 'Everything in the natural world that is weak for life will ineluctably [*i.e.* inevitably] be destroyed. In the last few decades, mankind has sinned terribly against the law of natural selection. We haven't just maintained life unworthy of life, we have even allowed it to multiply.'[61]

Notice all the value words for which evolutionary philosophy has no justification. Mankind is said to have *sinned terribly* against the arbitrary, subjective, and ever changing demands of the 'law' of natural selection. Whoever does not go along with Nazism's program is actually 'sinning terribly.' Darwinism as a worldview strove to

---

60. Weikart, ref. 25, p. 220.

61. Michael Burleigh, *Death and Deliverance: Euthanasia in Germany,* 1900–1945 (Cambridge: Cambridge University Press, 1994), p. 189. Cited by Weikart, ref. 25, p. 226.

explain morality and ethics on a natural (anti-supernatural) basis to achieve a scientific and progressive ethic. Moral relativism was the result of undermining the revealed moral standard of Scripture. The shift in worldviews meant that all sorts of atrocities could now be called morally good, but opposition to these atrocities was morally evil.

No wonder Hitler found a ready audience for his rhetorical skills. Many of the leading intellectuals had been advocating these ideas for years. Newspapers, political tracts, and even films promoted the evolutionary survival of the fittest among the common people. Instead of reacting to Hitler with words like, 'That is horrifying and repulsive' the more common response was more like, 'That's what I've always thought, but no one ever expressed it so well.' Weikart draws this conclusion from his extensive study:

> 'Darwinism by itself did not produce the Holocaust, but without Darwinism, especially in its social Darwinist and eugenics permutations, neither Hitler nor his Nazi followers would have had the necessary scientific underpinnings to convince themselves and their collaborators that one of the world's greatest atrocities was really morally praiseworthy.'[62]

Since a tree is known by its fruit, we may conclude that the evolutionary worldview is a bad tree indeed.

---

62. Weikart, ref. 25, p. 233.

CHAPTER 12

NATURALISM AND APOLOGETICS

A. THE RELIGIOUS NATURE OF NATURALISM

Evolutionists are fond of saying that their speculations are 'science' while the Christian view of creation is merely 'religion'. This is, of course, to prejudice the case by an *a priori* exclusion of anything supernatural. The result is a conclusion to the effect that if we exclude any possibility of supernatural activity, evolution is the best explanation of our origins.

Some creationists and those of the Intelligent Design movement have tried to level the playing field by posing the issue as 'creation science' versus 'evolutionary science.' This is an improvement, but it still does not reach the foundational level. At a presuppositional or worldview level the issue is between the religion, philosophy, or worldview of naturalism, versus the religion, philosophy, and worldview of biblical Christianity. For both the creationist and the evolutionary worldviews, the presupposed axioms of thought determine what is allowed as evidence and what constitutes proof or truth. The fundamental framework through which we look at all of life is our worldview. Naturalistic science is not free from bias; it is in fact defined by its prejudice against any supernatural activity. Only unintelligent causes may be considered.[1] When one is asked

---

1. Phillip E. Johnson, 'Introduction,' in *The Wedge of Truth. Splitting The Foundations of Naturalism* (Downers Grove, IL: InterVarsity Press, 2000), p. 14.

to believe that order came from randomness, intelligence from non-intelligence, life from non-life, and all the variety and vastness of the universe from an exploding speck, there is quite a need for 'faith'—in the sense of blind faith, not the reasonable faith required of believers in Scripture.

Many in the Intelligent Design movement declare themselves opposed to the philosophy of naturalism, but often make two false assumptions. One such assumption is that naturalism's entrance into science began with Darwin. The other is that issues like the age of the earth have nothing to do with the fight against naturalism.

The biblical revelation has given us at least three truths in the book of Genesis that are fatal to evolutionary worldviews.

1. God created the world, *ex nihilo*, by the word of His power, in six days, and all very good.

2. God judged the sin of mankind by sending a worldwide flood. This unprecedented global months-long flood could not help having a massive effect on the geology of the earth.

3. God gave us a chronological framework of history beginning not just with the very first man, but with the heavens and the earth.

These three biblical truths are enough to keep any Christian from attempting to compromise his worldview with that of evolution. These same three truths had to be attacked to make way for evolution. It is not coincidence that compromised Christian positions cannot accept the straightforward exegesis of *any* of these three passages. The only common denominator that explains all three incredible exercises in the eisegesis of cultural conformity—against all indications of historical-grammatical factors—is that the interpreters have been 'evolutionized.'

Failure to beware of naturalistic philosophy has had a devastating effect on biblical studies. For such a philosophy, all things including the Bible are to be explained in accord with the presupposed naturalism. This despite the fact that the Bible is obviously hostile to naturalism. As we have seen, Spinoza's (1632–77) naturalism was applied to the Bible to such an extent that he has been called the 'father of higher criticism,' denying the Mosaic authorship of the Pentateuch and the miraculous elements of Scripture.[2]

The Scottish philosopher David Hume (1711–76) continued Spinoza's skepticism. Hume, too, attacked the possibility of miracles. His argument follows this line:

1. A miracle is a violation of the laws of nature.

2. Firm and unalterable experience has established these laws.

3. A wise man proportions his belief to the evidence.

Therefore his

> 'proof against miracles...is as entire as any argument from experience can possibly be imagined...There must therefore be a uniform experience against every miraculous event...nothing is esteemed a miracle if it ever happened in the common course of nature.'[3]

Most Christians did not seem alert to what was happening. Evolutionists were calling for Christians to discard the Bible as a source of scientific theory. But their views of uniformitarianism and millions of years were not scientific in the usual sense of the word. In their conceding of the Bible's authority in so-called scientific matters, Christians were actually undermining the *historical* reliability of the Bible. The Bible plainly relates the historical event known as the Creation Week. The biblical record and the evolutionary speculation both purport to inform us of what actually happened 'in the beginning.' Neither creationist nor evolutionary cosmology involves empirical observation, experimentation or testing. The question of origins is ultimately an historical question.

---

2. Edward J. Young, 'Criticism, Old Testament,' in *Baker's Dictionary of Theology*, 1960, ed. Everett F. Harrison, pp. 150–51.

3. David Hume, *Enquiry Concerning Human Understanding* (1748), ed. Ernest C. Mossner (New York: Washington Square, 1963), 10.1.122f. Cited by N. Geisler, Ref. 4, p. 2.

The result of the intrusion of naturalism into biblical studies was a denial of all things miraculous, including predictive prophecy. Being naturalistic did not prevent them from pontificating on all sorts of theological issues. This was to be expected, since naturalism is a worldview to interpret all things, including the Bible. All prophetic predictions had to be either re-dated until after the event, or reinterpreted to refer to some current or past event. Rudolph Bultmann (1884–1976) followed Spinoza and Hume in skepticism and destructive biblical criticism. Bultmann turned the Bible's history into mythology, believing it would be intellectual suicide to accept the ancient cosmology that 'we now know to be false.'[4]

Proud of his modernity, Bultmann asserted that the Bible just could not be correct in the light of modern science. Of course, he meant naturalistic evolutionary philosophy rather than actual empirical science. While evangelicals in general have not bought into the metaphysical naturalism of Spinoza or Hume, they have been bedeviled with its offspring, methodological naturalism, both in science (by way of theistic evolution) and in biblical criticism.[5]

The philosopher Immanuel Kant (1724–1804) wanted to move us away from Hume's skepticism, but could only manage to get us as far as agnosticism. So fails every non-biblical worldview. Kant's 'god' is in the realm of the unknown and unknowable noumenal world, but we can know only the phenomenal world. Religion was reduced to a concern with morals. But Kant's metaphysics and methodology are from a non-Christian worldview; they do not belong in biblical studies. They are not qualified to serve as a handmaiden, let alone lord over biblical studies. Such philosophies are to be evaluated by Scripture, not the other way around. Christians who followed their own worldview were not deceived by Hume, Kant, or Bultmann.

The philosophical theory of evolution gained acceptance by donning the garb of science. Herbert Spencer (1820–1903), whom

---

4. Norman L. Geisler, 'Beware of Philosophy: A Warning to Biblical Scholars,' *Journal of the Evangelical Theological Society (JETS)*, March, 1999, p. 2. <findarticles.com/p/articles/mi_qa3817/is_199903/ai_n8837699>, accessed August 10, 2007..

5. Ref. 4, p. 3.

Darwin praised as 'our great philosopher,' set out the naturalistic tenets of evolutionary thought. As Geisler says, 'Spencer came upon his philosophy while meditating on the waves in a pond one Sunday morning—something that no doubt would not have happened had he been in church meditating on the Word of God!'[5]

The evolutionary worldview was naturally applied to the study of religion. Sociologists assumed that religion, too, 'evolved' from magic or animism, to polytheism, to monotheism. This is a total reversal of the true situation described in Scripture. Ecclesiastes 7:29 'Truly, this only I have found: That God made man upright, but they have sought out many schemes.' (NAS) The history of fallen man involves much de-volution from the original created state of righteousness to the present sin-cursed world. The denial of the Fall of man by every non-Christian system makes it impossible for them to understand history rightly.

Darwin did not hesitate to apply his evolutionary worldview to 'religion' as follows: 'The same high mental faculties...led man to believe in unseen spiritual agencies, then in fetishism, polytheism, and ultimately in monotheism.'[6] Why we are supposed to believe all that on his say-so, we do not know. Darwin was more open about his unbelief in the *Descent of Man* than he was in *Origin of Species*. His unbelief is even more obvious in his autobiography, which was not necessarily meant for publication. At this point we recall his statement revealing his naturalistic presuppositions:

> 'I had gradually come by this time to see that the Old Testament from its manifestly false history of the world, with its Tower of Babel, the rainbow as a sign, etc., etc., and from its attribution to God the feelings of a revengeful tyrant, was no more to be trusted than the sacred books of the Hindoos [*sic*], or the beliefs of any barbarian.'[7]

---

6. Charles Darwin, Chapter III 'Mental Powers,' in *The Descent of Man and Selection in Relation to Sex* (1871). (The Modern Library, (both *Origin of Species and Descent of Man*); reprint, New York: Random House, 1986), p. 470.

7. Charles Darwin, *The Autobiography of Charles Darwin*, ed. Nora Darwin Barlow (New York: Norton & Co., 1993), p. 85.

In short he says, 'I gradually came to disbelieve in Christianity as a divine revelation.'[8]

No one should have fallen into the deception that Darwin was just doing objective science and following the 'facts' wherever they might lead him. The sparks fly from Darwin's avid ax-grinding! We can understand why Adolf Hitler would welcome Darwinism, but it is an anomaly for Christians to give way before this anti-Christian philosophy. By what standard can we consider his assertions any more than arbitrary and subjective preferences? How can we prefer his unfounded assertions to the infallible Word of the Creator?

Attempts to compromise with rather than refute Darwinism have done great harm to the credibility of Christianity's worldview. Of course there have been otherwise good men and scholars who have attempted to reconcile evolution and Scripture. We could think of James Orr, A.H. Strong, the Princeton compromises, or the modern evangelical compromises. On the one hand it might be hard to understand why anyone would want to abandon the plainly revealed Word of the Creator Himself, and be so willing to twist the Scripture this way and that for the sake of cultural conformity and intellectual 'respectability.' Such scholars are fearful of contradicting allegedly scientific theories. But as Geisler says, 'some scholars have gallantly but futilely attempted to reconcile evolution with Scripture…only to do violence to the historical-grammatical method and to unwittingly undermine both human dignity and theological orthodoxy.'[9]

Since geology is not an unbiased objective search for truth, Christians must be aware of the presuppositions underlying that study and other allegedly scientific studies. Naturalism with its attendant uniformitarianism is a presupposition leading directly to anti-biblical conclusions. In other words, naturalism guarantees a false conclusion. The case for millions of years begins with anti-biblical presuppositions and very predictably ends with anti-biblical conclusions. The Christian apologetic then must challenge naturalism

---

8. Ref. 7, p. 86ff.
9. N. Geisler, 'Beware of Philosophy: A Warning to Biblical Scholars,' p. 4.

at its foundational presuppositional level. The unbelieving evolutionist does not simply need more evidence (although there probably are factors he has not considered). What is really needed is an entirely new framework within which to interpret the evidence. We must learn to separate the kind of science that calculates the next lunar eclipse, or analyzes the light spectrum, or sends men to the moon, from speculations about what might have happened in the historical event known as 'the beginning' or the origin of the universe.

B. CHOOSE YOU THIS DAY WHOM YOU WILL SERVE

Since the question of origins is an historical issue, the trite saying, 'The Bible is not a textbook on science' is not only trivial but also irrelevant. The Bible relates the various creative acts of God during the Creation Week. These acts actually happened and are therefore historically accurate and true. It is utter nonsense for compromising evangelicals to maintain that the account is theologically true, but scientifically false, since the latter would mean, by definition, that it is historically false. And the theology depends intimately on the history. Where could we find a more reliable historical source than God's Word? Which of these should we choose:

a) The God-breathed written records of the Creator himself preserved in the patriarchal *toledoth*. Or

b) The speculations based on naturalistic presuppositions, which are devised to fit the preconceived theory, and based on the theory that anything can happen given enough time.

There is no reason to prefer naturalistic presuppositions to biblical ones. Plainly an historically accurate account cannot be ignored when investigating an historical event.

The Intelligent Design school has pointed out the dominance of naturalism, but holds back from suggesting any alternative to the current evolutionary philosophies. To concede the millions of years is to accept naturalism in geology and astronomy, while professing to fight naturalism in biology.

We have seen the influence of the Galileo affair and how the modern church repeated the errors of Rome while professing to avoid them. We have also seen the statement of Francis Bacon on keeping the book of nature separate from the book of Scripture. There are two fundamental errors involved in this kind of thinking. First, it directs us to study certain subjects with naturalistic presuppositions. The Lordship of Christ the Creator is universal and accepts no human-imposed limitations. If the Word of the Creator makes a statement of truth regarding a 'scientific' subject, it is as unerring and infallible as always. No man has a right to arbitrarily limit the authority of the God-breathed Scripture. The Bible gives vastly more detailed instructions for all of life than merely 'how to go to heaven.' The failure to take into account the religious presuppositions of evolutionists has given them a totally undeserved reputation for scientific objectivity.

The second major error involved is that such statements are actually calling into question the historicity of the biblical account. In the rush to concede to so-called scientific claims, the very historicity of Scripture is called into question. The historically reliable Bible tells us that God created the world in six calendar days, by the Word of His power and all very good. It also tells us that there was a global flood sent as a judgment upon rebellious mankind. It also gives us a straightforward chronology, which is an essential element of history. Without a chronology, the events seem unreal. To reject the biblical chronology is to set oneself on the downward slide into regarding the account as mythology. The compromising evangelical claims it does not matter *when* the events of Genesis happened, and the next generation will say it does not matter *if* the events of Genesis actually happened! This is exactly the course that has unfolded from the milder Princeton compromise, to the 'Genesis as mythology' view that has infected Westminster East.[10]

---

10. This is not to imply that Westminster has in any official way adopted the mythological view of Genesis. There is serious opposition from within the seminary to the use of myth language to describe the Genesis historical narrative. But, as long as Westminster refuses to uphold the biblical chronology, the global Flood, and the six calendar days of creation, students will continue to be led away from considering Genesis 1–11 as real space-time history. It is misleading when professors are required to say they believe in 'six-day creation' but are free to redefine 'day' as they please, perhaps as six long ages, perhaps as six literary pictures in the upper register. This also subverts the meaning of 'creation' by changing the instantaneous supernatural acts of the Creator into a long process much like the evolutionary worldview demands.

Of course the Bible does not give us science in technical detail, but has left man to discover many things about how the creation ordinarily operates. Then too, the language of appearance is frequently used. Even in the twenty-first century we have no reasonable substitute for the terms 'sunrise' and 'sunset,' but without the intention to teach a particular cosmology. But the things we learn by observational, experimental science and technology are in an entirely different class from naturalistic speculations which pretend to do 'science' apart from observation and experimentation and critical analysis, and pretend to do 'history' while lacking or ignoring historical records and eyewitness testimonies. This is another indication that the naturalism is religiously held, not scientifically established.

There is a strong connection between holding a naturalistic philosophy and the kinds of assertions made about the age of the earth. As early as 1778 the French scientist Buffon published an estimate for the age of the earth of 75,000 years, based on his study of the rate at which hot metals cool. As a deist or secret atheist, he had no regard for the scriptural account of creation. Privately Buffon believed the earth was actually at least three million years old, but desired to blunt the edge of controversy by suggesting merely several thousand extra years.[11] It would be extraordinary blindness to suppose that his anti-Christian, anti-biblical worldview had no effect on his thinking! The atheists believed in millions of years, but first sought acceptance of merely thousands of years. Once Christians conceded that a few thousand extra years would not hurt the Bible's credibility, they had no solid foundation on which to resist the ever-increasing estimates that were forthcoming. As microbiology revealed the complexity of the cell and the increasing improbability of evolutionary randomness, evolutionists increased their age estimates to give evolution more time to work. Their faith commitment held that given enough time anything, no matter how improbable,

---

11. Terry Mortenson, "Philosophical Naturalism and the Age of the Earth: Are they Related?,' *The Master's Seminary Journal [TMSJ]* 15, no. 1 Spring 2004 available from <creation.com/naturalism-church> accessed 23 October 2008.

could and would happen. Randomness, they firmly believed, could eventually produce the appearance of amazing complexity. At this point some cry foul, claiming that the neo-Darwinian mechanism of mutation and natural selection makes evolution a non-random process. (The adaptation is specific, tailored to the environment.) But mutations are unguided, random genetic mistakes that may then be selected by whatever environment happens, by chance, to be there. Chance + chance = chance; evolution is at its core an unguided process that perfectly suits the needs of Epicurus, Lucretius and their modern-day counterparts.

Christians should have been much more skeptical about the truth claims of the militant atheists and unbelieving deists who were the driving force behind the promotion of 'old earth' speculation. The connected chain of thought from Hume to Hutton, to Cuvier, to Lyell led to the millions of years being presupposed. The misguided compromises from Buckland, Sedgwick, etc. only aided the evolutionary cause. Christians are not to try to refine the vain philosophies of unbelievers, but to consciously construct a biblical Christian worldview in every area of thought and life. To take the lazy way out and forsake this calling is to simply absorb, without critical thinking, the current cultural consensus. The biblical warning, 'Be not conformed to this world,' was woefully neglected by those scrambling for a compromise. We have no need for compromises of desperation, resulting in incredible eisegetical gymnastics. We have a God-revealed worldview by which to accurately interpret all the data of observation. We can do so because both we and the creation around us have a common source in our Creator. Being created in His image, regenerate man is able to think God's thoughts after Him within creaturely limitations. God is omniscient; man is not. We cannot know everything, but we can know some things truly as the God who knows everything reveals some things to us. God's word is of absolute authority; man's speculations are open to correction.

The inevitable fact of bias has been acknowledged at times by evolutionists themselves. They are especially likely to make honest acknowledgments either in private diaries of private correspondence, or in technical journals that they expect no one but the evolutionary faithful to read. For example, the private correspondence of Charles Lyell sets out his intention to overturn what he calls the 'Mosaic geology.' From a biblical worldview, there is no such thing as 'Mosaic geology.' For one thing there is no detailed technical analysis of rocks and fossils. For another thing, Moses is not the ultimate source of the Genesis record of creation. It is both God-revealed and recorded by the patriarchs preceding Moses. What Lyell and others really want everyone to do is to abandon the God-breathed historical account of the global Flood judgment upon sinful man. Lyell reacted precisely as the Scripture says the rebellious sinner will act: refusing to have God in his knowledge and suppressing the truth in unrighteousness. The weighty influence of his and others' hostility to God the Creator and His Word, the Bible, cannot be denied.

Hand in hand with the development of naturalism in science was the application of naturalism to the study of the Bible. For example, the Pentateuch was declared to be written long after the time of Moses and of no more authority than any other ancient writing. Those liberal higher critical scholars were naively uncritical of the contemporary naturalistic philosophy. Their advocating accommodation to naturalism only undermined the biblical foundations of the Christian worldview. They made their own area of study appear futile and even senseless. If the Pentateuch really was as they say it is, why were they wasting their time?

Evolutionists have made good use of the bait and switch technique in promoting their theory. After citing the advances in technology and the social benefits of operational science, they insist that the same respect be accorded to evolutionary speculations about a vaguely historical event known as the origin of the universe.

The Christian worldview recognizes that God's ordinary providence acts in ways that man can formulate into 'laws of nature.' We are obliged to accept only the supernatural events recorded in Scripture, recognizing that God upholds His creation by His providence. We recognize the obvious existence of secondary causes, but dare not ignore the extraordinary providence in supernatural acts. As an example, we can formulate laws of gravity describing the way things fall and accelerate in our everyday world. But that does not mean that God cannot act in an extraordinary way so that through the word of the prophet, He made 'the ax head float' (2 Kings 6:6 NET). If we ignore historical events like the supernatural acts of creation and global Flood, and other historical events like the Fall of man, and the historical records of the patriarchs, we are bound to come to false conclusions in our quest for the origin of the universe.

Much of the nineteenth century theology had a sentimental view of nature in which all was sweetness and light. The Fall of man and the consequent curse on creation were ignored. When Darwin and others noted the cruelty, waste, and death in 'nature,' Paley's case seemed to crumble. But a truly biblical worldview would take the Fall and the Curse into account. We cannot rightly understand the creation apart from the revealed historical truth found in Scripture. Indeed, one of the weaknesses of a 'mere design' viewpoint, as per the Intelligent Design movement, is its lack of history.[12]

Bertrand Russell repeated Darwin's faulty observation when he wrote:

> 'When you come to look into this argument from design, it is a most astonishing thing that people believe that this world, with all the things that are in it, with all its defects, should be the best that omnipotence and omniscience have been able to produce in millions of years. I really cannot believe it.'[13]

The so-called mainline liberal denominations were, of course, stumped by Russell's challenge. Liberal theology liked to think that this was the best of all possible worlds, getting better every day in every way. But there are several misrepresentations in the Darwin-Russell view of the world. One major distortion is to think that the world we now see is identical to the world God created. The perfect world is an eschatological expectation, not a present reality. Death and

12. See Jonathan Sarfati, *By Design: Evidence for nature's Intelligent Designer—the God of the Bible*, chapters 12, 13, Creation Book Publishers, GA, USA, 2008.

13. Bertrand Russell, 'Why I Am Not a Christian,' March 6, 1927, Drew University, http://www.users. drew.edu/~jlenz/whynot.html (accessed December 18, 2006).

suffering were introduced into the creation after man's sin. Of course, neither Russell nor his allies wish to acknowledge man's (especially their own) fallen depraved nature, or God's wrath and judgment against sin. Russell has a valid point against a deistic worldview, but not against the Christian worldview. Note too the assumption of an evolutionary framework of time. Russell's imaginary deity can't get rid of the defects even after millions of years. The biblical worldview says God created all things, in the space of six days, all very good, and a few thousand years ago. Honesty would force Russell to rename his article 'Why I Am Not a Deist' or 'Why I Am Not a Theological Liberal.' The old earth theories are theories about history, not operational observational science. Admission of unbiblical presuppositions resulted in faulty conclusions and weakened the foundation of Christianity. The weakened Christianity was ill prepared to resist the inroads of evolution. We must be done with the 'tranquil flood' and the 'tranquil fall' and trust God's word concerning a global Flood and a Fall with devastating consequences. Liberal theology's tranquil, local or non-existent flood left no traces in the real world; its mythical 'fall' had no effect on man or the world. They were indistinguishable from atheism's position of no flood at all and no fall whatsoever. A Christian worldview includes the reality of evil, but a synthetic worldview will be destroyed by the presence of evil that it cannot account for.

The embrace of naturalism as a controlling factor in science did not begin with Darwin as Phillip Johnson implies:

> 'What went wrong in the wake of the Darwinian triumph was that the authority of science was captured by an ideology, and the evolutionary scientists thereafter believed what they wanted to believe rather than what the fossil data, the genetic data, the embryological data and the molecular data were showing them.'[14]

It is true that the philosophy of naturalism is at the root of Darwin's error, but naturalism had already been accepted in geology and astronomy before Darwin applied it to biology. In fact, believing 'what they wanted to believe' began with the Fall of man, continued in Babel, was formulated as a cosmology in ancient Greece, and continues to this day. The time to resist and refute naturalism is when it first appears, not waiting until it invades biology and every other discipline. Naturalism gains access into Christian thought by careless lack of discernment. The following is so typical that dozens of similar quotes could be gathered:

> 'For Christians, the date of creation is not a primary issue of faith and should not be regarded as such, because the Bible does not specifically state a date of creation. This fact can be easily confirmed by reviewing sources such as The NIV study Bible, The Believers Study Bible, The New Geneva Study Bible, and evangelical commentaries.'[15]

Unfortunately, what some Christian scholars believe today is no proof of correctness. This is especially true as most Christians do not consciously construct a Christian-biblical worldview and tend to limit the relevance of the Bible to 'spiritual' issues. There is a great deal of difference between a Christian with an opinion, and a truly Christian worldview based on Scripture. If we take a more critical look at the presuppositions of modern geology, astronomy, biology, or any other area we would see that the so-called evidence for millions or billions of years is really only a naturalistic interpretation of the observed data. If the naturalism is removed, no 'evidence' remains. Because a person is a Christian does not mean he is thinking biblically. Going to Scripture 'on a mission' to make it fit naturalistic presuppositions of modern culture is to guarantee error. As Mortenson has said:

> 'The key is to oppose the accommodation of biblical revelation with naturalistic interpretations of the creation, which is what all old-earth reinterpretations of Genesis

---

14. Phillip Johnson, 'Afterward: How to Sink a Battleship,' in *Mere Creation: Science, Faith and Intelligent Design*, ed. William Dembski (Downers Grove, IL: InterVarsity Press, 1998), pp. 448f. Cited by Mortenson, Naturalism, p. 84.

15. 'Our Focus,' http://origins.org/articles/00site_ourfocus2.html (accessed September 5, 2007). Position statement of Origins, an Intelligent Design group.

are. The issue is not a vaguely defined theism's marriage with naturalism but rather the adulterous union of biblical teaching and naturalism...fighting naturalism only in biology will not work.'[16]

Creationist geologist John Reed has aptly summarized what must be our approach in forming a Christian worldview: 'An accurate translation, a valid hermeneutic, and a careful exegesis are the only critical issues pertinent to the interpretation of Genesis 1–11.'[17]

By sharp contrast, compromised views have already been determined apart from the text of Scripture. It is then presumed that a certain view must be true because so many scientists believe it. Therefore they see their task as 'interpreting' the Bible to fit that preconceived mold. These views require us to turn historical narrative into poetry or mythology so as to accommodate the evolutionary mythology currently believed in the culture. The Scripture has its own hermeneutic; it is not a nose of wax. Novelty and social conformity are over-valued and faithfulness under-valued in the modern theological scene.

As succinctly put by the Westminster Confession of Faith:

'The infallible rule of interpretation of Scripture is the Scripture itself: and therefore, when there is a question about the true and full sense of any Scripture (which is not manifold, but one), it must be searched and known by other places that speak more clearly.' (WCF. Chapter 1, section 9).

As creationist geologist John Reed has said:

'Throughout its history, the Church has allowed clear biblical statements to be folded, mutilated, and spindled

---

16. Mortenson, Ref. 11.

17. John Reed, 'John Reed Responds to David Campbell's Review of Plain Talk About Genesis,' December 4, 2000, Presbyterian Church in America, http://www2.pcanews.com (accessed June 14, 2007).

> to accommodate assertions derived outside of the Bible... much of the data presently applied to that interpretation [of Genesis 1-11] are not only external to Scripture, but are, in fact, alien to Scripture; being part of the antagonistic worldview of Naturalism.'[18]

The pattern historically has gone this way: The atheists (or sometimes politely known as deists or agnostics) come up with an explanation deliberately opposed to the God of Scripture, the God who holds people accountable. The majority of Christians, instead of doing the work of critical thinking and constructing a thoroughly biblical worldview, glibly accept whatever the current 'scientific' consensus says, and quickly add that it was just in this very way that God did His work of creation. The unbeliever is not challenged in his worldview; neither is he about to 'add God' to his scheme of evolution because the very reason for its invention was an attempt to escape from God. The Christian's worldview must be built from the ground up using God's own materials. We must stop trying to construct a worldview made mostly of scraps left over from anti-Christian worldviews. The Bible tells us clearly that the ungodly suppress the truth in unrighteousness. We must stop the neutralist thinking that refuses to see the influence of evolution's religious, but anti-Christian, presuppositions. Every unbeliever, scientist or not, will in their unbelief attempt to suppress the truth of a Creator God who holds every person accountable. We cannot pretend otherwise. There are no neutral areas of thought because God has revealed the only correct framework of interpretation of all data that we may observe. There is no 'unimportant' area in which the Lordship of Christ can be abandoned. The omniscient God has from eternity known infinitely more about science, philosophy, or any other subject than any boatload of scientists can ever hope to know.

Here is the fork in the road for the contemporary Christian Church: Choose this day the worldview by which you will consistently think and live. Compromise ends in surrender, faithfulness leads to victory.

---

18. Ref. 17.

Romans 12:2: And do not be conformed to this world, but be transformed by the renewing of your mind, that you may prove what *is* that good and acceptable and perfect will of God.

Here then is the way to overcome compromise:

1. Regeneration, in which a person is thoroughly transformed, ends his rebellion against the living God. The issue is foundationally a moral and spiritual issue rather than a so-called scientific one.

2. Sanctification, by the renewing of the mind, that we may learn how absolutely trustworthy is the Word of God and how He has spoken with penetrating clarity.

3. That we resist the temptation to interpret Scripture in a way that makes it agree with the anti-Christian naturalism of cultural consensus. Instead, we discipline our minds to evaluate and interpret all things by the God-breathed words of Scripture.

4. The critical need is biblical evangelism and an ongoing, sanctifying reconstructing of our thoughts and worldview. Thus our goal is conformity, not to the world, but to the specific God-breathed words of Scripture.

APPENDIX

POTASSIUM-ARGON DATES IN ERROR

Historic lava flow	Actual age of rock sample in years when estimated (round figures)	Potassium-Argon estimate in years	Overestimation factor
Hualalai, Hawaii c.1800	200	1,600,000 +/- 160,000 1,410,000 +/- 80,000	8,000 times 7,050 times
Mt. Etna, Sicily 122 BC	2,100	250,000 +/- 80,000	119 times
Mt. Etna, Sicily AD 1792	180	350,000 +/- 80,000	1,950 times
Mt. Ngauruhoe, New Zealand 1954	45	<270,000 1,300,000 +/- 300,000 3,500,000 +/- 26,000	0–5,000 times 26,000 times 70,000 times

This chart was compiled from information in two *Creation* magazine articles by Ph.D geologist Andrew Snelling, see 'More and more wrong dates', *Creation* **23**(3):24, 2001 <creation.com/rubble2>, also 'Radioactive "dating" failure', *Creation*22(1):18–21, 1999, <creation. com/NZvolcano>.

NOTES:

- Most fossils are not dated radiometrically, as they seldom contain the necessary radioactive isotopes. Volcanic rock and ash often do, by contrast. So to date a specimen, one may try to find an associated volcanic sample.

- In such radiometric dating, of which Potassium-Argon is the most commonly used, the 'clock starts ticking' from the moment when the lava solidifies into rock. So a rock formed from a lava flow 50 years ago should not give an age older than that.

- Samples from the same lava flow can vary greatly, e.g. the three Mt. Ngauruhoe samples. Are they 270,000 years, or 3.5 million years old? Actually, 54 years old.

- As seen in the two Mt. Etna basalt samples, Potassium-Argon dated the 2,130 year old sample 100,000 years younger than the sample that was only 216 years old.

- The plus or minus numbers often represent a significant percentage of the total. There are several assumptions at work. These include the original amounts, the presupposed uniformitarian rate of decay (now under serious challenge by the findings of the RATE project—see <creation.com/rate>).

- Almost all estimates overestimate by reporting ages from 1,000 to 70,000 times the actual known age.

- If one cannot trust radiometric dating whenever rocks of *known* age are dated, why should one trust it when dealing with rocks of *unknown* age?

- The geological column with its millions of years was largely set in place, based on uniformitarian assumptions that rejected the biblical Flood, prior to the discovery of radioactivity. If a radiometric 'date' disagrees with the assumed geological date, the radiometric date is always assumed to be in error. For example, if a sample in a rock associated with dinosaur fossils were to give an 'age' of 10 million years, it would be rejected and another sample sought. Because 'everyone knows' that dinosaurs had died out tens of millions of years earlier.

ABOUT THE AUTHOR

Donald D. Crowe
Ph.D. American University of Biblical Studies
M.Div. Pittsburgh Theological Seminary
B.A. Asbury College

Dr. Crowe served as a pastor, Christian school teacher, and is presently Professor of Biblical Languages at American University of Biblical Studies and Christ Theological Seminary.

He is the book review editor for *The New Southern Presbyterian Review.* He has also written articles for the Atlanta Center for Apologetics and is a member of the newly formed Atlanta Creation Group.

He and his wife Carol have two married children and three grandchildren.

AUSTRALIA
Creation Ministries International
P.O. Box 4545,
Eight Mile Plains QLD 4113, Australia
Phone: (07) 3340 9888
Fax: (07) 3340 9889

CANADA
Creation Ministries International
300 Mill St, Unit 7,
Kitchener, ON
N2M 5G8
Phone: (519) 746 7616
Fax: (519) 746 7617

Subscriptions and orders only:
1–888–251–5360

NEW ZEALAND
Creation Ministries International
P.O. Box 39005, Howick,
Manukau 2145, New Zealand
Phone and fax: (09) 537 4818

SINGAPORE
Creation Ministries International
P.O. Box 195, 911207, Singapore
Phone and fax: (65) 9698 4292

SOUTH AFRICA
Creation Ministries International
P.O. Box 3349,
Durbanville 7551, South Africa
Phone: (021) 979 0107
Fax: (086) 519 0555

UK and EUROPE
Creation Ministries International
15 Station Street
Whetstone
Leicestershire, LE8 6JS
United Kingdom
Phone: (44) 0845 6800 264

USA
Creation Ministries International
PO Box 350
Powder Springs, GA 30127, USA
Phone: 1-800-6161-CMI
Fax: (404) 420 2247

OTHER COUNTRIES
Creation Ministries International
P.O. Box 4545,
Eight Mile Plains QLD 4113, Australia
Phone: (+617) 3340 9888
Fax: (+617) 3340 9889

Email: mail@creation.info